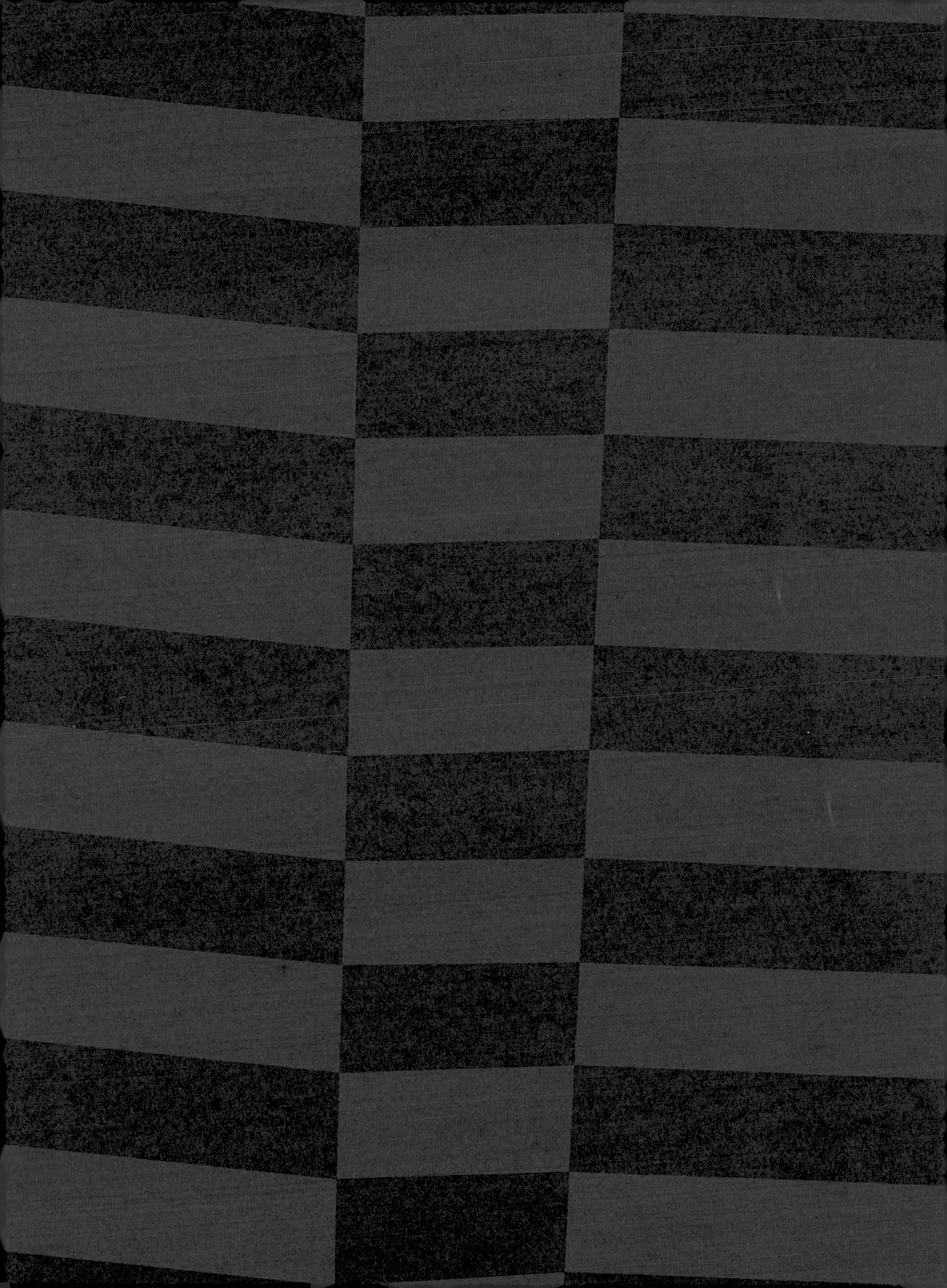

Nathan Coley

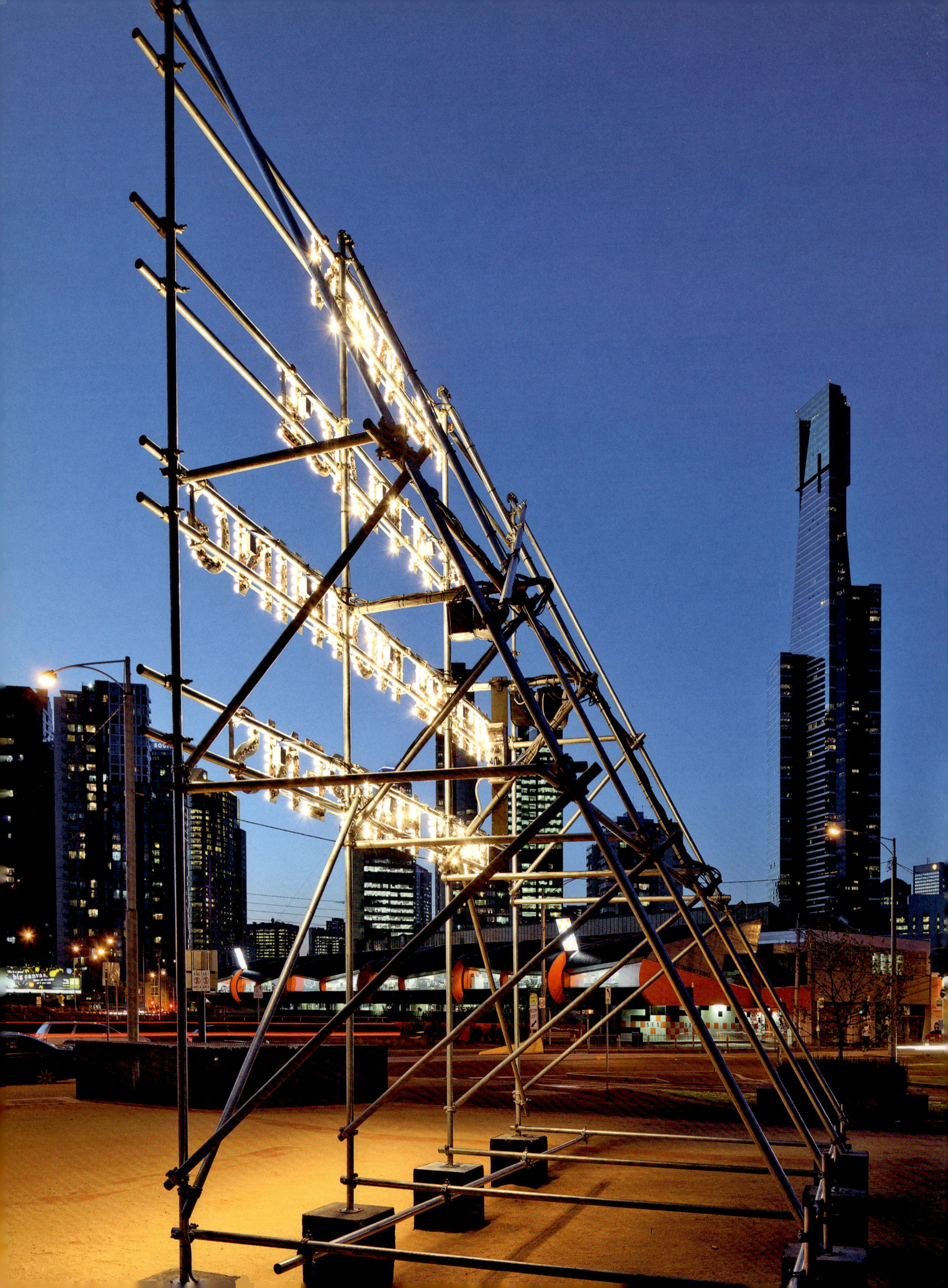

Nathan Coley

With texts by Katrina Brown, Celia Davies, Brian Dillon, Juliana Engberg, Jes Fernie, Jonathan Horrocks, Tom Hunt, Caroline Käding, Tanja Karreman, Lisa Le Feuvre, Rory Mitchell, Darren Pih, Nigel Prince, Michael Rooks, and Andrea Schlieker

HATJE
CANTZ

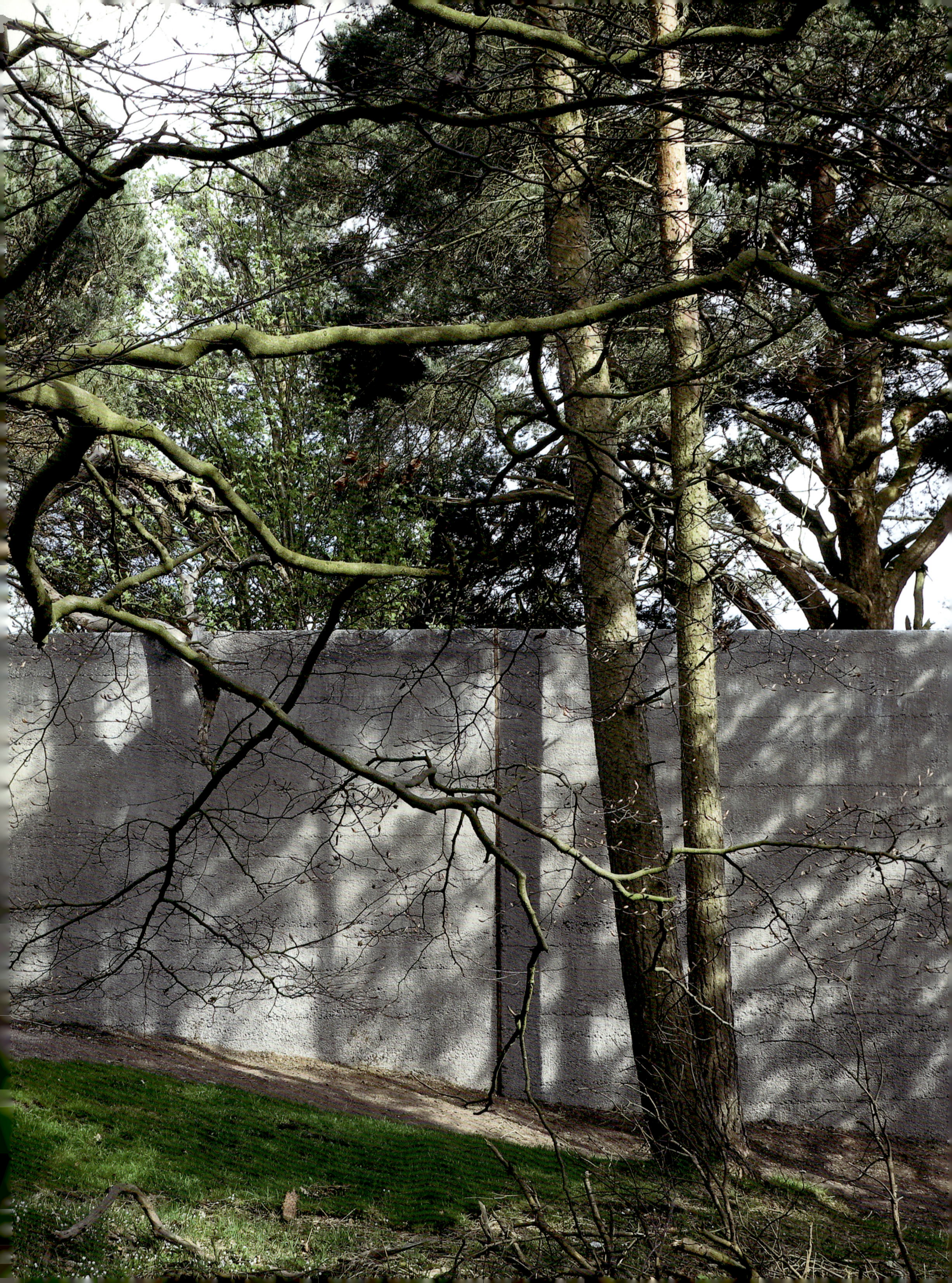

Contents

Frontispiece:
Heaven Is a Place Where Nothing Ever Happens, 2008
Installation, Australian Centre for Contemporary Art, Melbourne

Opposite:
In Memory, 2010
Permanent sculpture, Jupiter Artland, Edinburgh

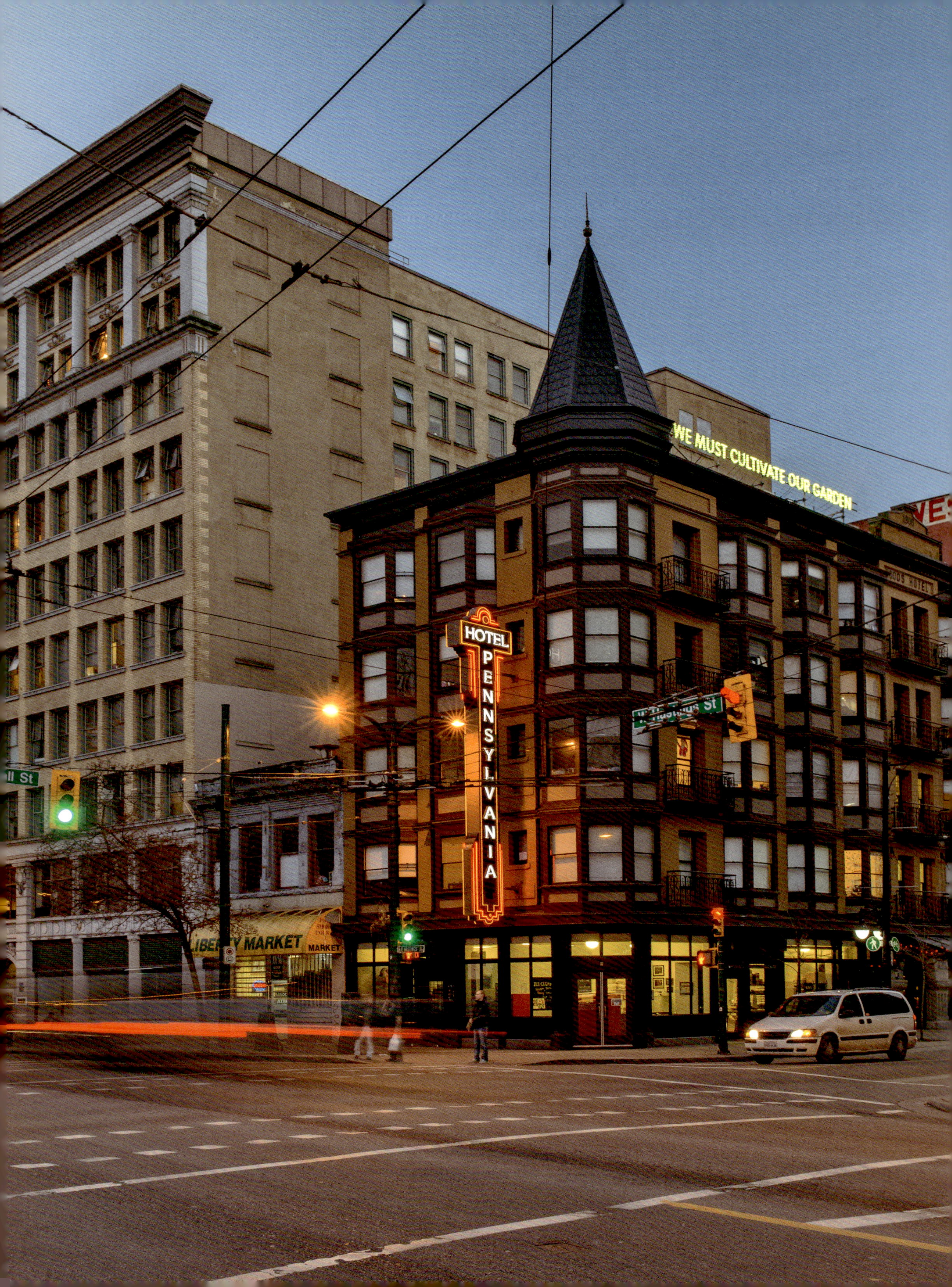

HOTEL
PENNSYLVANIA
WE MUST CULTIVATE OUR GARDEN
LIBERTY MARKET
MARKET

Introduction

Nathan Coley's practice centers on examinations into the social aspects of our built environment, working across a diverse range of media. Interested in public space, the artist explores how architecture comes to be invested—and reinvested—with meaning, and how through the competing practices of place these claims and significations come into conflict. For Coley, buildings are empty vessels given significance by their social history: by the communities that populate them. He is interested in this politicization of place, especially in the current pluralist climate of enforced equality. Fiona Bradley, in the last publication on Coley to bring together a series of individual projects, comments, "The gap between the city as built and as experienced, as it exists in the world and in the mind and memory, resonates throughout Nathan Coley's practice . . . [he] conjures cities, metaphorically dismantling them."

This publication draws together a selection of Coley's significant body of work—exhibitions, commissions, and public works—created since 2004. The occasion of his two recent solo exhibitions—*Knowledge, Kindliness and Courage* at the Contemporary Art Gallery, Vancouver, 2012, followed by Kunstverein Freiburg early in 2013—were both developed as expansive presentations examining the multi-faceted nature of his practice, and signaled a high degree of investment in bringing Coley's work to fresh audiences and constituencies in North America and Europe. Such a moment seemed a most appropriate juncture in which to address his ongoing artistic propositions through an in-depth examination setting these newer projects in the context of related works from the past eight years.

Both exhibitions included recent and existing work alongside new commissions. In Vancouver, Coley's first solo show in North America, *Unnamed (Vancouver)* formed the centerpiece, the exhibition title a quotation from "Why I Am Not a Christian," a 1927 essay by the British philosopher Bertrand Russell, considered as one of the most influential texts of the twentieth century in its "devastating use of cold logic" to articulate his atheist position. This made for a powerful statement, the ideas it embodied being felt across the city through the equally strong presence of Coley's large-scale illuminated text work *We Must Cultivate Our Garden* presented off-site. Its message and meaning, so pertinent to our contemporary lives, continues to resonate in Vancouver.

In Freiburg, Coley's public sculpture *Bandstand*, unveiled in November 2012, is a raw concrete structure which can be seen as both a formalistic sculpture and a functional public platform for performance and other leisure activities. It is situated in a suburban field. Steps lead up to the raised floor with a circular aperture through which a fruit tree grows. Coley's subsequent exhibition at Kunstverein Freiburg, his first solo presentation in Germany, opened in January 2013. It was conceived in conjunction with *Bandstand* and its themes.

The contributors to this publication add their voices to the critical examination of the complexity of these and other individual works presented here. Each brings insight into particular projects and the various aspects of Coley's practice, enabling a considered and nuanced overview to emerge. These texts help reveal that claims to public space in postmodern society, one marked not by national cohesion, but fragmentation, are made by groups of people who have different ideas on how it should be used. The structures they erect manifest these desires, values, and beliefs, revealing the unconscious of the architecture and cityscapes Coley interrogates, investigating social as much as physical constructions.

Caroline Käding
Director, Kunstverein Freiburg
Nigel Prince
Executive Director, Contemporary Art Gallery, Vancouver

We Must Cultivate Our Garden, 2006
Installation, Carrall Street, Vancouver

In Flagrant Contradiction

Lisa Le Feuvre

When is belief needed? On a very general level, it seems to be required most when doubt is at its strongest. Every person can cite their own examples, every fiction uses oscillation between doubt and belief to drive narrative tension, and all holders of power, whether individual or institutional, affirm their status through a negotiation with faith and hesitation. Belief is part of the invisible landscape of knowledge. Belief can be an explicit declaration. And it is a complicated term to address. Belief opens a box of leaping and squirming groupings of consensus and conflict, not to mention suspicion and sentiment. To believe is to place weight, value, and emphasis on something. It is a process that pulls the fiction of the straight line of objectivity into oblique subjectivity. All these problems come before this word has even been tied to a referent or wrapped around a subject or object.

Nathan Coley's subject is *belief*, not *belief in*. He conducts his research through the making of objects. Belief and art are coupled through the powers of doubt and wavering agnosticism, be it the polychromatic wooden sculptures of medieval Silesia telling stories of hell and damnation in a preliterate era or the exquisitely smooth surfaces of John McCracken's other-dimensional blocks of pure color. Removed from their own times, both examples instruct each other: paired, they offer registers of visual excess that privilege the phenomenological encounter to initiate belief. In a 1998 interview, McCracken described:

> For a long time I was more directly interested in cosmology than in aliens. But in the last few years I started reading more about them, and I became convinced that there really are UFOs and aliens all around us. Aliens are elusive and hard to pin down because of their other-dimensionality; their medium of travel is time, as far-fetched as that seems. I think there are actually thousands of extraterrestrials—and other entities that you wouldn't call extraterrestrials—flying and running around, looking at us, studying us. While they may think we're kind of cool in some way, even brilliant, I think they wonder how we can be so opaque, why we don't see them more than we do. It's amazing that we don't really see what's going on. But I think we're purposefully "programmed" in that way. I think there is a reason for our forgetting where we originally came from; so we could focus on things here. But now, I think, there's a reason for us to remember where we came from so we can integrate that with what we've learned since we've been here, so we can get the perspective we badly need. Then we can more effectively set about the business of moving on—and up. The whole thing adds up to a very provocative idea that I think impinges in important ways on humankind's development.[1]

Replace "alien" and "UFO" with the word "belief" in the above passage. What results is an anthropomorphization of a feeling and with it a discussion on why humans need to believe is opened. Pause to think about what it means for art to be committed to something outside of convention—be that the consensual skepticism of art from the first decade of this century, or the rational truth that humans are the ultimate intelligence. There is nothing so unusual about looking outside the assumed structures of knowledge in the realm of art. Hilma af Klint developed abstract thinking though anthroposophy, Kazimir Malevich was committed to theosophy, Piet Mondrian to spiritual order; more recently, Joachim Koester seeks the mystical to discover the rational, Carol Bove studies Aleister Crowley to release ideas from fixed meaning, and Nathan Coley mines the nature of belief to consider how we might understand our place in the world. McCracken's interlocutor then asks, one might suspect hesitantly given the wild belief system he had just claimed, what led him to speak on the record about these issues. He responds: "Even before I did concerted studies of UFOs, it helped me maintain my focus to think I was trying to do the kind of work that could have been brought here by a UFO. I liked imagining that these cool, advanced beings might zip here in their time-space vehicles and leave objects for us to look at. I like the idea of making objects that are equivalent to such things." To stand before a McCracken plank is an experience not to be underestimated: it is a moment of reflection that stretches beyond known horizons of perception.

1. Conceptual artists are mystics rather than rationalists. They leap to conclusions that logic cannot reach.
2. Rational judgements repeat rational judgements.
3. Irrational judgements lead to new experience.
4. Formal art is essentially rational.
5. Irrational thoughts should be followed absolutely and logically.

These are the first five points Sol LeWitt makes in his "Sentences on Conceptual Art" of 1969. This is a declaration concerned with many things, including belief. A mystic believes in something outside of human rationality, outside of language and judgment, in order to enable a pondering of imponderables. The attempt to concretize inner belief through art, both contemporary and historical, feels its way noisily through current exhibition practices. The mainstream belief systems Coley turns to, like these more esoteric systems of ordering the world, are a reflection of the times within which humans operate, and, as such, need to be unpacked to understand a particular present.

This knotted impossibility is central to the artistic practice of Coley. His sculptures study the nature of language, architecture, and assumption in order to suggest that we consider paying greater awareness to how we understand our place in the world. For two decades he has been consistently mining belief as a concept, be it through architecture, law, superstition, religion, or the authority of the lecture, the conduct of humans, the distribution of information, the representation of memory, or belief in art itself. His research is conducted by using language that already exists in the world—commands, conversations, platitudes, and conventions. It could be an overheard exchange between friends, a radio program, or the recounting of a historical reference. Each example uses language to represent an event, feeling, or opinion produced by the peculiarities of a specific frame of time. Coley finds these resources rather than seeks them out; he is a listener. In his hands, words become images, and objects are placed in the public to be read.

The cover of this book announces: *A Place Beyond Belief*. This single-sentence sculpture takes the form of a freestanding scaffolding sign, the sans-serif text written in point size, four lights by eight, conceived to be tested in a potentially limitless number of sites. As discussed in Caroline Käding's text, it was shown in the small town of Freiburg, Germany, in 2013, displayed within a Kunstverein, viewable above from a balcony or from below by gazing up at the towering edifice from floor level. In 2012 it was shown in a city square in Pristina, Kosovo, unveiled on September 11 by city authorities. Day, night, sun, rain. Crepuscular light, electric light. Ignored, examined like a painting. It does not matter to this indifferent structure—the light is illuminated for twenty-four hours with no heed to what reactions it causes. The work responds to its site

A Place Beyond Belief, 2012
Installation, National Gallery of Kosovo, Pristina

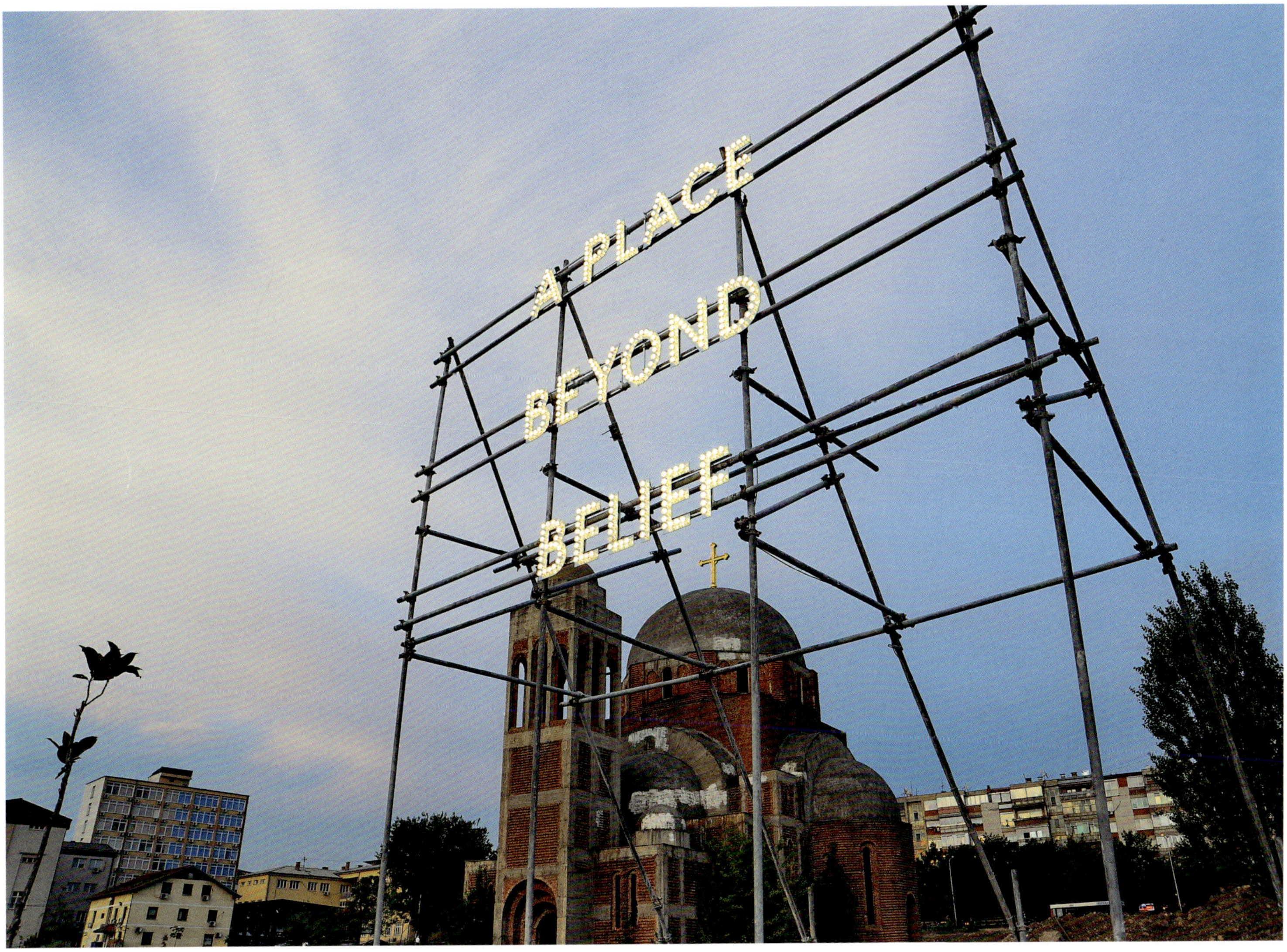

and to the particularities of each encounter—be that the histories of Kosovo or the recent production and reception of contemporary art.

"Place" is a site that has been named; "a place" is one among many. "Beyond" is outside of a territory of knowledge, be that intellectual, geographical, or ethical. "Belief" is just difficult. "A place beyond belief" is a vernacular phrase, used generally when describing a deeply disturbing event that has occurred in a specific, named location. Coley picks up phrases as ready-mades from private and public sources. This is the ground from which his sculptures grow. They observe the belief, balance, order, control, fiction, and illusion we use to try and interpret the world we have created. Coley considers the ways in which experience is fixed and distorted by language and its attendant inferences. In discussing the word "heaven," for example, the artist moves from dictionary definitions to the reception and distribution of Led Zeppelin's rock classic "Stairway to Heaven," to the eponymous film directed by Tom Tykwer; cotton sheets, a farm in the south of England, a gay night club, the lyrics from a Talking Heads song stating "heaven is a place where nothing ever happens." This phrase blazed in 2008 in the seaside town of Folkestone, a place that has been grand, run down, and gentrified. Illuminated day and night, on a high street of cut-price shops, it pointed simultaneously to somewhere else and its own present, a shopping street filled with art and beach tourists, retired and disenfranchised locals, those looking for something better or mourning something worse. The origin of each of Coley's works is the surrounding world. His sculptures are

There Will Be No Miracles Here, 2006
Installation, Scottish National Gallery of Modern Art, Edinburgh
Collection of the National Galleries of Scotland, Edinburgh

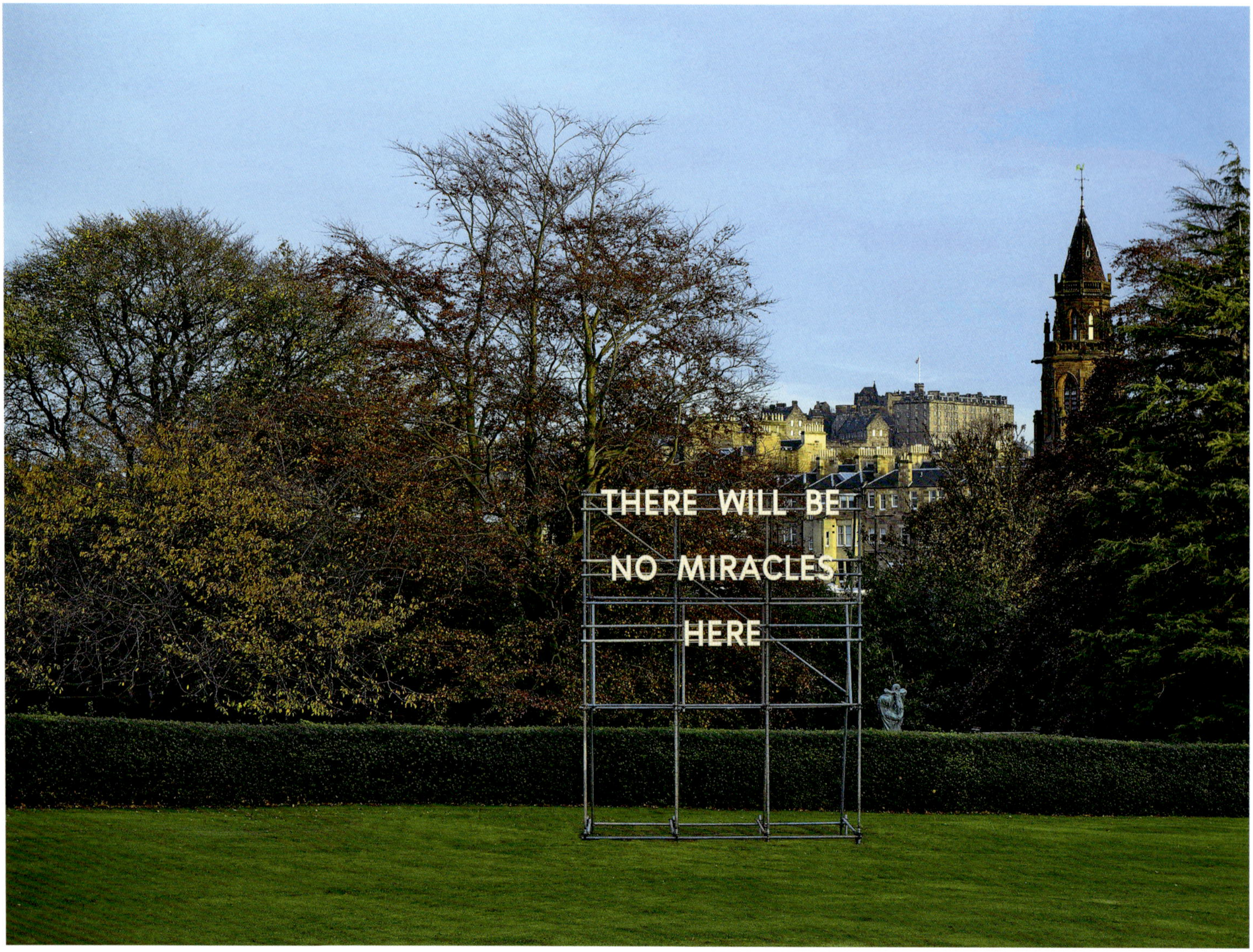

manifestations open to be misread and ignored as much as any other activity. Coley's works are always generated by an invitation, with the flight from production to realization compromised and influenced by those encountered during the process.

A radio program, listened to as background noise, where personal memories of the atmosphere in New York following September 11 were shared, initiated the sculpture *A Place Beyond Belief*. Such memorial programs are emotive, as they communicate the subjective nature of perception. When an event becomes an anecdote it changes; it becomes edited to work as a story with impact. Coley's possession of this story through claiming it as ready-made material for an artwork also distorts it through distribution—in this very book a number of such stories are repeated as each writer seeks out the source of the work in an attempt to grapple with Coley's sculpture. This one goes: a young woman sits in a New York subway carriage a number of days after the terrorist attacks on the twin towers. It is early morning, and the city is grudgingly back at work. Like many of her fellow passengers, she is tired, emotionally fragile, confused, and angry—still trying to come to terms with what has happened to her city. A Sikh man sits opposite her, wearing a bright orange turban. There is a strong tangible sense of hatred from the passengers toward the man—a feeling of raw anger and disgust. The man's eyes are averted, the commuters stares un-replied. His head is bowed, he is sobbing. The train travels on, stopping at the next station, the doors open and close, passengers get on and off. After a few stops and more torturous minutes, the man gathers his belongings and gets up to leave. Standing by the exit is a young black woman with a newly born baby. As the man approaches, he reaches into his pockets and takes out a handful of dollars. Without saying anything, he shoves the money into the folds of the baby's clothes and exits the train. The doors close, and the remaining passengers burst into tears. At that moment, the woman realizes that for New York to get past the attack, to move on and rebuild itself, it has to think anew, it has to look again. It has to get to a place beyond belief.

This story is shocking. It is beyond belief. Why was this told on national British radio? Is it true or embellished? What difference does placing the money, without an invitation, make? Why do we need to know the woman's skin color? Who has the right to judge another? Does telling this tale of prejudice teach anything? Could this happen in another place? Could it happen here, now? These questions can only be raised as the distance from the specifics of the event widens. Coley is an editor of the world—what he presents may be there already, but his compilations question. Rather than explain, this story inscribed into a sculpture operates as a report from elsewhere—somewhere as unknown as McCracken's references. Something personal is not universal, it only becomes an applicable generalization once comparisons are made and commonalities sought out. What Coley himself believes in is irrelevant and undisclosed. His subject is neither personal nor private: it is public belief—a drive that formulates the origination of society. His concern is with the general, or, in Ludwig Feuerbach's terms, the species rather than the particular or individual. Indeed, Coley's own religious or moral opinions have never been shared either in the work or in public interviews.

Coley's work is a private study of public proclamations, a million miles away from commentary. In another text work a phrase states: *There Will Be No Miracles Here*. This sculpture has been seen widely and written about extensively, because, very simply, it is a significant work central to Coley's investigations and to considering art today. Like all his works, it does not stand still, it moves with its times, in tune with the personal and the political. The site of encountering Coley's work is created by the nature of cultural reflection, be it encountered in a gallery, museum, or public space. The work is mobile: it rests in one site before moving elsewhere, driven by the flow of the international art world, driven by the desire for economic and knowledge capital outside of any artist's control. Each work operates in time as much as it does in space as every presentation leaks into what has come before and what follows in an echo of the production of history.

There Will Be No Miracles Here began its journey in 1998 when Coley created a series of posters of appropriated signs, presenting plain black text with red emphases: "The village and surrounding heathland *is* private property"; "Persons creating a noise or disturbance in or near this public street are guilty of *a misdemeanour* and are likely to a fine and imprisonment"; "There will be *no miracles* here. *By order of the King*." When first shown in a gallery, photographs of the posters in public sites were accompanied by a voice speaking these admonishments that offer unspecific threats. Why *is* and not *are*? What is a *miracle* and who is *the King* to abolish them? What is a *misdemeanor*? It depends on the circumstances, on what has been deemed correct conduct. Jean-Luc Nancy makes an important distinction between "politics" and "the political": the former is the administration of the latter, which consists on a dissensual gathering of individual positions.[2] It is in this realm of the social that Coley's sculptures unpack the bureaucracies of politics. Like the word belief, these phrases are charged terms that have power without qualification. The former phrases are familiar, an ungrammatical formal legal language that appears in sites where trouble, whatever that may be, is expected. Perhaps outside a late night bar, or on a street corner—the sign, perversely, inviting misdemeanors because it is expected.

The architectural historian Mark Cousins relayed the third phrase to Coley. His anecdote, repeated and warped in retellings, describes how this text appeared on a sign in a mediaeval French village named Modseine, following a period of inexplicable mass hysteria. In an attempt to assert control, the conduct was named "miracle" by local administrative powers. Once classified, it could be legislated. Presumably, the illiterate peasants would read this sign and they then complied by curbing their miracles, resulting in the harvest being completed as the unrest ceased. A "miracle" is a word for something unknown within language. A miracle is an effect or extraordinary event in the physical world surpassing known human and natural powers, ascribed to a supernatural cause or a god to rationalize irrationality.

This open and consistent concern with the encounter between objects and language opens the door to two useful references for considering Coley's wider artistic practice. First, the artist Lawrence Weiner, who understands art as an examination of "the relationship of human beings to objects and objects to objects in relation to human beings."[3] We make objects to try and find a place in the world—objects make life easier, present problems to be solved, embody thought. They are negotiated in the realm of the social. Objects ask questions of other objects that have already become familiar. Weiner's and Coley's work is profoundly sculptural, interactive, and material. Metaphor has no place; as Weiner states in the 2007 short film *Turning Some Pages*: "Art is not a metaphor upon the relationship of human beings to objects and objects to objects in relation to human beings, but a representation of an empirical existing fact. The world needs to be re-presented to make it mystical, unknown, and outside the taming properties of language. It does not need to stand for anything that it is not already, as it is complicated enough by itself."

To talk of objects in the context of belief evokes the nineteenth-century philosopher Ludwig Feuerbach, particularly his 1841 treatise *The Essence of Christianity,* a humanist study of why we have the desire to believe. Religion is a sphere of belief Coley frequently addresses. *Fear of Death (for Bertrand Russell)* (2009) consists of a series of denuded larch trunks, standing nearly two and half meters high, painted rust red. The titular reference is to a talk, subsequently distributed in a pamphlet, by Bertrand Russell in 1927, delivered under the auspices of the National Secular Society that concludes with the statement: "religion is based, I think, primarily and mainly upon fear." Around each tree a phrase had been hammered into the surface, giving reasons why humans turn to religion: "Fear of Death"; "Fear of Defeat"; "Fear of the Mysterious." Larches are often founds in cemeteries, a site where language, memory, and belief intersect.

Feuerbach notes that above all other animals, humans possess self-consciousness. This quality is enabled through acts of perception, "the ability to distinguish one sensuous object from another."[4] Through this, "man becomes conscious of himself through the object that reflects his seeing; man's self-consciousness is his consciousness of the object."[5] Perception involves a reflection *on* and production *of* values, producing what Feuerbach calls a "species consciousness" that gives humans an understanding of the infinite, bringing with it an admission of personal fallibility. The ideal being in this scheme holds qualities of wisdom, rationality, love, and benevolence as the highest ambition. Feuerbach suggests religion fulfills human needs by suggesting that human desires for an ideal can be realized, with the notion of a Christian god based on the outward projection of man's inward nature, a fluid ever-shifting definition. Religion, he asserts, changes as human life does—the building of temples mirrors the concept of the home, for example. In his 1843 "Preface to the Second Edition" of *The Essence of Christianity,* Feuerbach states that religion was out of step with his experience of the modern world. God had become superhuman, removed from daily life and distanced from the actual practice of being human: "Christianity has in fact long vanished, not only from the reason but from the life of mankind, that it is nothing more than a *fixed idea,* in flagrant contradiction with our fire and life assurance companies, our railroads and steam-carriages, our picture and sculpture galleries, our military and industrial schools, our theatres and scientific museums."[6]

As the world sped up, industry and culture could provide the feeling of the infinite; belief moved from God to somewhere else. Both Weiner's and Feuerbach's meditations on the object locate it in the realm of the social.

Sculptors traditionally make work by removing or adding: carving into block, building up from dust. Coley does both. *Unnamed* from 2012 folds language, emotion, site, and memory into sculpture. A collection of re-cycled headstones sit in the gallery, propped just above the floor using ready-at-hand building materials—recently, in Vancouver, standard two-by-four red cedar blocks, while in London lacquered steel sections of a similar size. The names of those to whom these stones belong have been taken away. All that is left are dates and sentiments. Some die young, others old; some in circumstances known to history, others pass unconnected to world events. My dear husband; forever in our hearts; in loving memory. What does it mean to bury a daughter or a prisoner of war. To think of it is enough to pull tears. How can one find the words to express a loss? It is impossible, any activation of regret is a platitude, and any platitude can be an emotional trigger—sometimes actual, other times projected as we test out what it might feel to experience loss. Gathered together with no names, these stones become civic rather than personal.

In a three-part series of altered photographs, Coley again addressed memory though reduction. Color removed, the images appear to be of another time. All were taken by the artist while traveling for other reasons than specifically making this work; rather like the aforementioned anecdote collection while half-listening to the radio, distraction enables an unconscious gathering of material. *The Honour Series* (2012) captures figures protesting or celebrating in an urban environment, gold leaf applied to remove specific allegiances written on handmade placards and banners. The shapes of these signs are, in another work titled *Choir* (2012), formed into a mass of white abstract sculptures, sized to be held in the hand and displayed sitting on a table covered with a flattened cardboard box. In a sister project, *The Honours Series* (2012), the volumes of statues in cityscapes are, in a vertical figure-ground exercise, filled with gold, while around them they are ignored—in one by a man on a mobile phone, in another overlooked while another sculpture gains attention.

Familiarity creates disappearance. In these protests or examples of civic commemoration, speeches and memorial gestures are made to a disinterested or absent crowd. A lack of knowledge leads to projection that this must be happening in an elsewhere—another time when protest meant something, another country where statues were more than park decorations. An event becomes attributed to honor, respect, and privilege so that it can be heard. Civic space is created for its citizens to possess, or at least to believe they do.

A pair of photographs of the Square of the Three Powers in Brasília taken by Coley, while making the artist book *Urban / Wild*,[7] stayed pinned up in his studio for seven years before becoming the work *The Square of the Three Powers* (2011). In Coley's reworking, the sky in one image has been

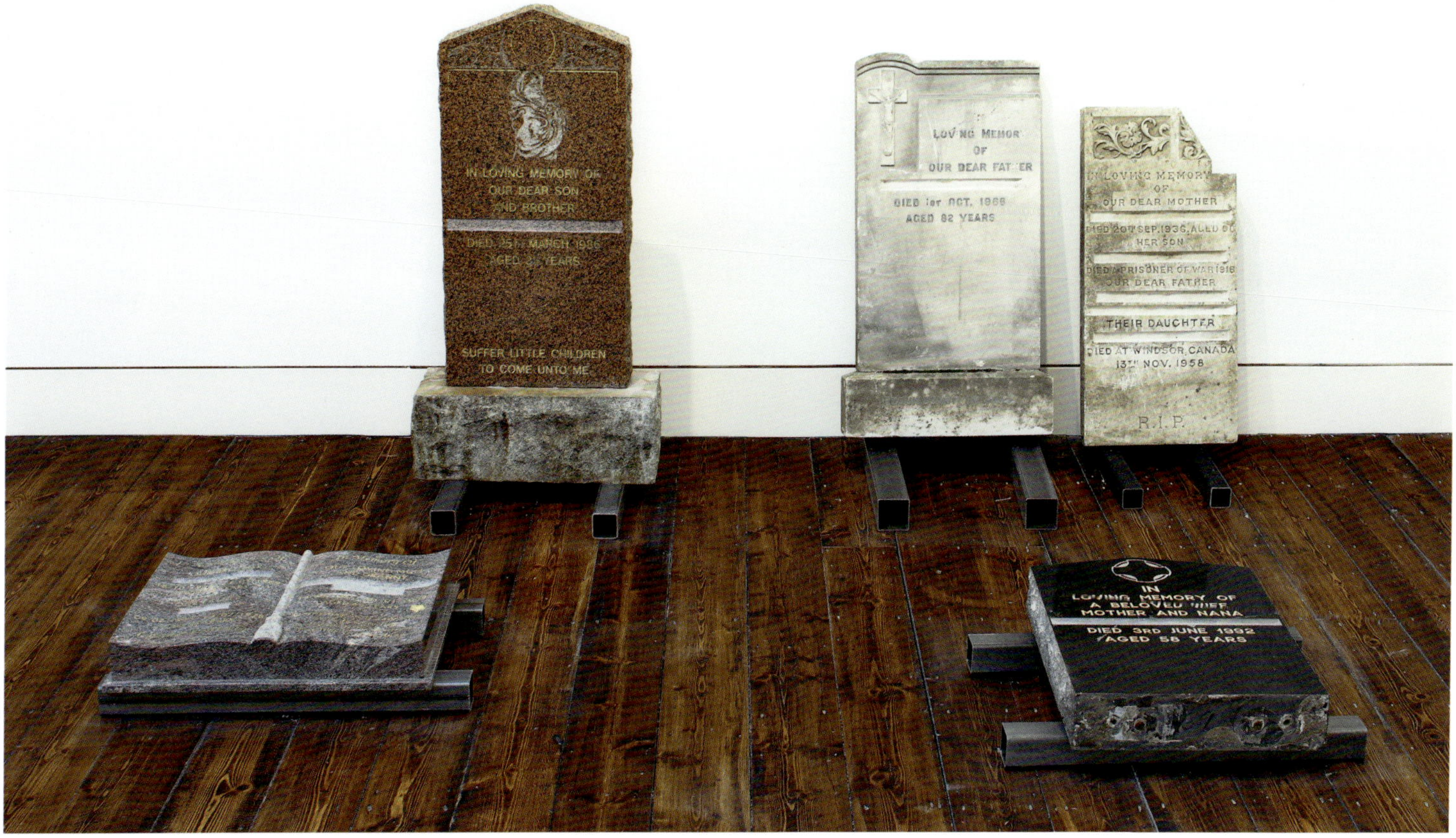

Unnamed, 2012
Installation, Haunch of Venison, London

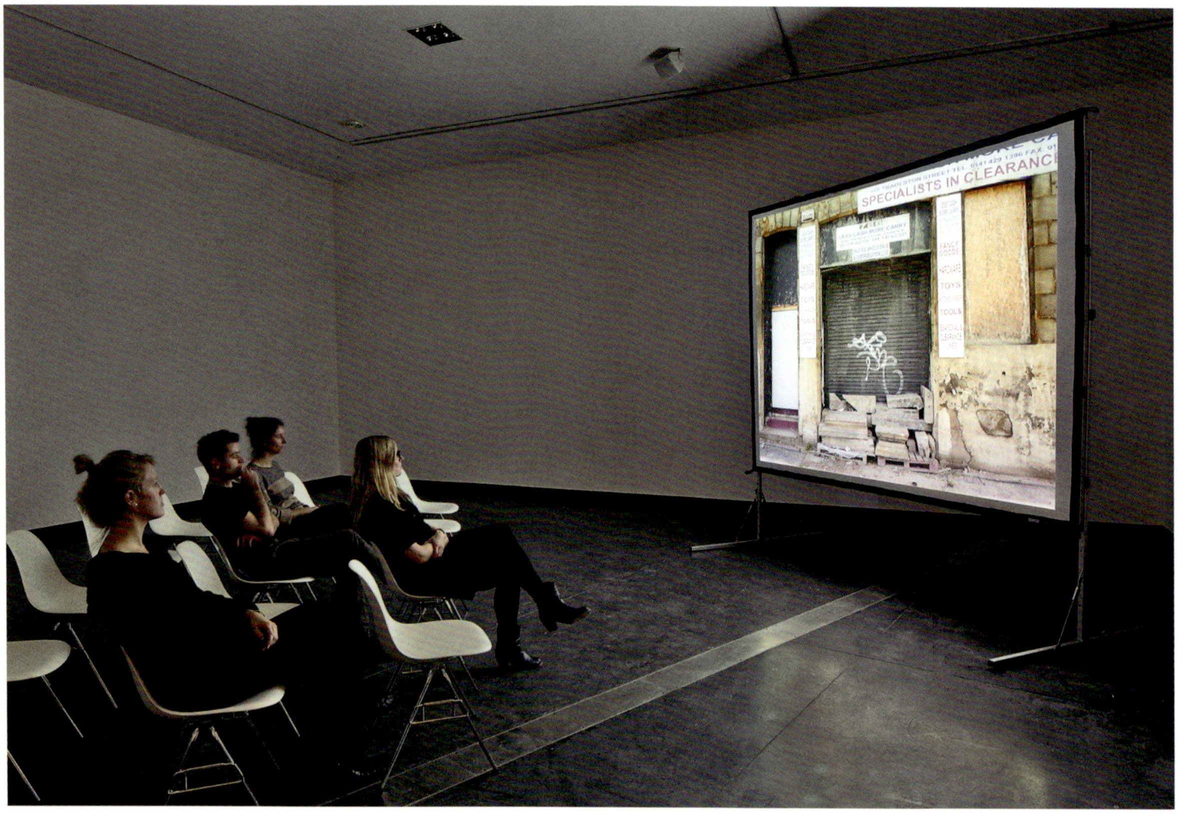

filled with gold leaf while a trio looks upward and a man sits alone staring into space. This site and its surrounding administrative buildings were among the first public spaces completed for the inauguration of the new Brazilian capital in 1960, designed by Oscar Niemeyer to hold literally and symbolically the power of the legislature, judiciary, and the executive. Four steps lead to an elevated platform in the center, an invitation to speak and to listen, the basis of political exchange, as it is for tourists and office workers to gather and sit for lunch. Coley himself created a platform a year later, *Bandstand* (2012). This permanent sculpture in Rieselfeld, Germany too has four steps, this time with a built-in backdrop, a screen to block out the landscape and fill the field of vision with the potential performance. Both *Bandstand* and *The Square of the Three Powers* invite public declarations to be imagined, if not made. For speech to hold authority it must be listened to.

Authoritative language is consumed by the ears as well as by the eyes. Coley uses spoken and written words, as described above in the first iteration of *There Will Be No Miracles Here*. The lecture is a pedagogical convention striving to produce knowledge, but not all words are to be trusted. In her 2008 spoken word performance and album *Homeland,* Laurie Anderson told a tale of a time when she taught an art history evening class on a topic she know nothing about—so she made her own version up. The students learned, but not what they thought. When the "truth" was discovered Anderson was fired. Coley's *Another Lecture* (2011) is a PowerPoint presentation of images of the left-behind parts of Melbourne and Glasgow. Unfinished fences, piled up paving slabs, boarded up buildings awaiting development are the backdrop to a confident voice that, like many practiced public speakers, describes in detail the carefully planned space with an over-familiarity of the spoken words which serve to widen the gap between the dry authority of the rhetoric of city development and the plain facts. Which is fiction, which is to be believed?

In the late nineteen-nineties Coley made four other lecture pieces, these using now obsolete thirty-five millimeter slides. *Lecture* (1996) shows unfinished buildings in Glasgow set to a voice expressing a desire to humanize and beautify the city. *Villa Savoye* (1997) brings together a historical text giving a weighty detailed description of Le Corbusier's masterpiece, with images a world away from the suburban demonstration of the five points of modernist architecture embodied in his Villa Savoye. Instead, it is a different machine for living as that which fills the screen, a Barratt Home, a particular genre of British housing stock that is quick-build, low cost. Not unpleasant, these buildings fulfill the idea of what a home might be and enable a

British desire to have a home, no matter what toll such an economic commitment might play some two decades later. Both lecture sculptures allude to the language of permanent architecture, of a modern wish for a future better than the present, while pointing to the fact that cities rise into ruin rather than fulfill the imagining of a single vision. Cities are tangible products of ideological positions. In design, compromise produces unsatisfactory consensus.

When Coley pays attention to an architectural landscape it is always constructed through a singular gaze, sometimes directed where the buildings meet the ground as one walks through the streets, other times looking up or down at the buildings designed to stretch up to their full height, like enthusiastic children in a schoolroom, urgently wanting to say their piece. Architecture fulfills and produces desires, perhaps most explicitly seen in places of production, power, worship, and memory. *The Lamp of Sacrifice (161 Places of Worship, Birmingham)* (2000) and *The Lamp of Sacrifice (286 Places of Worship, Edinburgh)* (2004) track sites of institutional devotion using the Yellow Pages in two cities—a reference tool nearly as obsolete as the rhythmic sound of the analogue slide lecture. The title points to John Ruskin's 1849 book *The Seven Lamps of Architecture,* the sacrifice in the first chapter being a human dedication to craft as a means of providing a visible proof of love and respect for God. In the following sections, Ruskin outlines the lamps of truth, power, beauty, life, memory, and obedience: all terms that wind their way through Coley's wider artistic practice. These two works consist of models filling the exhibition spaces: a model is an example to reproduce. Coley's, though, reproduce what is already known but not necessarily seen. He makes us look anew.

Palace (2008) is another model, this time a saloon timber façade from the eighteen-seventies, nearly black, and familiar from the genre of Western movies that repeat inaccurate stories of the American Civil War's aftermath. This version of America is one of hard drinking and suppliant women,

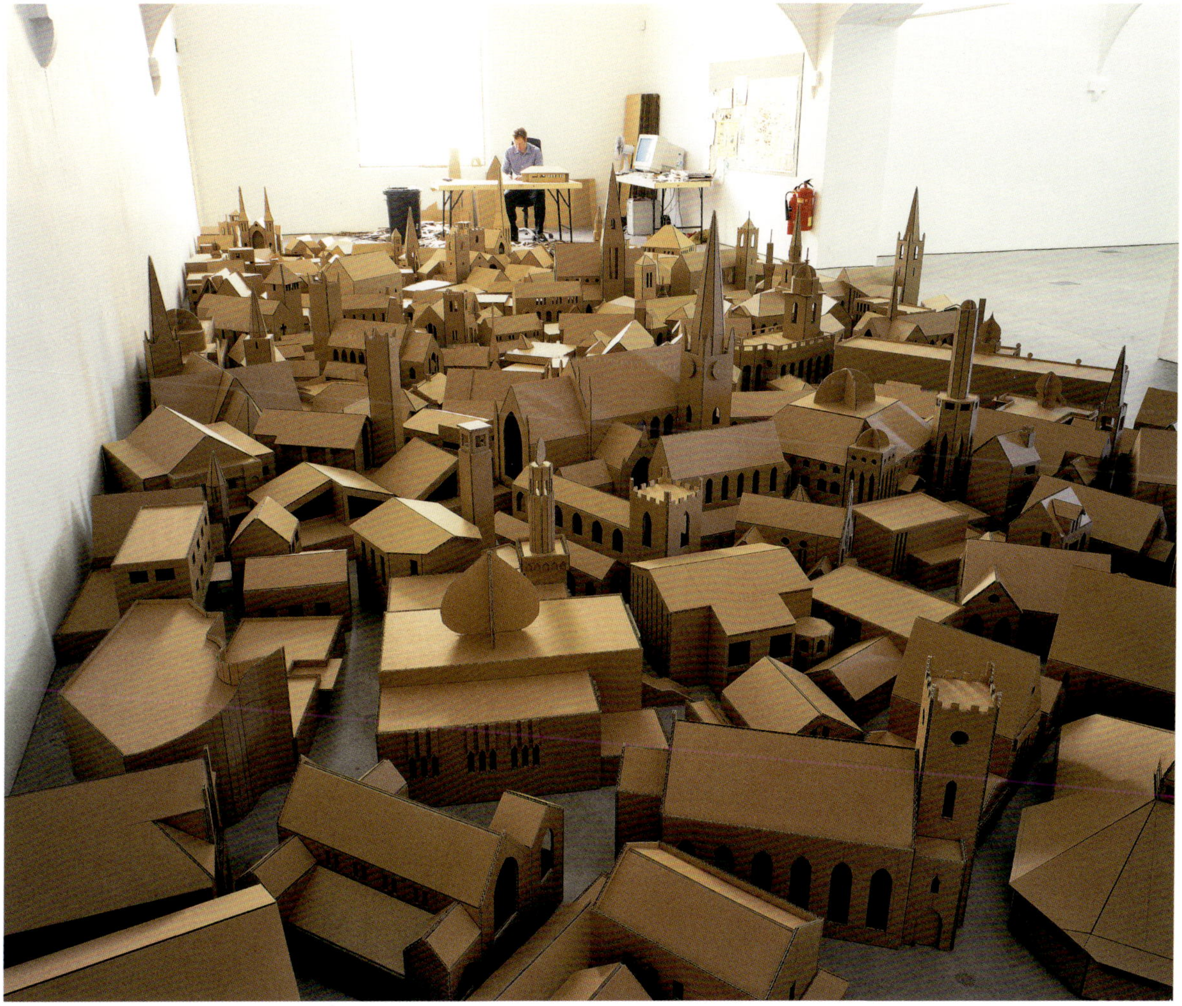

Opposite:
Another Lecture, 2011
Installation, Australian Centre for Contemporary Art, Melbourne

The Lamp of Sacrifice (161 Places of Worship, Birmingham), 2000
Installation, Ikon Gallery, Birmingham

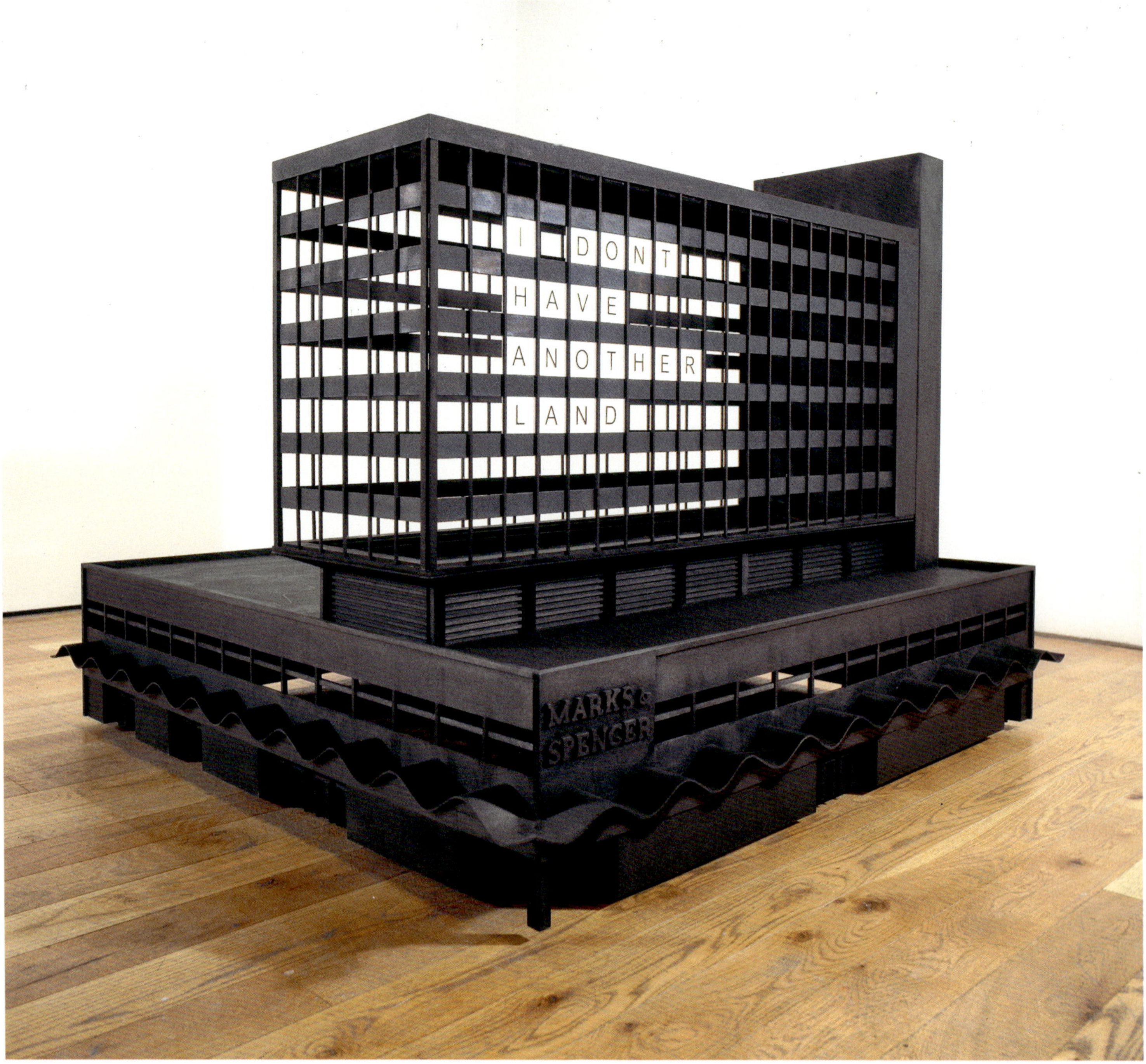

of racist stereotypes and fast running horses, of frontiers and a dysfunctional legal system played out in the saloon. Like a movie set, this sculpture is all façade, propped up like Coley's light-signs. When we see his illuminated signs in photographs the reverse is rarely shown but, like all sculptures, when engaged with fully they need to be seen in the round. Documentation of artwork is only theater, what really matters is the phenomenological encounter.

The encounter with *Palace* is an invitation to walk behind the set and across a platform that reverberates footsteps through this structure. Drilled into it are the words "land," "belief," "wealth," "life," "mind." These are concepts fought over in a search for power and control, often under the auspices of balance and utopian democracy. In form it echoes *I Don't Have Another Land* (2002), this sculpture a model of the Marks & Spencer building in Manchester bombed in 1996

I Don't Have Another Land, 2002
Stained wood and mixed media
130 × 160 × 160 cm
Collection of The New Art Gallery Walsall

by the IRA. Like *Palace* it holds a text, in this case fitted into a grid of windows rather like contemporary signs offering offices and parking spaces for cheap in empty buildings. The phrase "I don't have another land" is another found example of language by Coley, an utterance in common usage, seen written on a wall in the Occupied Territories. How is the statement understood? It depends on the position of the reader. As the Manchester bombing recedes into history, other struggles over land thefts, rarely mentioned, raise their hands. Coley is not suggesting a position, rather transposing a specific struggle on to another—the values are waiting to be made by the reader as the specific becomes opened out into the general to be snapped into whatever place one chooses.

If the first decade of the twenty-first century was the time of the "whatever," the teens are chasing doubt and failure as something to hold on to. A study of the methods of narrating the experience of the present issues a license to cut through assumptions. The general notion that this is an age where agnosticism is the primary position cannot be true as belief is found everywhere. It is hard to believe in revolution, in capitalism, communism, the church, the government. Yet, there is still belief in taking a position. Belief in failure may not be a rosy future; however, the consensual notion that "we are all doomed" has comforting warmth that makes the future, perversely, seem safer. This is not an era when all is thrown out of the window and hedonism prevails—that would be a retrogressive position out of step with the now—it is a time to examine what possibly might drive us to believe. It is impossibility that makes Coley's work so consistently pertinent for the present.

---

[1] Frances Colpitt, "Between two Worlds: John McCracken," *Art in America* (April 1998).
[2] Jean-Luc Nancy, *The Inoperative Community* (Minneapolis, 1991).
[3] Gerti Fietzek and Gregor Stemmrich, eds., *Having Been Said: Writings & Interviews of Lawrence Weiner 1968–2003* (Ostfildern, 2005), p. 123.
[4] Ludwig Feuerbach, "Introduction to The Essence of Christianity," in *The Fiery Brook: Selected Writings*, trans. Zawar Hanfi (London, 2013), p. 97.
[5] Ibid., p. 101.
[6] Ludwig Feuerbach, "Preface to the Second Edition," *The Essence of Christianity*, trans. George Eliot (Oxford, 1881).
[7] Nathan Coley, *Urban / Wild* (London, 2004).

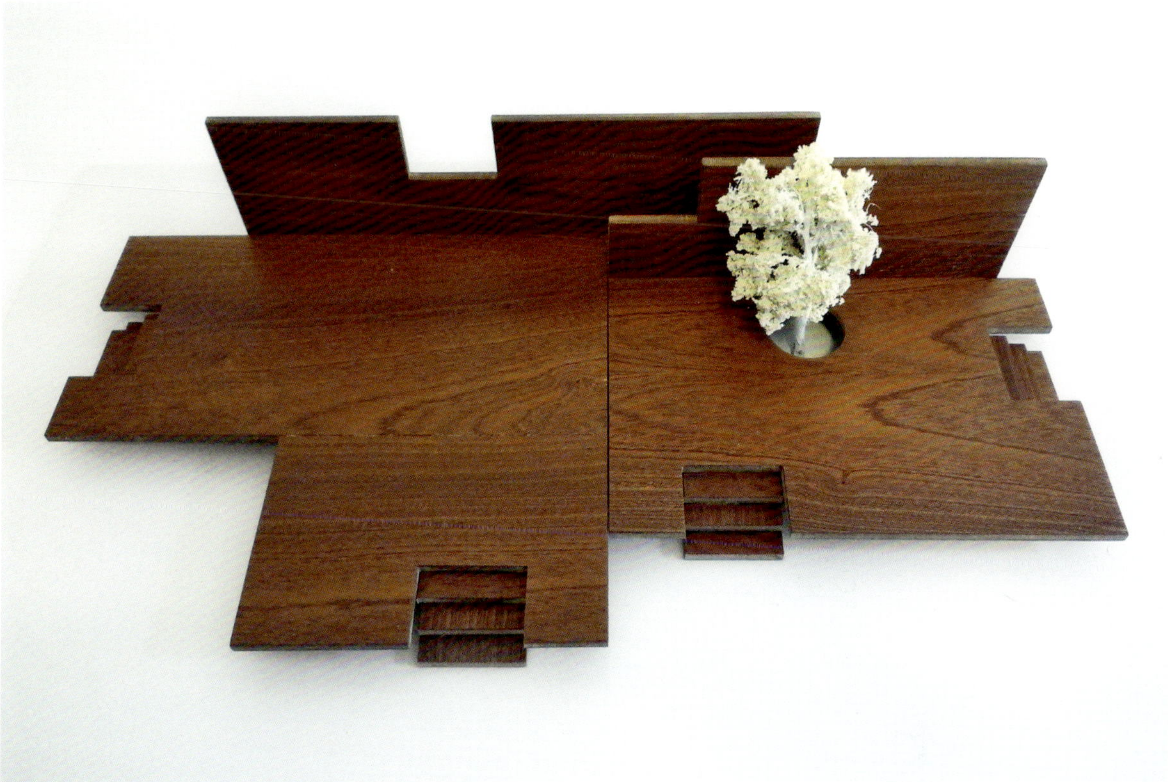

Bandstand (model), 2012
Plywood and mixed media
14 × 44 × 26 cm

Selected Works

Bandstand / Untitled (Cardboard Wall Sculpture)

From Abstraction to Allusion: Nathan Coley's Bandstand

Bandstand consists of a monolithic piece of concrete, poured on site, whose surfaces create a particular spatial arrangement. In front of two parallel, overlapping, and room-high vertical walls, a horizontal surface "hovers" approximately forty centimeters above the ground. It is composed of two rectangles of about the same size as well as a smaller one, which are all placed together to create a single orthogonal shape with protruding and receding elements. At the front and on each side, the surface can be accessed by a set of four concrete steps, which are set into the horizontal plane. Another set of steps are found at the rear and leads in between the two back walls running across the surface, set apart from each other but overlapping at roughly the middle of the raised platform. To a viewer standing in front of the sculpture, these two back walls, the front one shorter than the back one, form a single plane, whose smooth surface bears the rhythmic vertical markings of the structure's casting joints.

The artist placed the sculpture at the narrow back end of an elongated area of greenery, set against a row of trees located a short distance behind it and bordering the park. On the other side of the park, across from the row of trees, is a foot and bicycle path, which runs parallel to the town's main tram line. Fruit trees stand at irregular intervals on the grassy area.

In the center of the sculpture, protruding through a circular hole in the concrete slab, another tree stands. One wonders whether it was already growing there before the sculpture was created around it. In any case, through this tree, the sculpture is rooted to the piece of land on which it stands and thus also to the landscape.

Bandstand produces a multi-dimensional frame of references, opening up the possibility of critically reflecting the historical precedents of the sculpture. The work makes direct reference to an existing piece of architecture Coley came across whilst visiting Brasília in 2004, a fifty-square-meter concrete platform hovering in the city's Square of the Three Powers. Probably poured in the nineteen-fifties, Coley photographed this "landing" along with the few lingering people who were viewing it.

This hovering surface in Brasília is constituted by the formal language corresponding to the architecture of Oscar

---

Bandstand, 2012
Poured concrete and apple tree
3 × 15.5 × 7.9 m
Permanent sculpture, Rieselfeld, Freiburg
Commissioned by the City of Freiburg im Breisgau

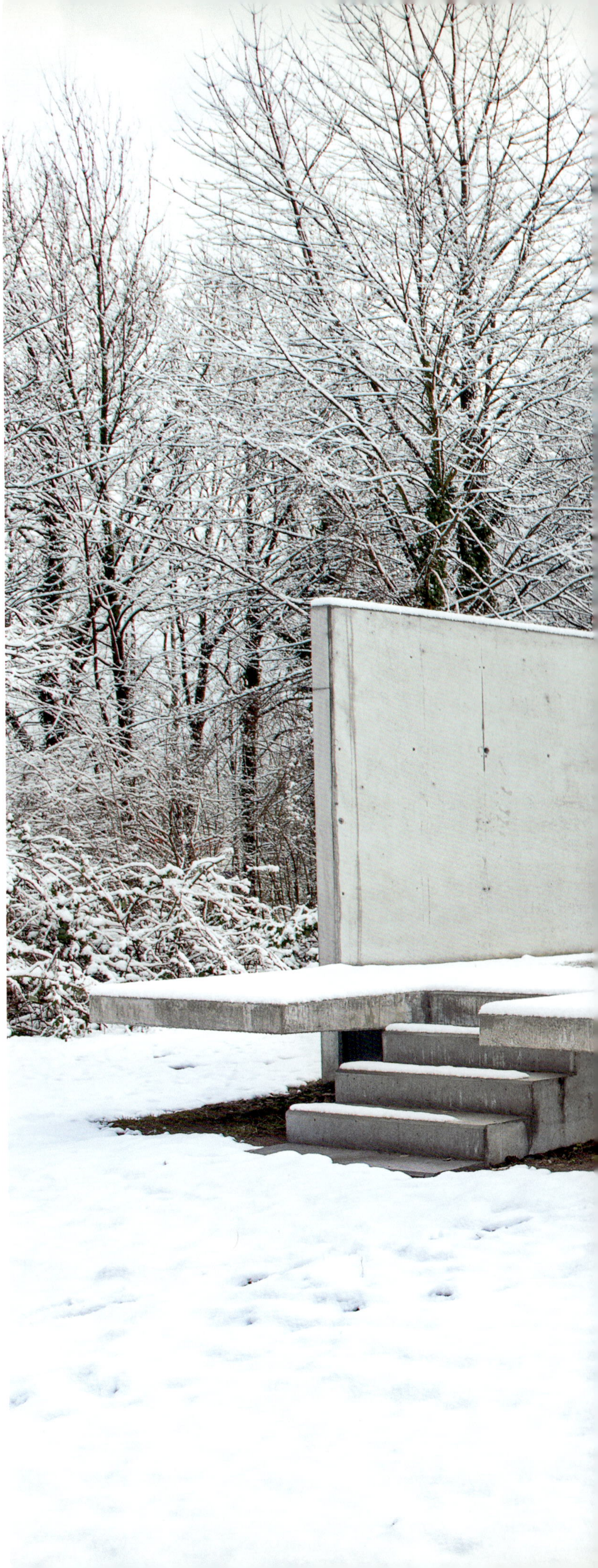

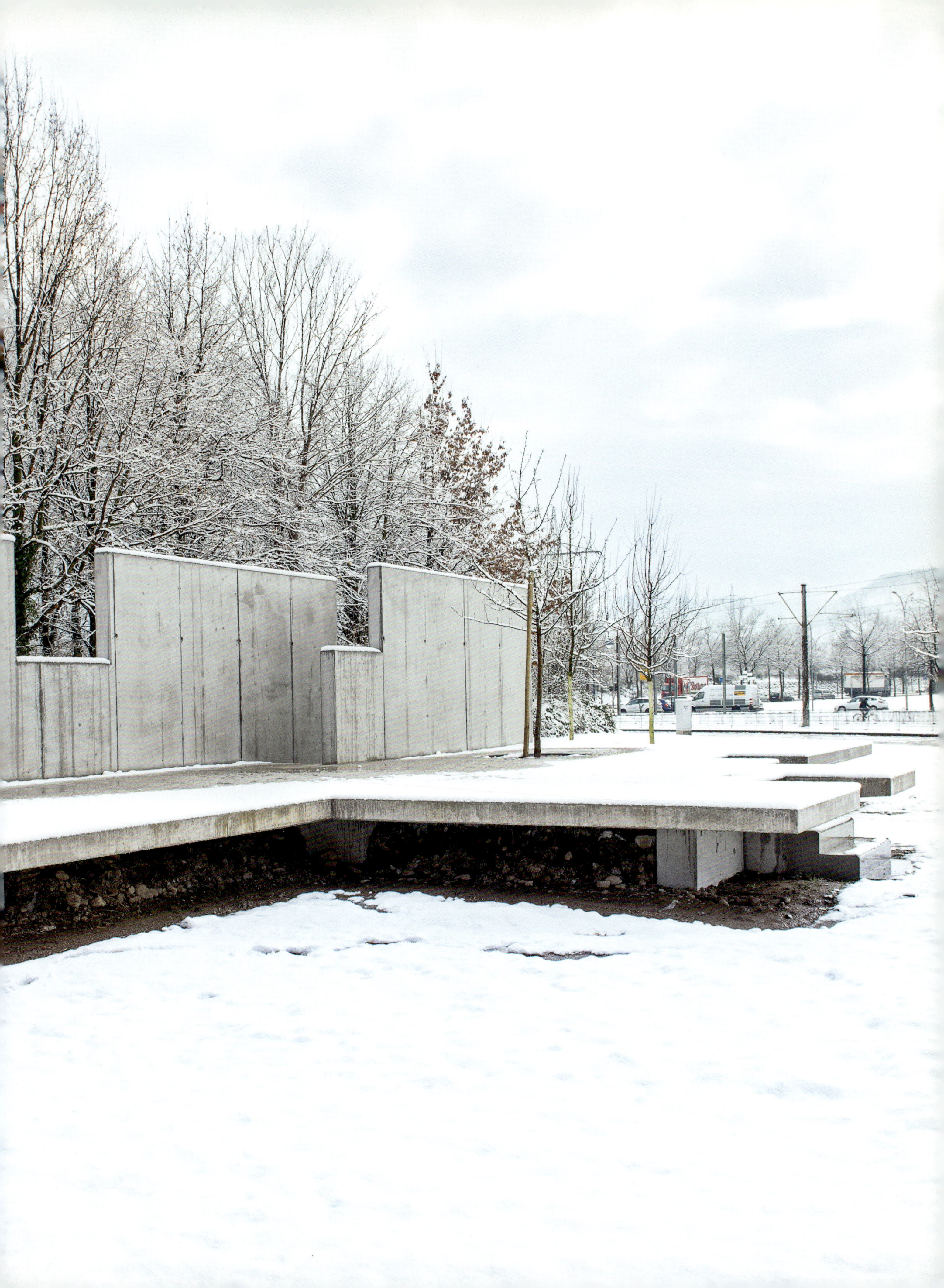

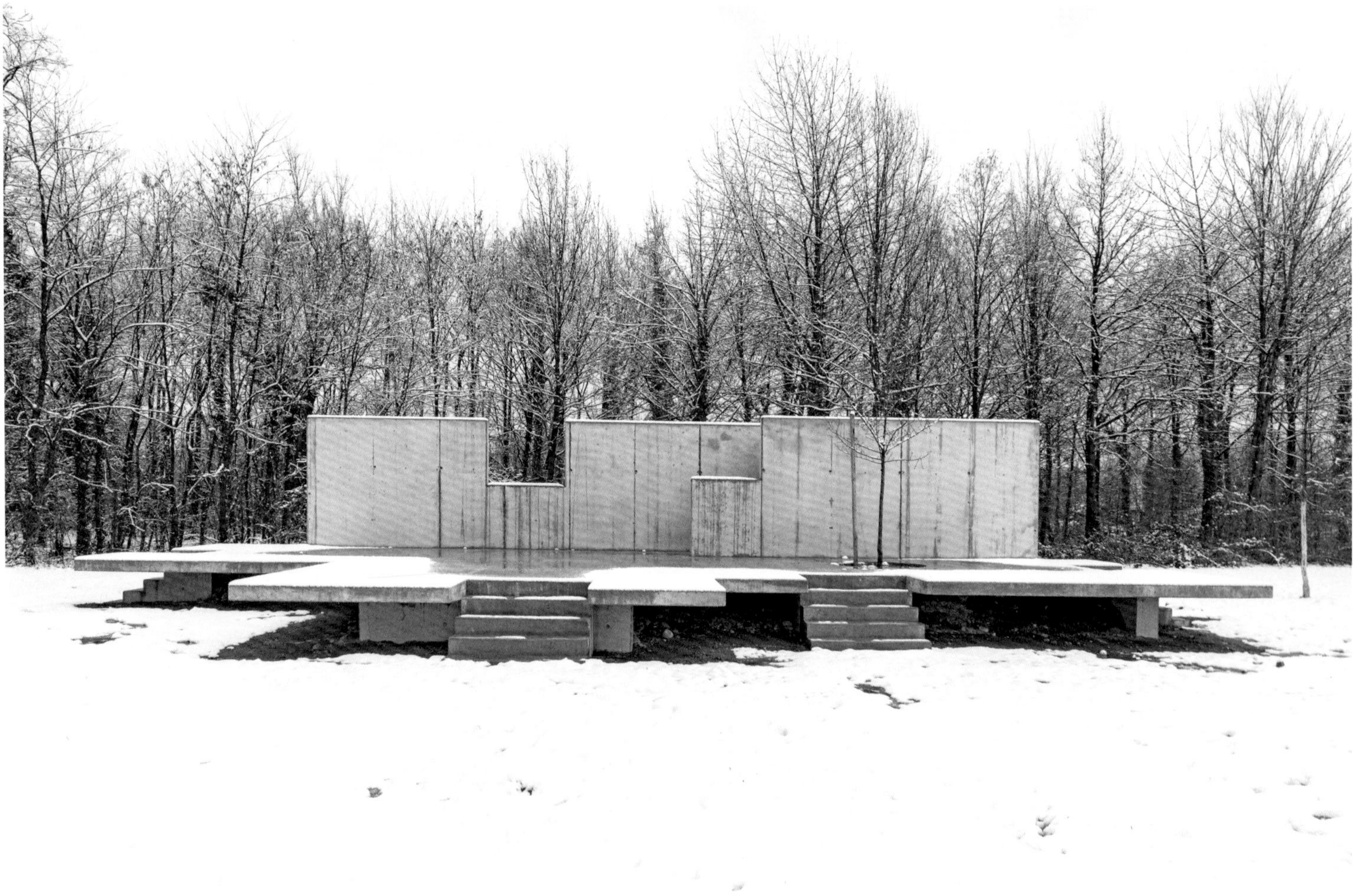

Niemeyer. His expressive, futuristic reinforced concrete constructions definitively shaped the aesthetic of the public buildings and squares of Brasília in the nineteen-fifties and sixties, one of the heydays of modernism. Like the structure in Brasília, *Bandstand* has the quality of being perceived as an aesthetic work of art while simultaneously being usable. Or its usability is not overtly expressed, since it has been placed in an insignificant park area beside one of the city's main thoroughfares, a place where people pass through and don't spend much time. This is less suggestive of a function than the elevated cement platform on an urban square in the middle of the Brazilian capital. In addition, the vertical surfaces of *Bandstand,* which are absent on the object in Brasília, lend Coley's piece a sculptural rather than functional dimension. The two works are undoubtedly different to the extent that the surface in Brasília is a relic from the epoch of modernism, while *Bandstand* in contrast functions as a sign that points to this past.

The capacity of *Bandstand* to take up and recall a specific work from a bygone era stands in clear opposition to its formalistic sculptural language. This is due to the fact that in terms of the use of this formalistic language there is an obvious difference between explicitly incorporating modernism into a work and using a work to establish a specific reference to an epoch. Reworking the Brazilian original and creating it in another form, even if altered, is fundamentally antithetical to the original aims of modernist abstraction, which serves as the conceptual foundation of *Bandstand*. From the nineteen-nineties into the early years of the twenty-first century, young European artists who became well-known in this period often explicitly referred to works of modernism and reinterpreted the premises and process of this epoch in different ways. The work of Nathan Coley is characteristic of this generation, whose works portray the legacy of modernism through an abstracted formalism and thus comment on modernism itself. Such an approach makes evident the gap in time and the shift in underlying concepts and ideals. Since the nineteen-nineties, abstraction no longer has the connotations it once held—instead it has been carried over into a referential function.

In *Bandstand,* the ambivalence of formalistic abstraction and representation (in terms of the physical similarity with the hovering platform in Brasília) is obscured; in a figurative sense this obscuration means that both form the base and the window at the same time, and this is what defines this work. The formal aesthetic of the sculpture is both opaque and transparent. Coley supplemented the sculpture that he happened to discover in Brasília through the specific local context of his *Bandstand.* Located on the outskirts of Freiburg, Rieselfeld is a young neighborhood, largely inhabited by families and was built in the nineteen-nineties. The last phase of construction coincided with the erection of the artist's sculpture. The concrete shells of the buildings that were built here strongly resemble the vertical components of the work, giving the impression that *Bandstand* is incomplete. In this context, the indicated window opening in the left back wall seems to be symbolic. It is not only a presumed quotation from the new buildings that are being constructed around it, but also offers a view through the otherwise non-transparent concrete surface to the row of trees behind it. The opening penetrates the robust material and thus serves as a conceptual statement. As if one could look through the work into other eras, the opening formally offers passage into the past and to another place (such as South America), while also offering an open view of the immediate surroundings in this young neighborhood.

With the English title *Bandstand,* another conceptual element comes into play, which points toward Coley's native country—Great Britain. Seen today, these bandstands have deeper roots in the culture of Great Britain than that of Germany. This form of concert pavilion came into fashion in the Victorian era and can be found in many public parks as a remnant of the period. As a rule they take the form of a narrow and high tent, have a roof, and often have a decorative wrought-iron railing running along the edge of the elevated platform. The only thing that a concert pavilion

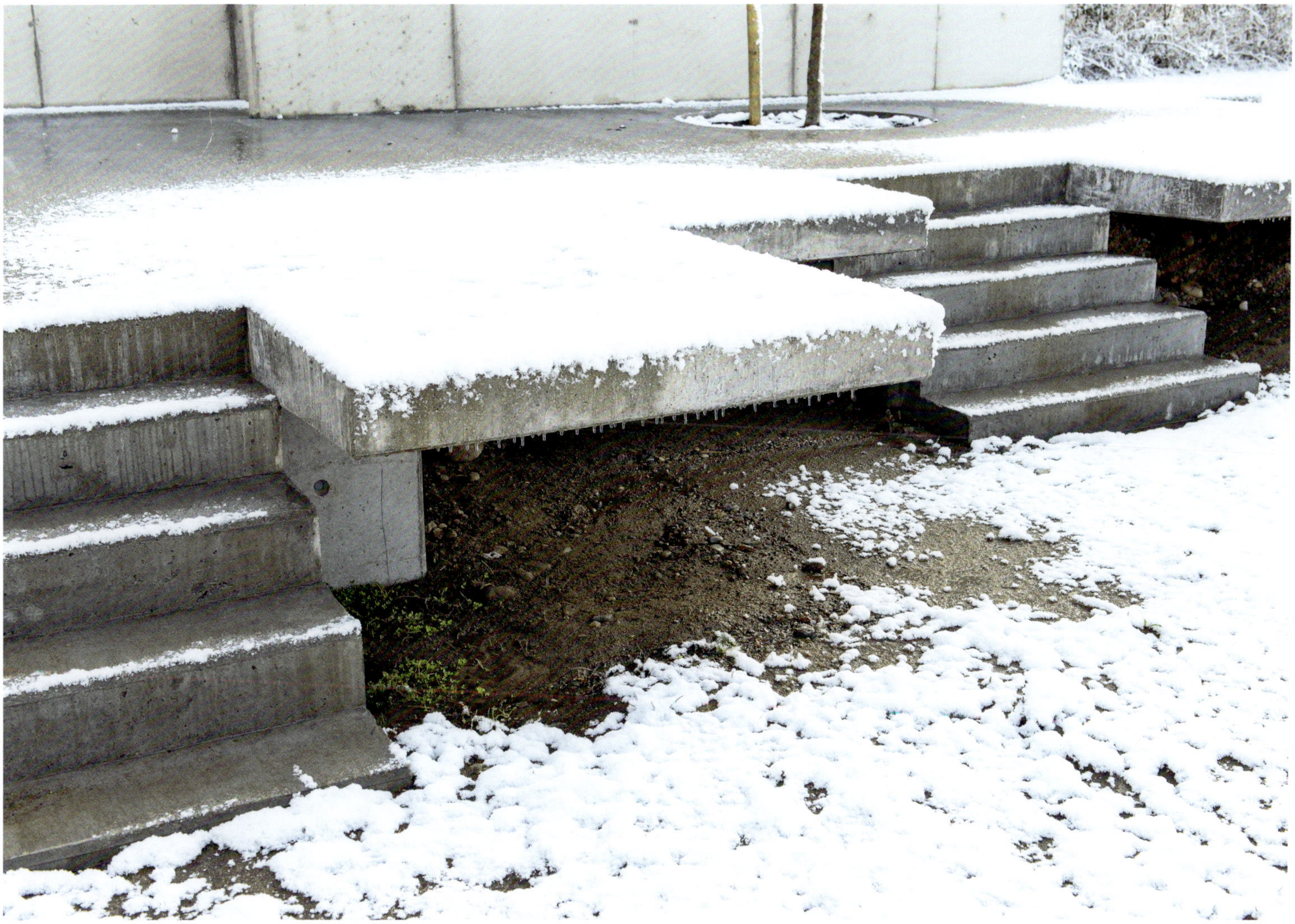

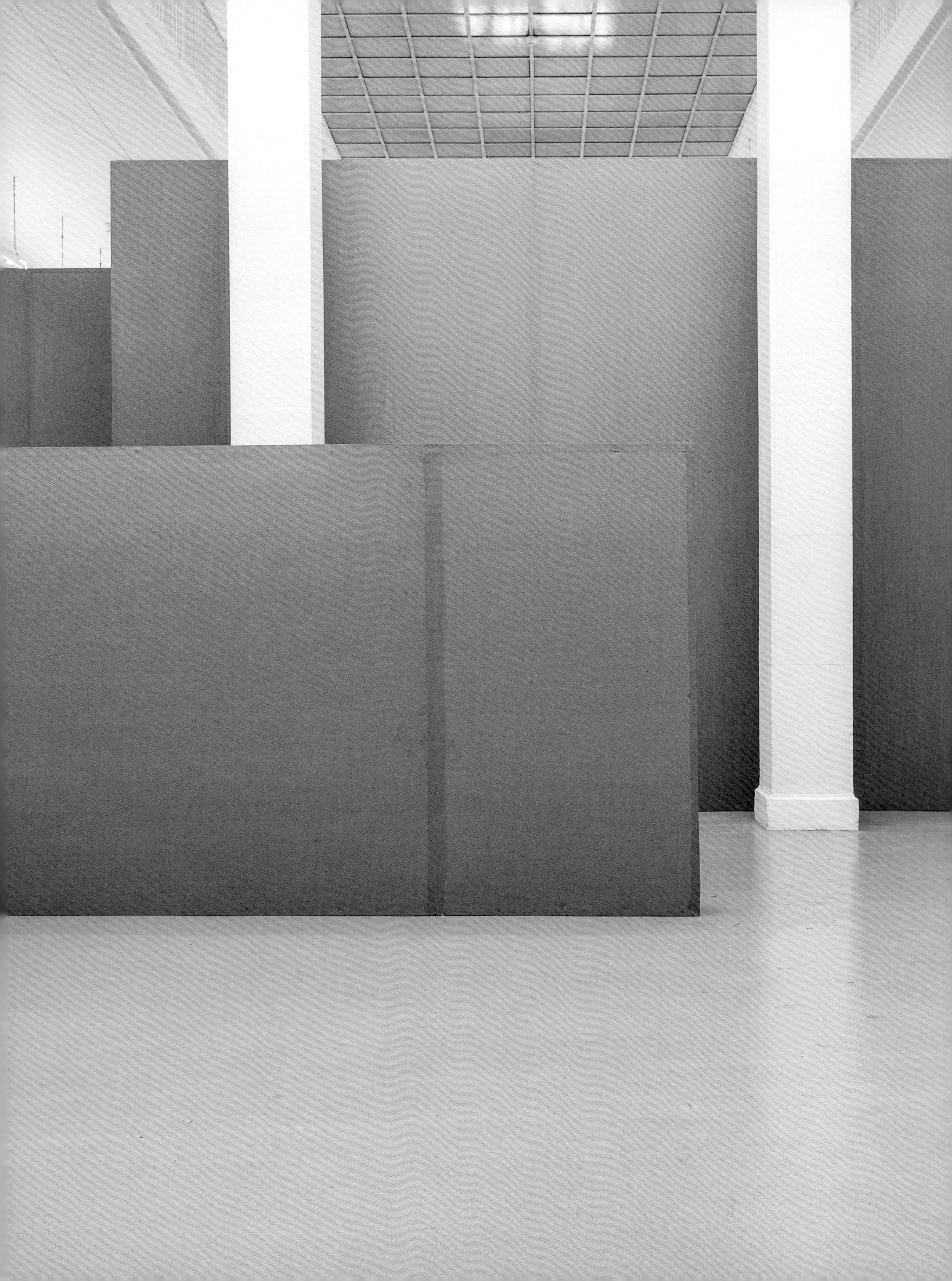

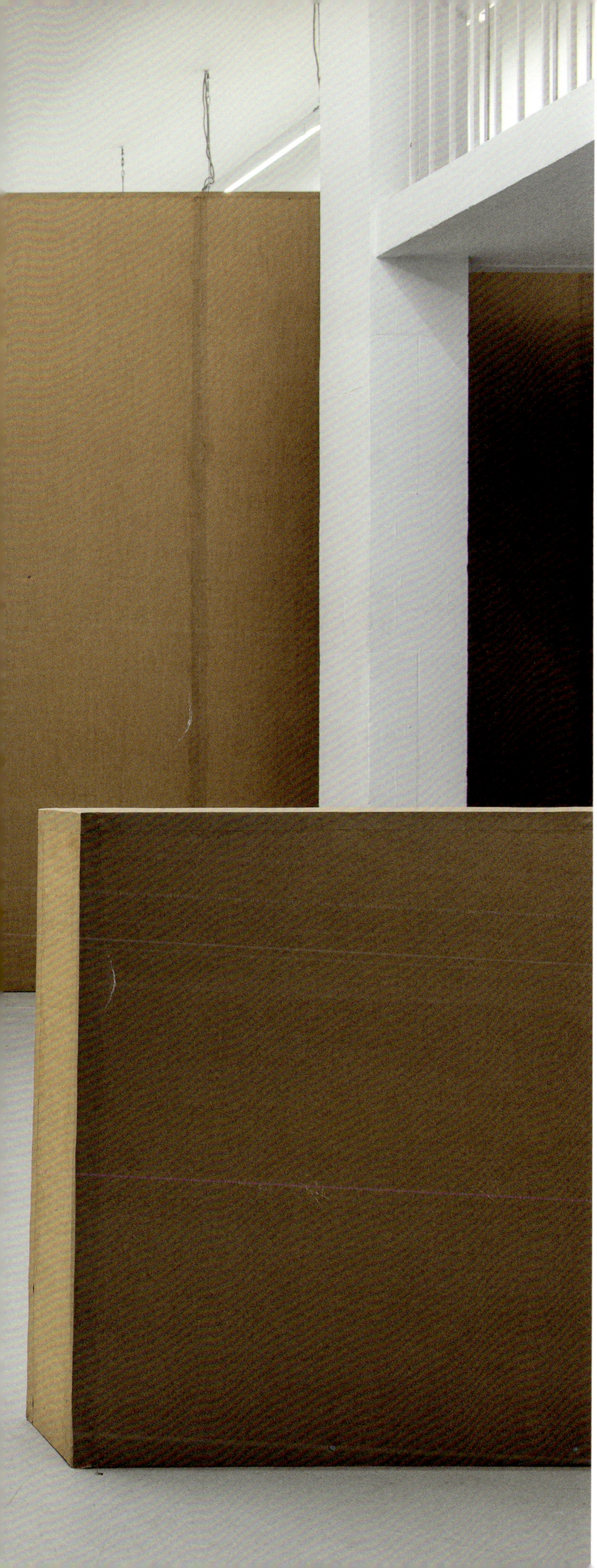

and the sculptures in Brasília and Rieselfeld share is that all are communal platforms, which anyone can access. On the weekends and holidays, concerts used to take place on these bandstands. They were also often the place of political gatherings, meetings, and demonstrations, recalling the Speakers' Corner in Hyde Park in London. Although they are used less today, they are perceived as relics of another time instead of sculptures. Coley's *Bandstand* does not make reference to this structure through its composition but only through its title. Due to the artist's conceptual approach, *Bandstand* has a global scope as it incorporates references from South America and Great Britain as well as allusions to other countries and cultures. In the process, no specific country is represented; the artist brings this distant place into a site-specific work for Rieselfeld.

For the period of Nathan Coley's solo exhibition at Kunstverein Freiburg in the spring of 2013, these various referential trajectories were supplemented by an additional location, the building of the Kunstverein—a distance of just under six kilometers from the suburb of Rieselfeld to the exhibition space on the edge of Freiburg's city center. The exhibition was developed in association with *Bandstand*. The gaze of the viewer—which normally passes from the five-meter-high anteroom and down the full length of the large, simple exhibition hall framed by an upper gallery and topped with a continuous glass at a height of eight meters—was obstructed by Coley's installation *Untitled (Cardboard Wall Sculpture)* (2013). Designed for the entry area, this multi-part work at first gave the impression of a single wall made out of large-format sheets of cardboard. However, the individual freestanding wall components were placed against the side walls of the foyer so as to offer a meandering path into the main gallery space. Three of these walls, which were placed one behind the other and staggered in height, were of similar proportion. The vertical rhythm created by the large sheets of cardboard created a similar effect as the vertical surfaces of *Bandstand*. In particular, the roughness of the brown packing material used for the walls in the gallery corresponded in its quality as an everyday and untreated material to concrete that is exposed to the open sky. In this manner, the elements of the installation made direct reference, both formally and aesthetically, to the sculpture in Rieselfeld.

In addition, the installation confronted the viewer with similar ambiguity, which leads to a dialectic of pure aesthetic observation and functionality, as in *Bandstand*. The functional aspect was manifested in the cardboard wall element that was constructed to protrude furthest into the hall and was shaped like a reversed "L" of which the longest side was placed just in front of the right side wall of the gallery. Hung on this surface were two collages, *The Square of the Three*

Powers (East) (2011) and *The Square of the Three Powers* (West) (2011), framed black-and-white photographs that Coley himself had taken of the sculpture in the Square of the Three Powers during his visit to Brasília. On both photographs he covered and thus obscured certain elements of the image with gold leaf. By installing these works on the final wall element of the installation, the cardboard wall sculpture "slipped" into acting as exhibition architecture similar to temporary partition walls. This arrangement is similar to the way in which the single planted fruit tree vibrates within the poured concrete sculpture of *Bandstand* in Rieselfeld, cementing the object to the landscape and surroundings. In this sense, a functional approach is asserted in both works of art.

The collages are comparable to windows; they permit a view through the otherwise opaque cardboard walls and to another place—a visual device that is repeated in the opening in the left back wall of *Bandstand*. Here the use of gold leaf could be interpreted as a quote from the Middle Ages or early Renaissance. On an immaterial level it could be seen as an opening of the self to another time or as a means of hiding information—contrary interpretations of the kind that repeatedly appear in Coley's work. The link to the square in Brasília occurs directly through the photographs in the exhibition, since they show two views of the monument in the city. In contrast to *Bandstand* this connection is an associative one, since the allusion to the object is integrated into the structure as a citation but is not immediately apparent as an image.

Coming from the relatively narrow and dark passageway at the entrance as part of *Untitled (Cardboard Wall Sculpture),* visitors are initially drawn into the installation and then, after a meandering path, reach the last, long wall in order to be let out into the brightly illuminated exhibition hall. The last segment of wall extends a bit further and then opens up into a light-infused hall, where Coley's sculpture *A Place Beyond Belief* (2011) occupies the back end wall and encompasses the full height of the space. The light sculpture essentially consists of three lines of text that seem to be floating in space. The phrase is written in large letters composed of dots of LED lamps, which further underscore the abstract nature of the letters. The three lines of text were mounted onto the framework of five-meter-high scaffolding. On a conceptual level, this work includes all the aspects of the dynamic driving the content of *Bandstand* as well as references or allusions cloaked in abstraction. The direct meaning of the words originally heard by Coley in a radio report on September 11, 2001 in New York can suggest an interpretation meaning a place that evades the imagination or a concept of plausibility or possibly just the opposite, a place where both definitively exist.

Through the collages, the concrete sculpture in Brazil, and ultimately through the title *Bandstand,* Coley also adheres to the theme of referring to other places in *A Place Beyond Belief*. Like many of his works, this sculpture offers a possibility to reflect on various allusions in a work of art. Common to the other arenas that Coley refers to in his works is that they can be considered public space: highly frequented places, areas that people move through; places that imply a range of different cultural exchanges. The conceptual and formal language of his works directly relies on the original references, which, however, remain remote. Correspondingly, Coley's works are never completely assimilated into their surrounding context—whether this is the exhibition space in which *A Place Beyond Belief* shiningly asserts itself, the institutional architecture in which *Untitled (Cardboard Wall Sculpture)* is placed, or the area where *Bandstand* is situated, whereby each of his works retains its own critical autonomy.

— *Caroline Käding*

Untitled (Cardboard Wall Sculpture), 2013
Cardboard and timber
Dimensions variable
Installation, Kunstverein Freiburg

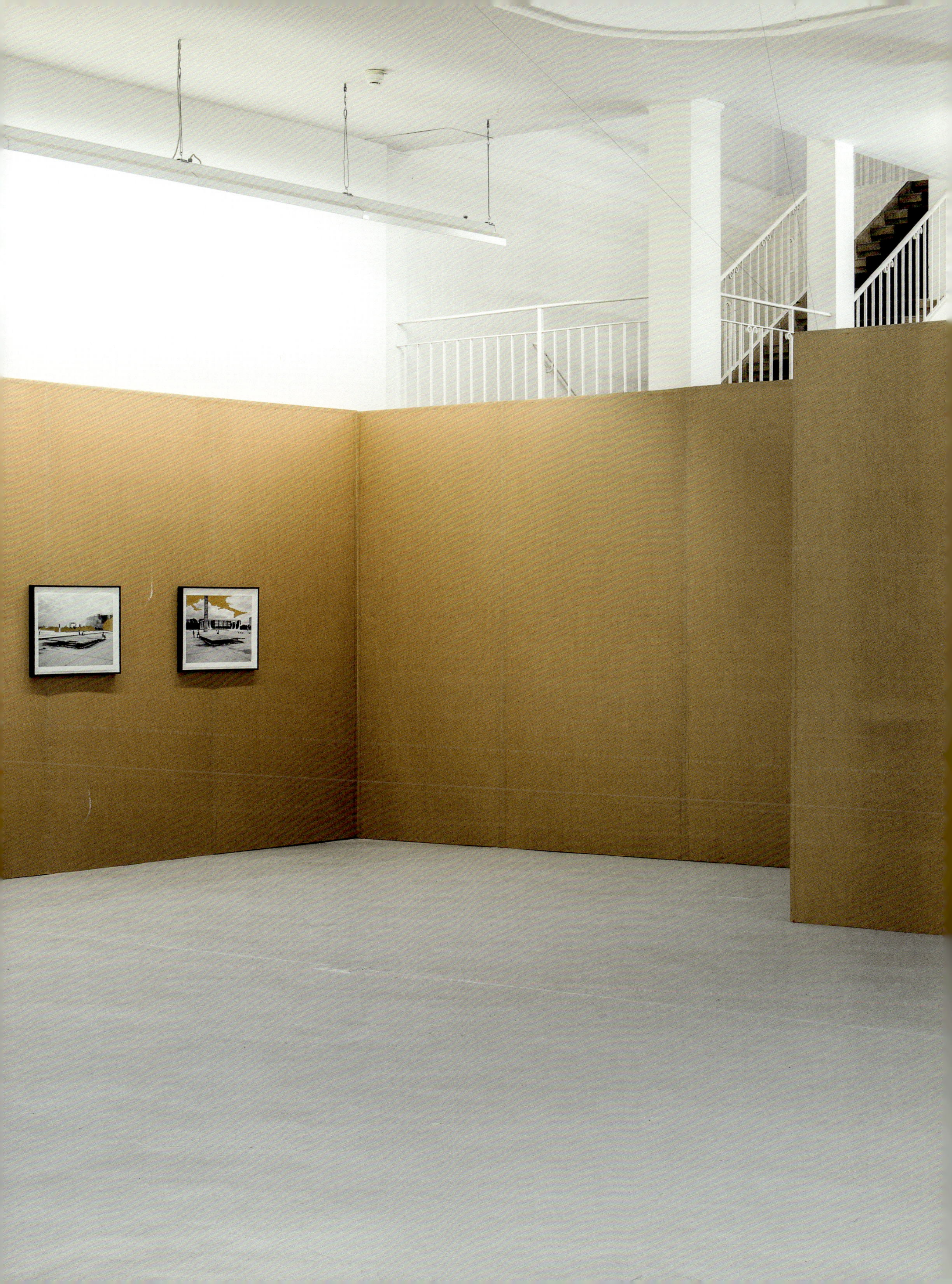

A young woman sits in a New York subway carriage a number of days after the terrorist attacks on the twin towers. It is early morning, and the city is grudgingly back at work. Like many of her fellow passengers, she is tired, emotionally fragile, confused, and angry—still trying to come to terms with what has happened to her city.

A Sikh man sits opposite her, wearing a bright orange turban. There is a strong tangible sense of hatred from the passengers toward the man—a feeling of raw anger and disgust. The man's eyes are averted, the commuters stares un-replied. His head is bowed, he is sobbing. The train travels on, stopping at the next station, the doors open and close, passengers get on and off. After a few stops and more torturous minutes, the man gathers his belongings and gets up to leave. Standing by the exit is a young black woman with a newly born baby. As the man approaches, he reaches into his pockets and takes out a handful of dollars. Without saying anything, he shoves the money into the folds of the baby's clothes and exits the train. The doors close, and the remaining passengers burst into tears.

At that moment, the woman realizes that for New York to get past the attack, to move on and rebuild itself, it has to think anew, it has to look again. It has to get to a place beyond belief.

A Place Beyond Belief

The fifth in Coley's ongoing series of illuminated text works consists of a brief stanza:

A PLACE
BEYOND
BELIEF

Four words stacked on three lines: indefinite article + noun / preposition / noun. The text is not a complete sentence, it has no verb, no punctuation, and it is written entirely in sans-serif capitals. As with the other works in the series, fairground lights describe the letters in lines and arcs.

This is a large sculpture whose subject is mounted on scaffolding bars that have been fixed to the wall or anchored to the floor. The physical nature of the work is paradoxical: its rudimentary construction suggests a temporary roadshow advertising the latest ride or quack scheme or the vehicle for erecting something permanent. However, the simplicity of its structure and its lack of adornment carries its own authority, endowing the glowing script with the inviolability of a calling or a promise. Without incidental effects, the gnomic phrase is suspended in isolation like a mantra to be digested and learned. Yet this axiomatic quality is itself at odds with the nature of the text whose precise meaning remains beyond reach.

"A place beyond belief." What does this text / sculpture describe? Where is the place designated by the title—*this* place the viewer shares with the sculpture, or *that* place, "the hill beyond the hill you can see," as Coley has referred to it? Does it exist already or is it utopia, a hypothetical place that will never exist.

The work consists of metal poles, nuts and bolts, a transformer, and some lightbulbs, though its primary concern is with the non-plastic oral tradition of storytelling and communication via words. Continuing Coley's ongoing engagement with the ready-made, the source of this sculpture is a phrase edited from a verbal testimony he heard.

Listening to the radio on the morning of the tenth anniversary of the World Trade Center attacks he was struck by a woman recounting an experience on the subway a few days after the towers fell. She described the collective, implicit hostility of her fellow New York commuters toward a Sikh man also on board the train, highlighting raw prejudices that cast a man in a turban as an outsider to be feared and loathed. Recalling her shame at their treatment of this man, she describes knowing that "to move on, New York needed to become a place beyond belief."

Echoing the ideological split that was projected between an outsider "you" and an insider "us" on the subway carriage, Coley's sculpture is concerned with belonging and community. Its three lines, "A Place," "Beyond," "Belief," each separately relate to concepts of in- and ex-clusivity, whether physical or ontological, and take up a theme that runs throughout Coley's practice: the notion of personal identity in relation to the group.

In his work, the viewer is repeatedly addressed by a voice assuming authority and asked either to believe or reject what is pronounced. In certain cases, this directive offers a simple choice: *There Will Be No Miracles Here* (2010); *Heaven Is a Place Where Nothing Ever Happens* (2008); *We Must Cultivate Our Garden* (2006). In *The Honour Series* (2012), the viewer's response to the demonstrators depicted across the photographs in different locations and supporting various causes, is complicated by the concealed slogans on their placards. *A Place Beyond Belief* (2012) is more ambiguous again because its offer is so enigmatic, to the extent of it being barely understandable as a choice or ambition at all. Whether, in the terms of Coley's re-contextualization of the phrase, the idea of *A Place Beyond Belief* is either conceivable or desirable remains moot. But the work is not blind or deaf. Conceived by having listened to a stranger tell their story via airwaves transmitted from one continent to another, the work speaks from and for the human collective. To quote Roland Barthes's "Death of the Author," it has been "drawn from the innumerable centers of culture" and "its unity lies not in its origins, or its creator, but in its destination or its audience."
— *Tom Hunt*

A Place Beyond Belief, 2012
Illuminated text on scaffolding
6 × 6 × 3 m
Installation, Kunstverein Freiburg

Overleaf:
A Place Beyond Belief, 2012
Installation, National Gallery of Kosovo, Pristina

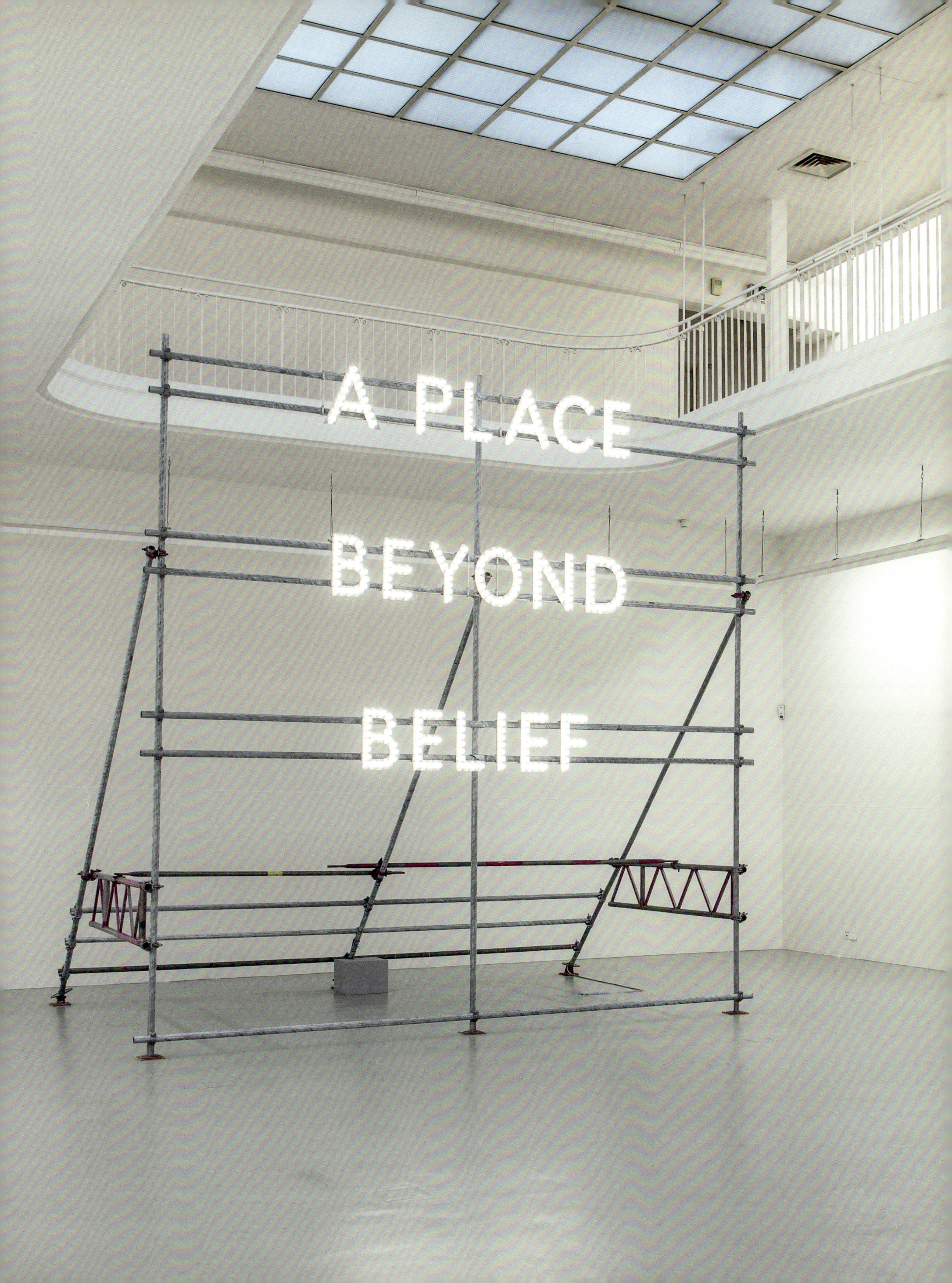
A PLACE
BEYOND
BELIEF

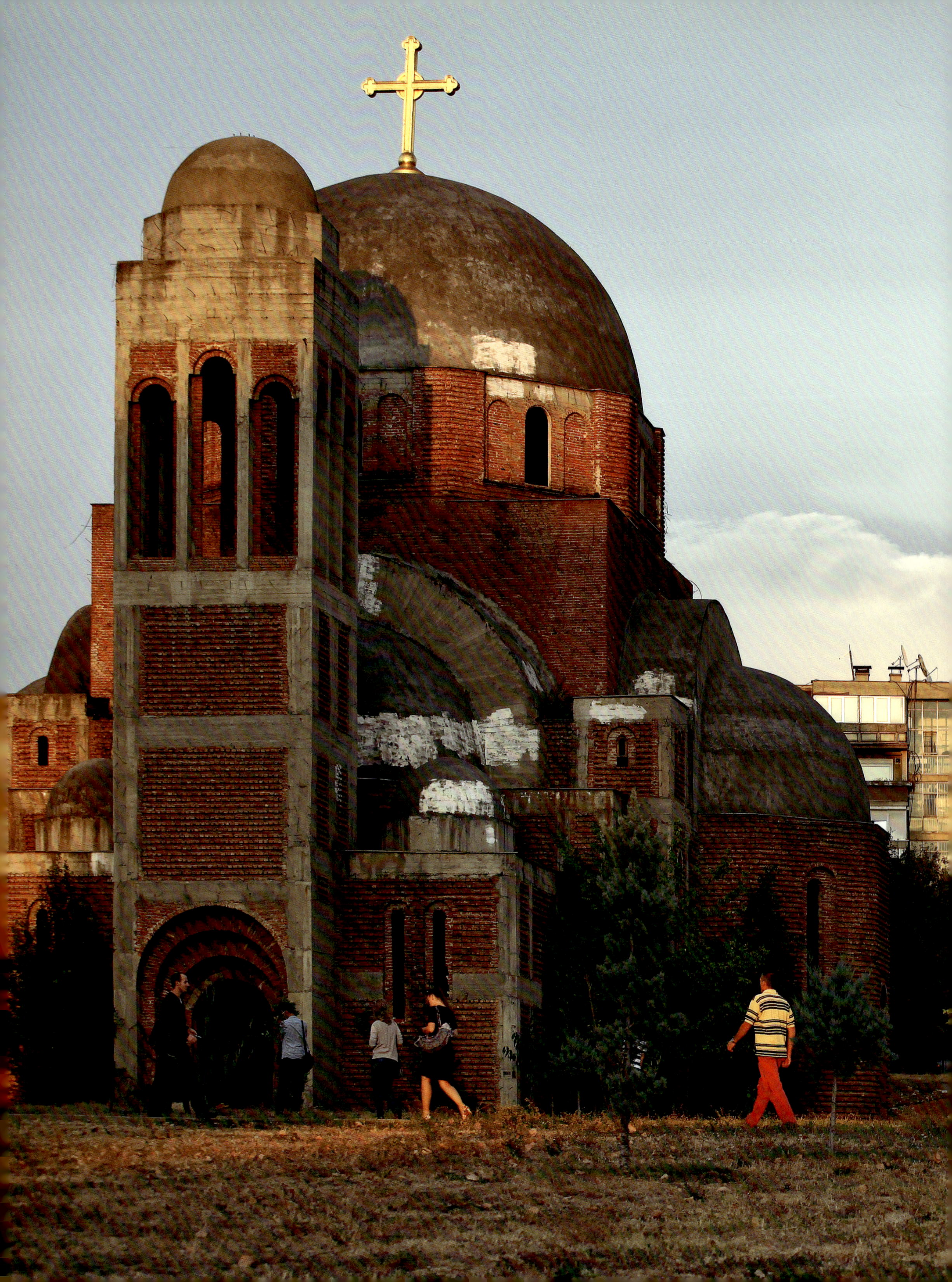

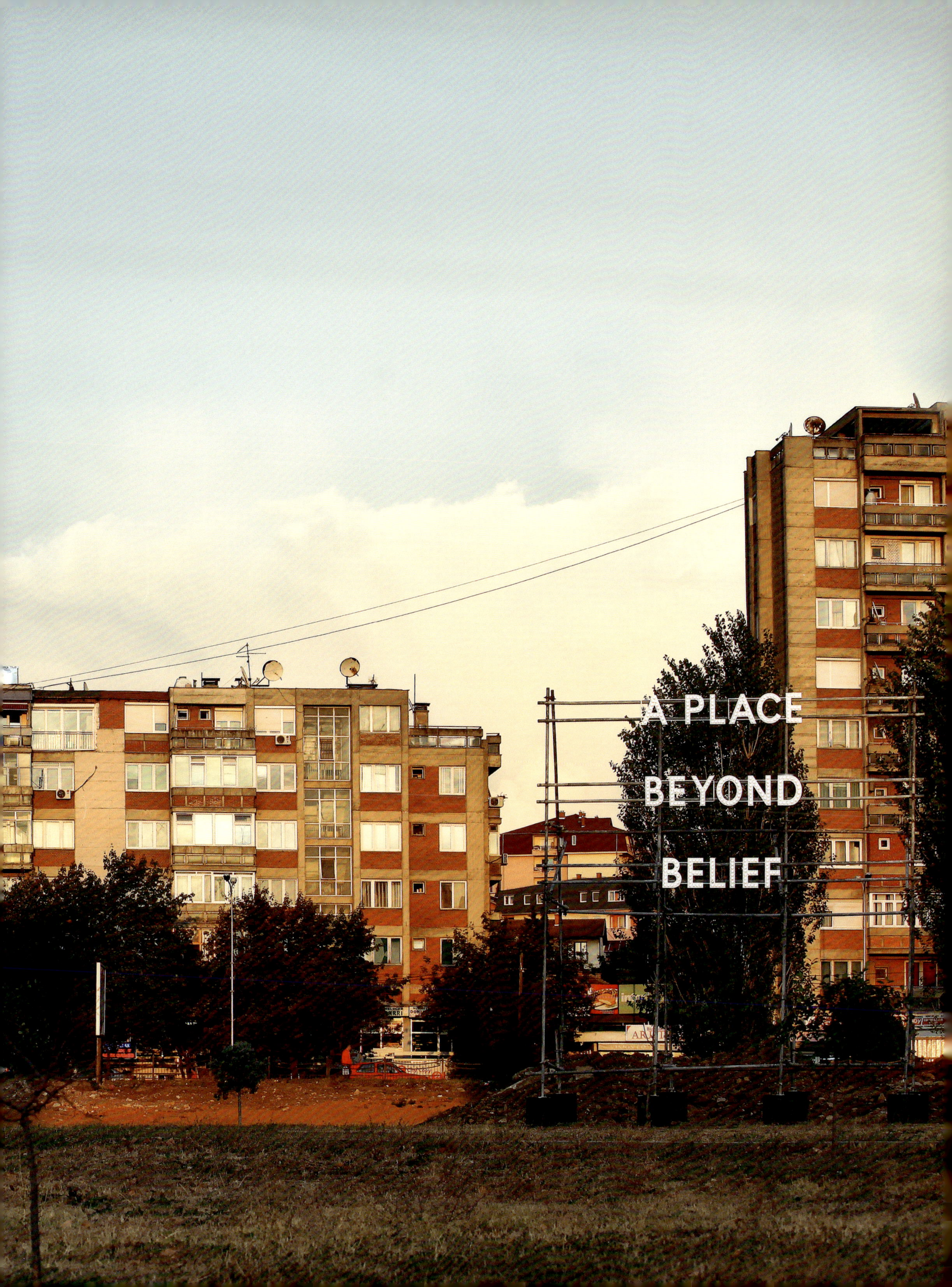
A PLACE
BEYOND
BELIEF

Unnamed (Vancouver)

Coley's practice revolves around investigations into the social aspects of our built environment, of what attributes might be considered to constitute public space and the values inscribed within them.

Unnamed (Vancouver) was commissioned to form the centerpiece of *Knowledge, Kindliness and Courage,* his exhibition at the Contemporary Art Gallery, Vancouver, in 2012. Just as previous works have looked at how buildings might be seen to symbolize systems of belief—specifically places of worship—this installation advances the thematic questioning by using found headstones, collectively telling stories of different patterns of history, immigration, and the politics of societies. If we understand these objects as an embodiment of some notion of community, then we might argue their significance reaches far beyond that as mere records of social history, insofar as they demonstrate a political demand on place.

For Coley it is important the stones are acquired, not newly made. Consistent within his practice, they are ready-mades; de-commissioned markers given a new context and life, in much the same way as phrases are unearthed and used for his text-based works. To reflect on faith, or more generally belief, as a notional intangible, then how might a concrete expression reveal itself? While there is a quite literal weight to these objects, there is also an immediate and tangible feeling of gravitas metaphorically embedded within the installation. The silence of these modified tomb-stones when manifested as an artwork produces a powerful aura far beyond the reverence that might be typically anticipated for such forms. Where have they come from, how did they get here, and therefore crucially, what do we make of them now. *Unnamed (Vancouver)* causes us to ask what occurs when private is made unexpectedly public, how the forms themselves come to be invested—and reinvested—with meaning.

Gathered throughout the gallery, supported on stout cedar batons, the seemingly informal, provisional nature of their installation—stacked, leaning against walls, placed in small groupings—creates a sense of being in transit, of yet to find a home, suggestive of a dislocation from their actual site, temporarily in limbo. The wooden blocks act as both plinth and an evocation of pallet systems characteristically used to transport grave markers by monumental masons. And yet these simple forms operate too as a formal device—

Unnamed (Vancouver), 2012
Re-cycled headstones and red cedar
Dimensions variable
Installation, Contemporary Art Gallery, Vancouver

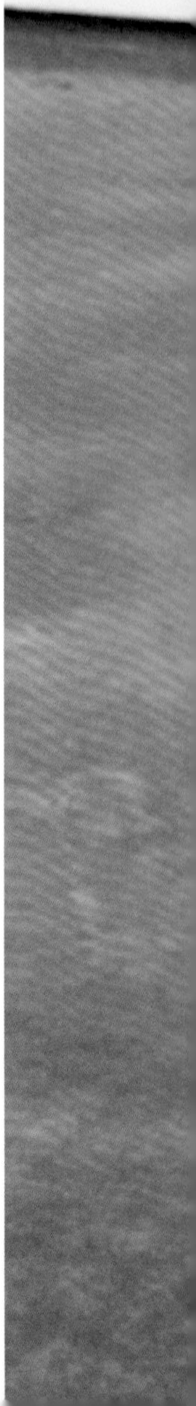

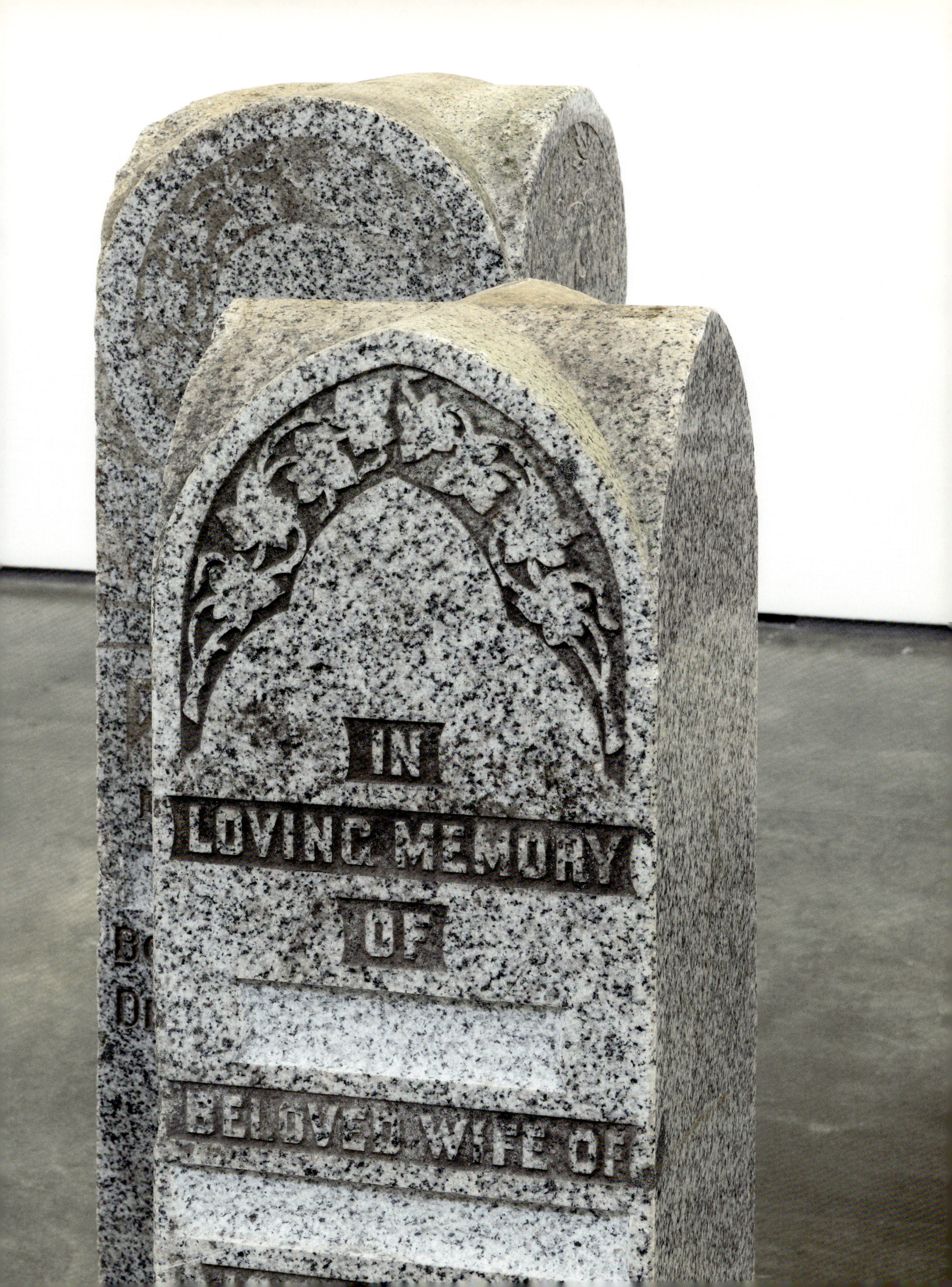
IN
LOVING MEMORY
OF
BELOVED WIFE OF

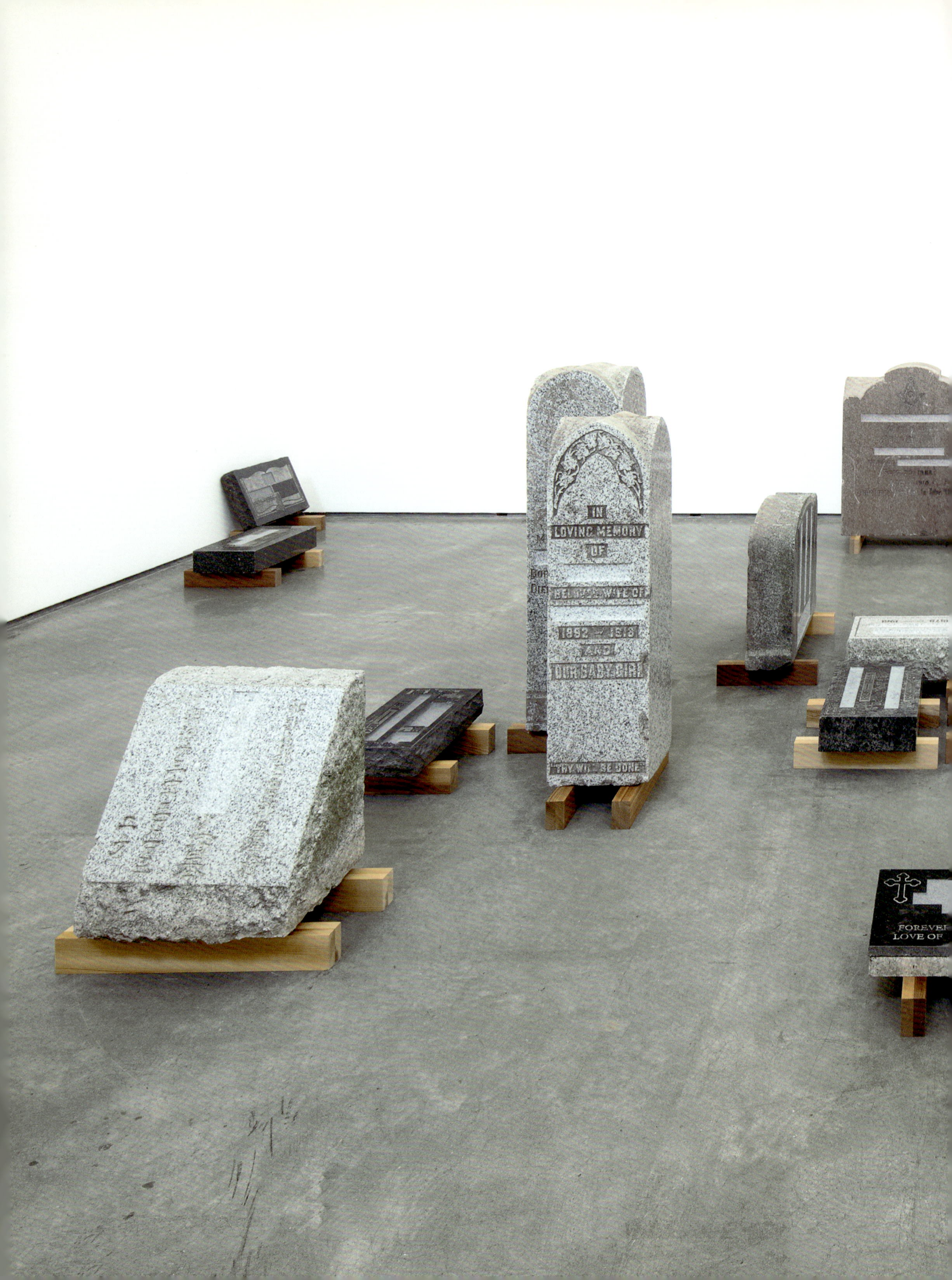
IN
LOVING MEMORY
OF
AND
OUR BABY GIRL
THY WILL BE DONE
LOVE OF

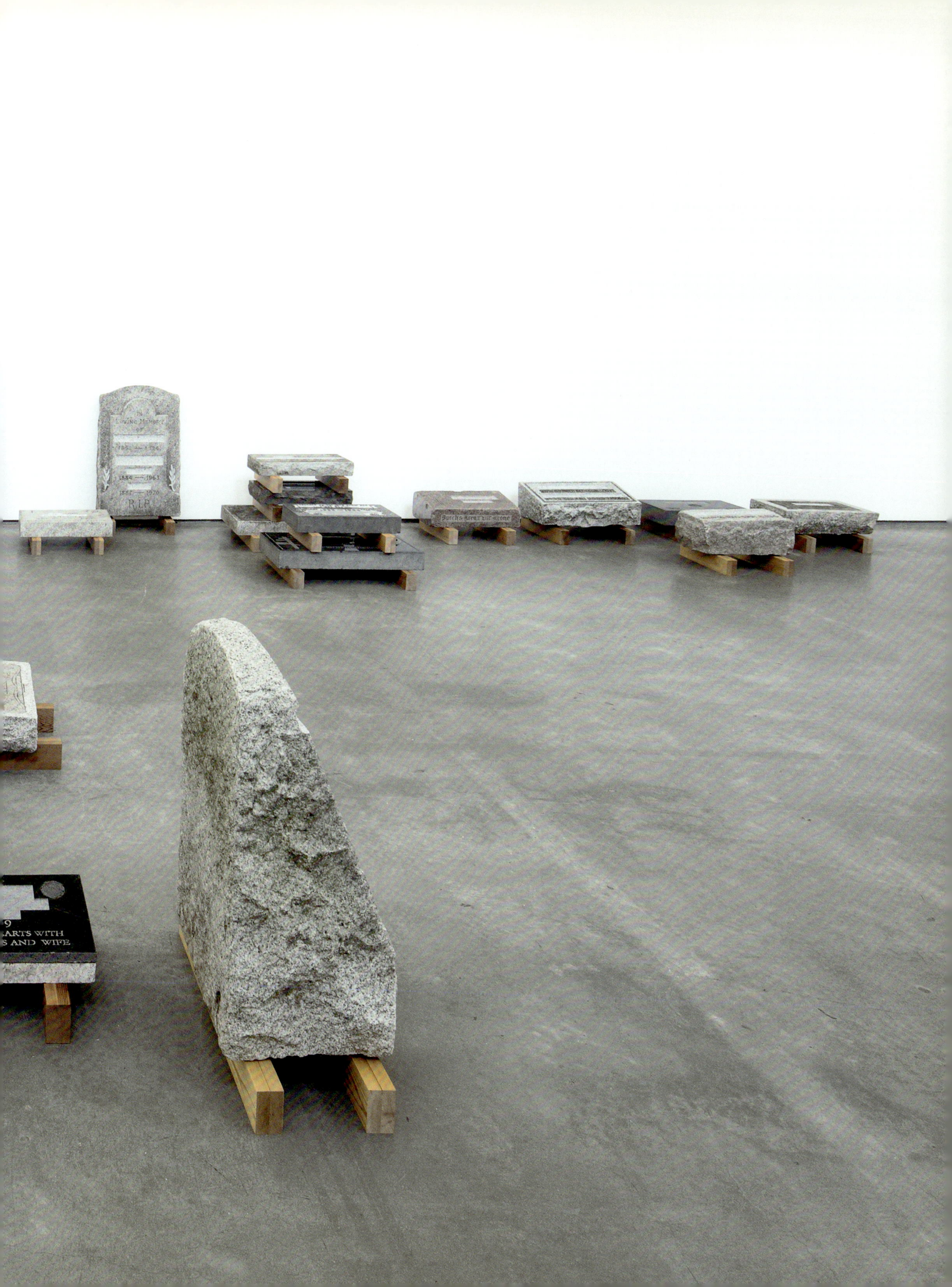
1884 — 1963
R.I.P.
ARTS WITH
S AND WIFE

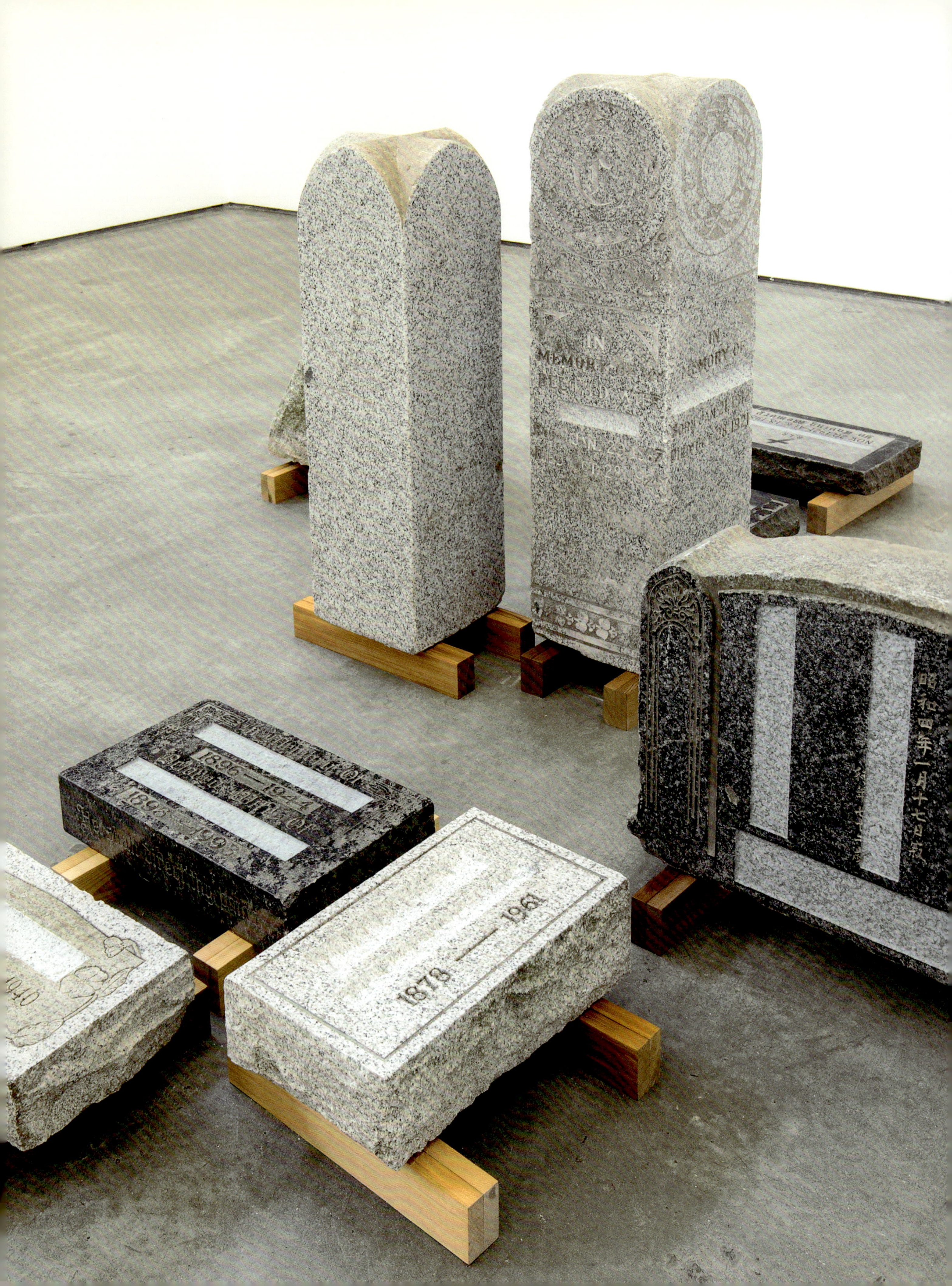
IN MEMORY OF
1878 —— 1961

warm against cool, color against none, soft against hard. Furthermore, in elevating the headstones off the ground we become even more aware of their physicality and the profundity of meaning that might be suggested by this act in relation to their former function. The batons also reference other art historical standards, their visual consistency and cross-section a unifying presence throughout the work, reminiscent of plays on seriality and modular form within minimal and conceptual practices. Within the visual logic of the piece, too, they echo where names once were, now deep rectilinear troughs of newly cut granite in contrast to the otherwise weathered surfaces. De-individualized, what remains are the conventions: dates of commemoration, mention of place, decorative features, inscriptions which indicate the gender of or relationship to a person, as well as more usual epitaphs of mourning and dedication. Languages are various: English, Chinese, Portuguese, Korean, Italian, Japanese, German, and Vietnamese. Many appear to be civilians; some honor soldiers, victims of war and internment. Yet with names removed, identity is opened out for us to consider a more wide-ranging and expansive series of issues, a very real sense of presence in something that has previously implied absence. The memorials speak to the broader notions concerning how we mark lives lived or events passed, and raise the issue of morality in using these loaded objects in such a way. Some of the stones document alarming brevity, some a ripe longevity, nonetheless still disturbing. Erased names notionally create a further space, which is now filled with a different understanding, one that makes the familiar unfamiliar. As with the day's turning, these monuments retrieve time but also signify a continual state of flux, a fundamental understanding of the inevitability that the structures we inhabit and the lives we lead will undoubtedly be outstripped by the environment that surrounds us.

— *Nigel Prince*

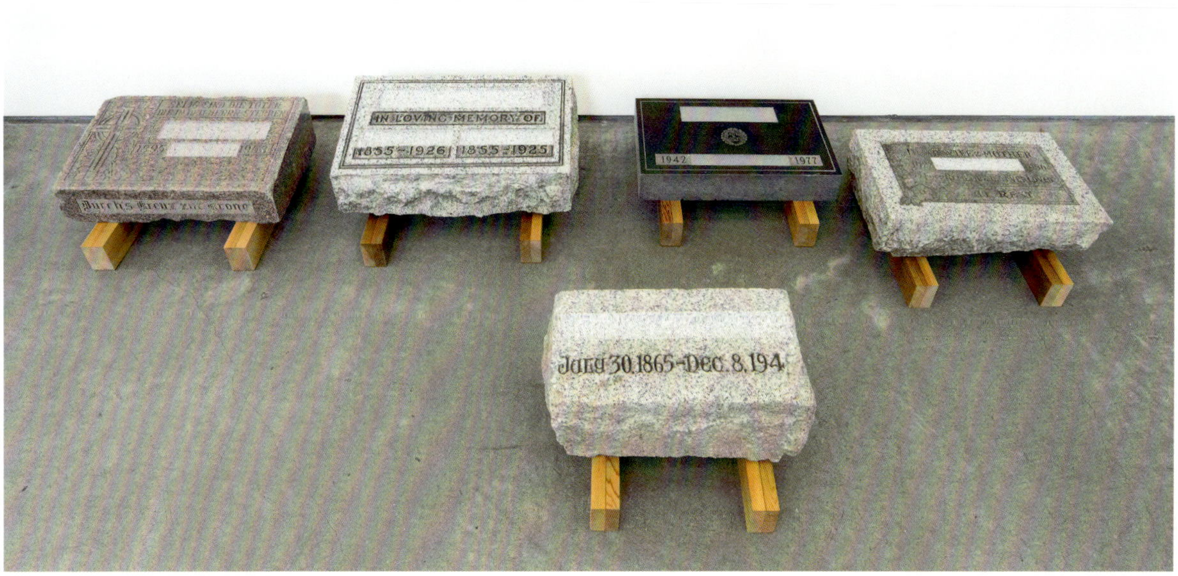

Burn the Village, Feel the Warmth (Utrecht)

During the summer of 2011, the streets of London were witness to a series of violent riots in which young protesters ran amok within the city. In the aftermath of the devastation, social networking sites used the phrase "burn the village, feel the warmth" to describe the feeling of discontent which sparked the rioters' anger. Taken from an African proverb, the phrase acts as a caution, warning mankind of the possible destruction which might ensue if the young are estranged from society. In particular, Nathan Coley was interested in how this phrase was appropriated from the spoken word to the written word—from oral history to being "texted" on a mobile phone.

Subsequently, the artist used the proverb as the starting point for a new illuminated text piece to adorn Hoog Catharijne shopping complex in Utrecht. Re-contextualizing the phrase, the artist generated a new reading of the proverb. While his text pieces are usually aligned horizontally, *Burn the Village, Feel the Warmth* (2013) sprawls vertically down the side of the shopping center's façade like that of a hotel sign. However, the sign acts as a warning rather than an advertisement. Splitting the proverb into two, and displaying the resultant halves back to back, Coley exploits this form of display to accentuate the condition of cause and effect stipulated within the text. The work's location is particularly poignant in light of the fact that numerous shops were looted and burned down during the London riots, thus lending the work a sense of foreboding.
— *Jonathan Horrocks*

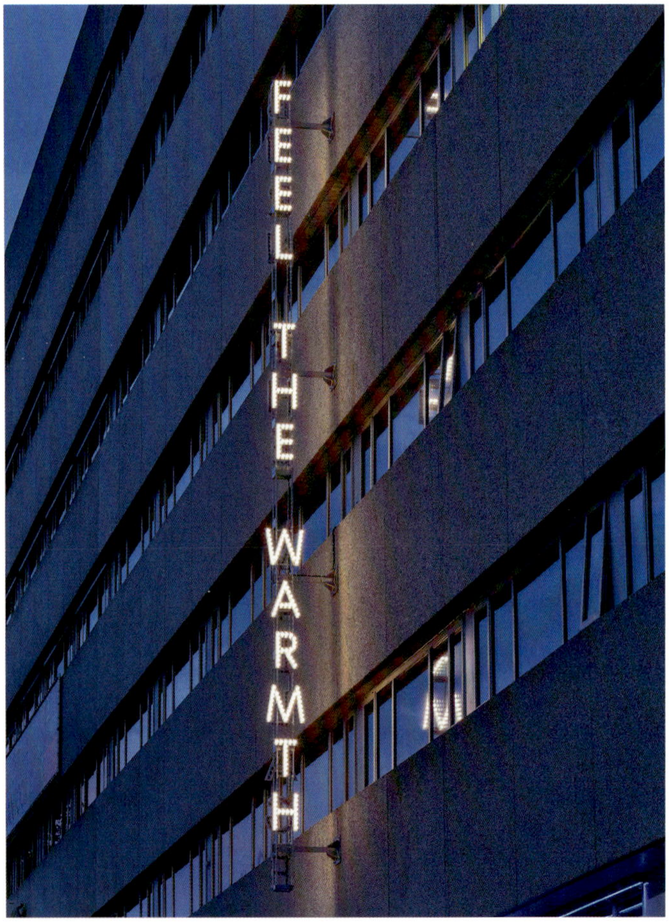

Burn the Village, Feel the Warmth, 2013
Illuminated text
10 × 0.4 m
Installation, Hoog Catharijne, Utrecht

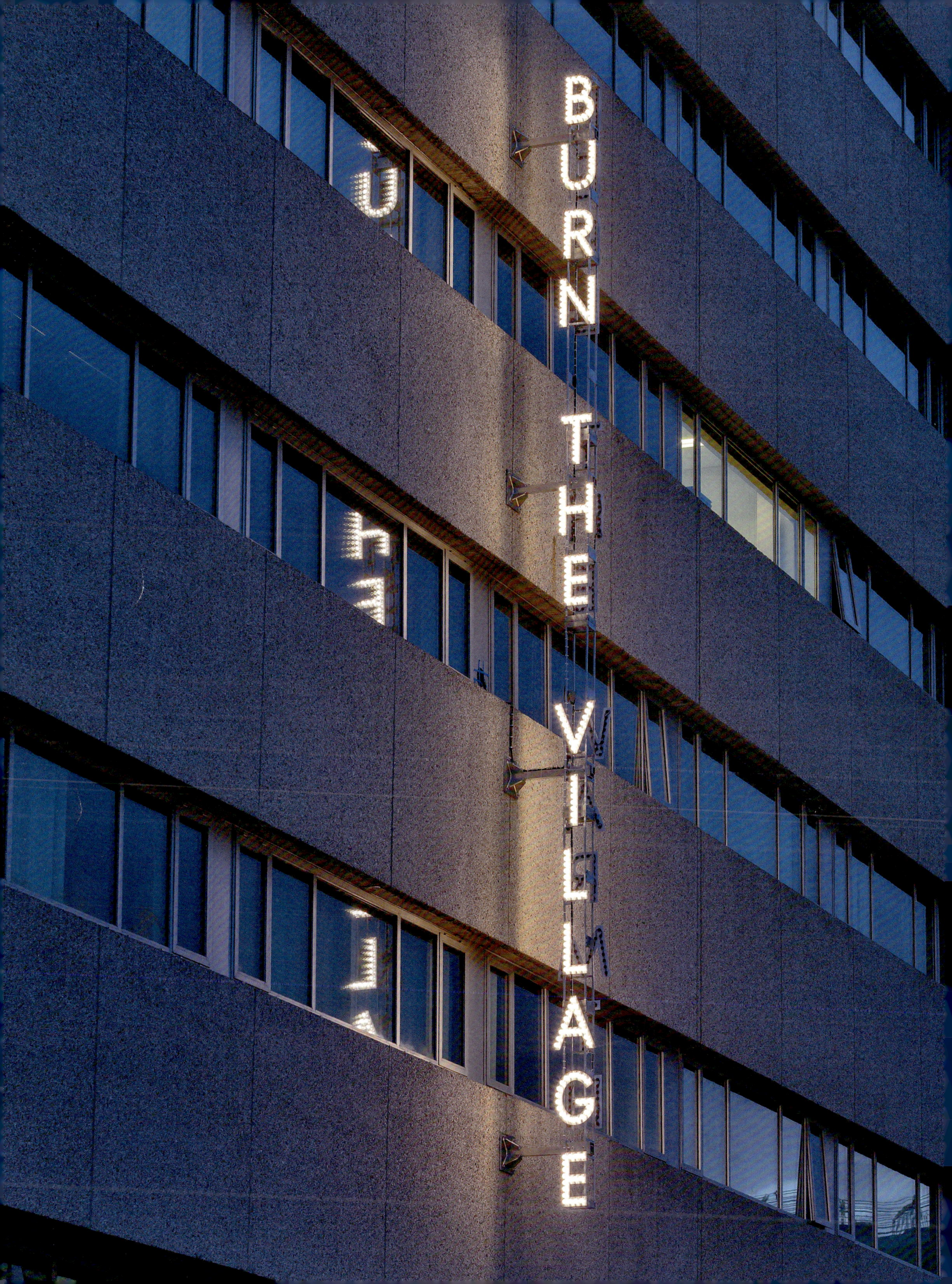
BURN THE VILLAGE

The Honour Series

An ongoing series of work consisting of black-and-white photographs, each partially obscured by one or more blocks of hand-painted gold leaf. Coley's photographs have been taken at sites where the public pay respect to God, to art, to national history, and to their own code of ethics. The series is defined by the contradiction between the impartial, documentary mode of gathering source material and the censored nature of the resultant work

The masking of the conventional subject of the image—Auguste Rodin's *The Burghers of Calais* or *Christ the Redeemer* in Rio de Janeiro, the particular causes of street demonstrations in locations across the world—contrasts with the legibility of tattoos, T-shirts, street signs, and other incidental information. In each case, part of the image has been screened from view, thereby charging the remaining mise-en-scène with the picture's content. If homage to a famous statue or endorsement for an ideological principle is being denied, the viewer is asked, to what then do these works pay honor?

When René Magritte thwarted the viewer's cognizance of the subject of a portrait by placing a bunch of flowers or an apple in front of their face (*The Great War on Façades* and *The Son of Man*), he was interested in the way humans hide things, especially themselves, from public consumption, whereas Nathan Coley's *The Honour Series* (2012) celebrates public performance as a form of collective faith. Despite obscuring the conventionally understood "message" of these works, Coley shows the event itself, the gathering, to be of central significance.

Coley has identified the series as being "social" rather than "political" and the "Honour" of the title indicates the nature of work, whose interest lies in the urban environment as an arena for discourse and the citizen as an agent within it. Paradoxically, in blocking the particular ideological content of a demonstrator's placard, Coley illuminates the substance of their gesture into a universal signifier of liberty and empowerment.

— *Tom Hunt*

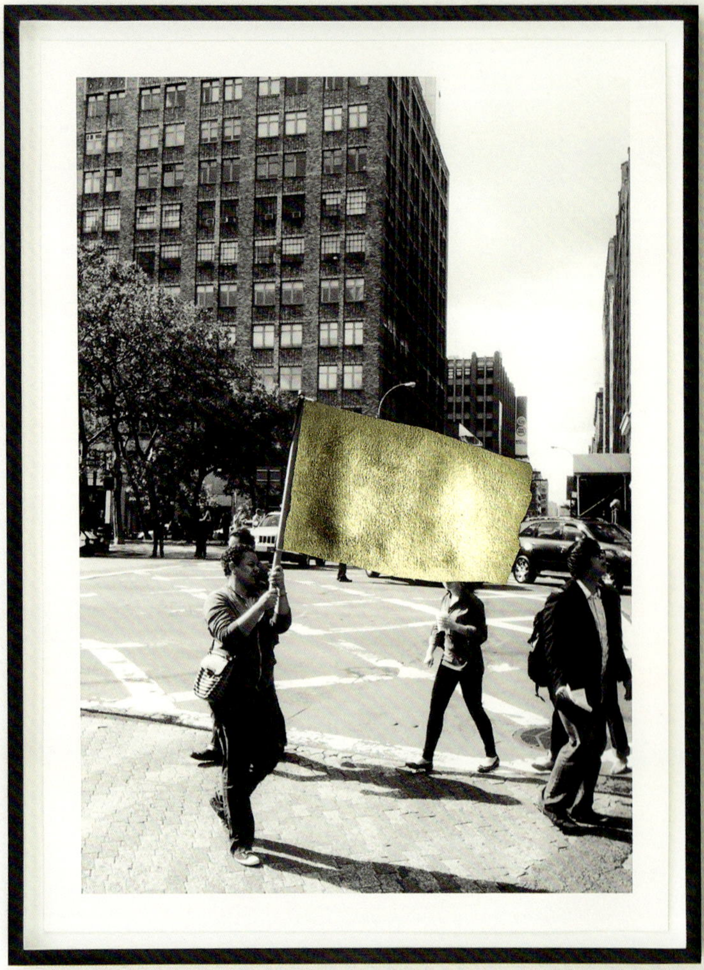

The Honour Series, 2012
Gold Leaf on Giclée prints
70 × 50 cm each

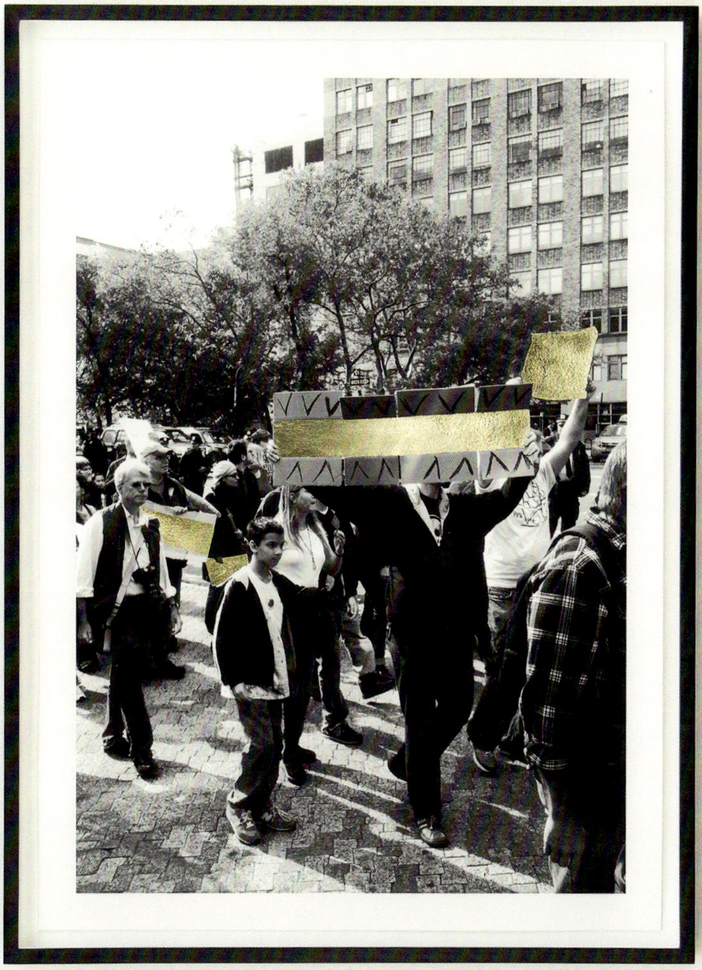

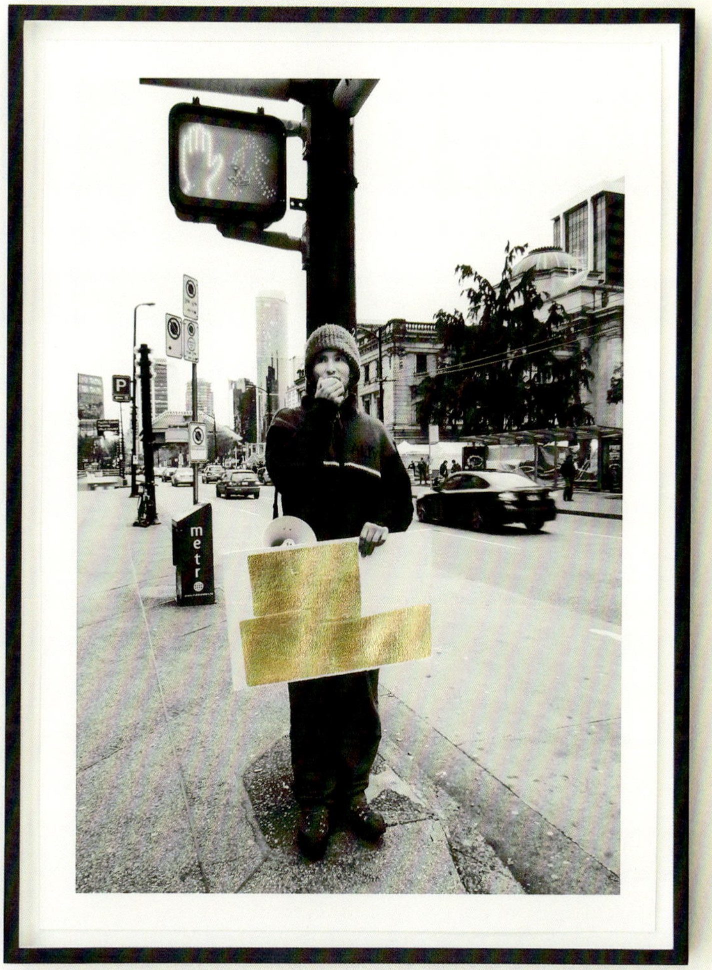
P
metr

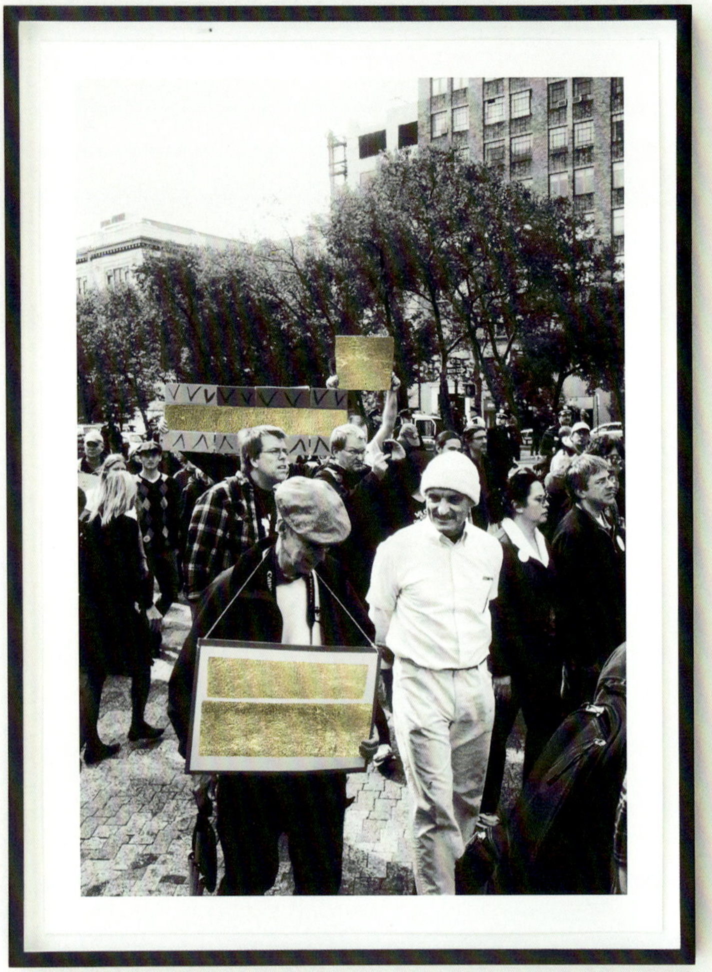

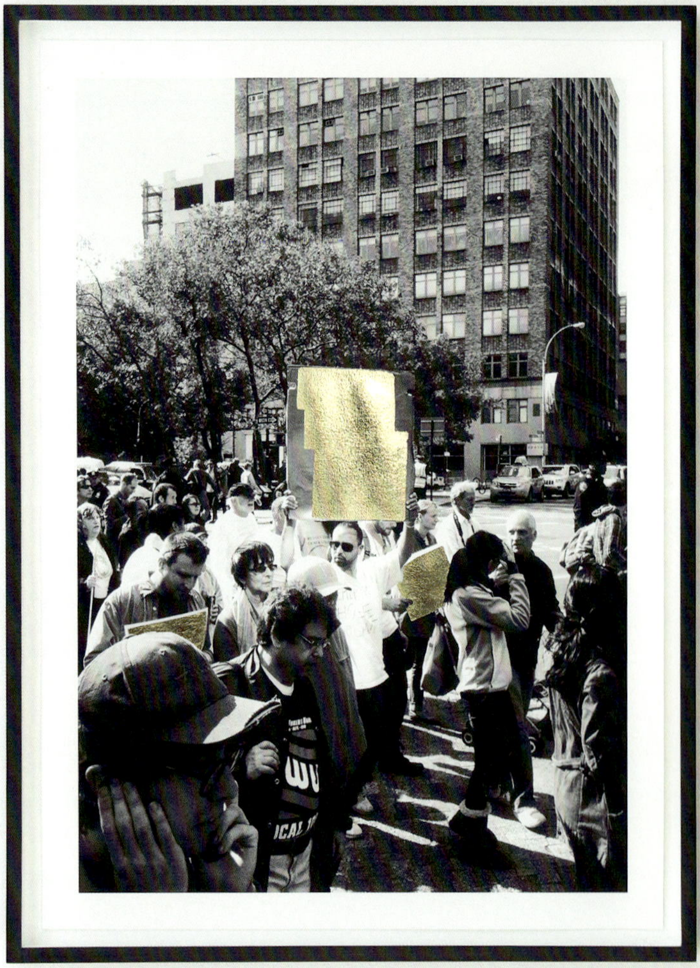

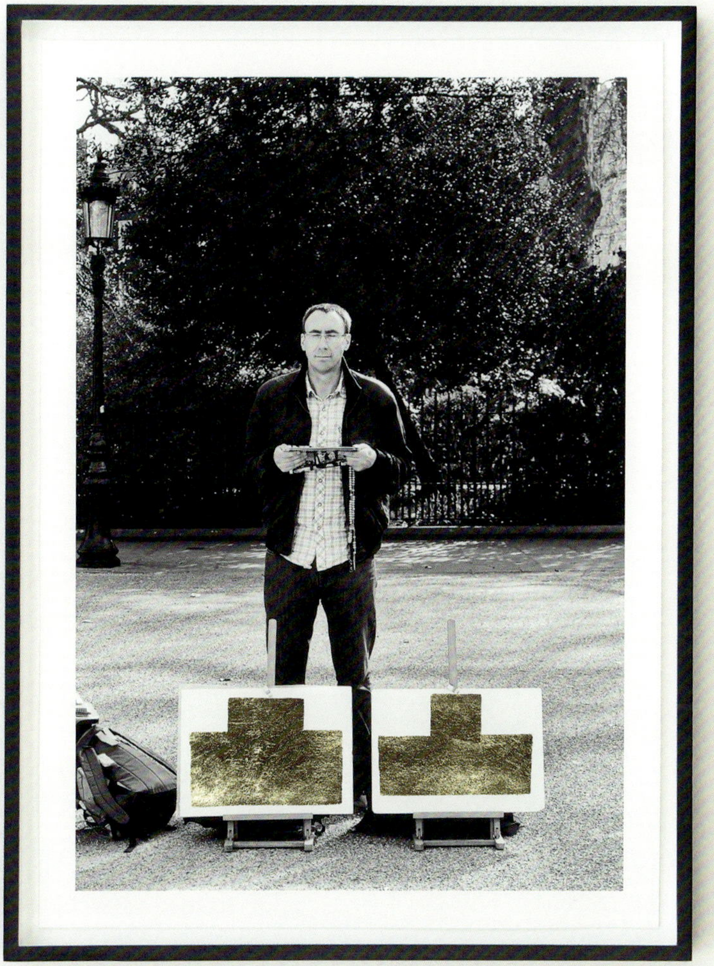

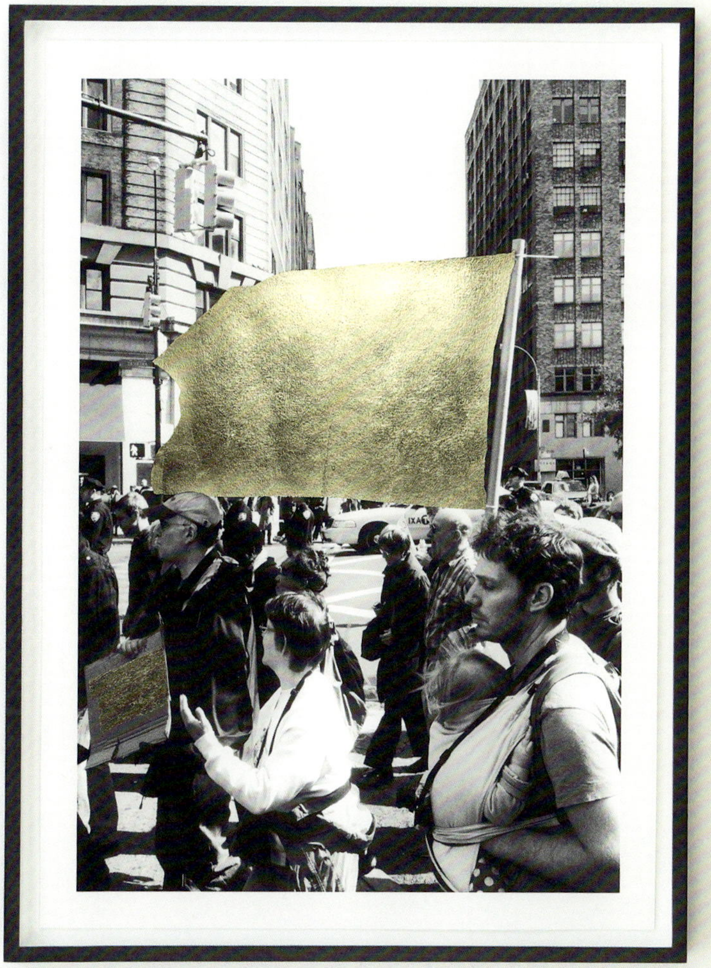

Choir

A crowd of sculptures, presented on a tablecloth of cardboard. The steel forms take their shape from the placards found in the images of *The Honour Series* (2012).

In this work, cheap second-hand packing material meets the heavy cool weight of powder-coated steel. Blocking your view, *Choir* (2012) becomes a forest of shapes, a crowd of personalities, a trophy collection without slogan, cause, or competition.
— *Nathan Coley*

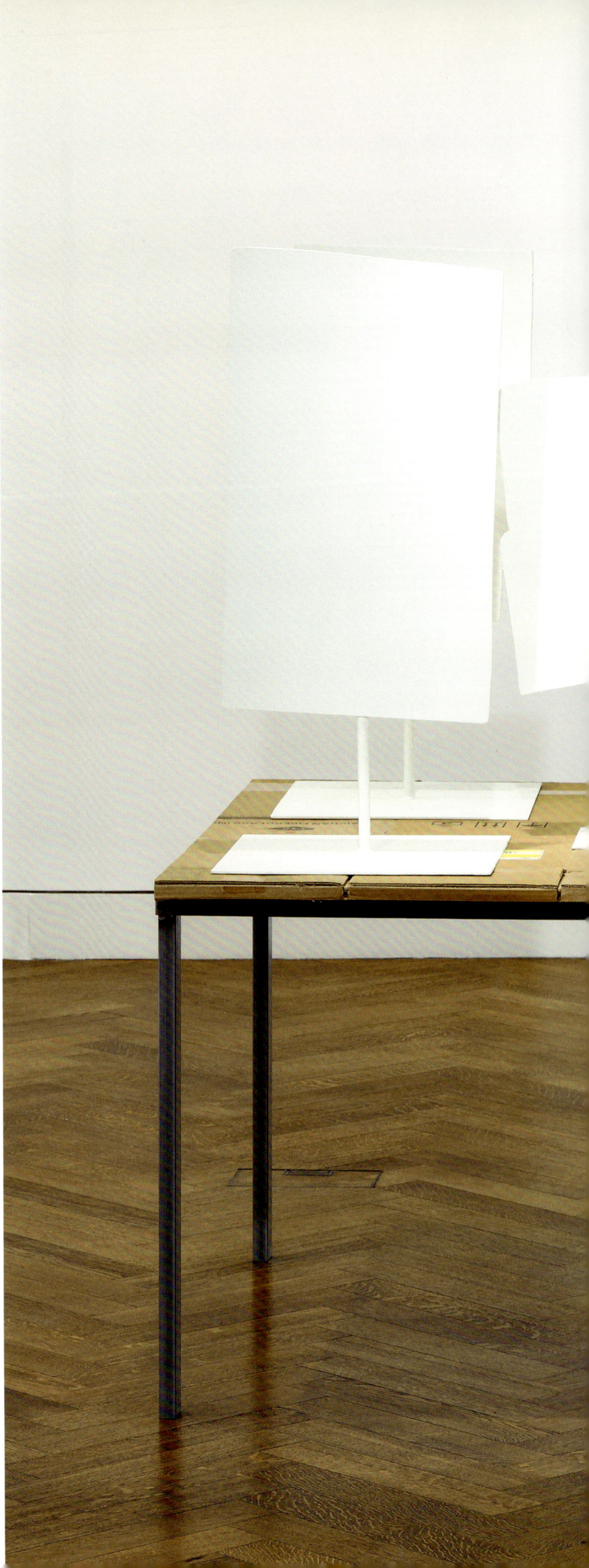

Choir, 2012
Steel, 9 powder-coated steel elements and cardboard
164 × 219 × 112 cm
Installation, Haunch of Venison, London

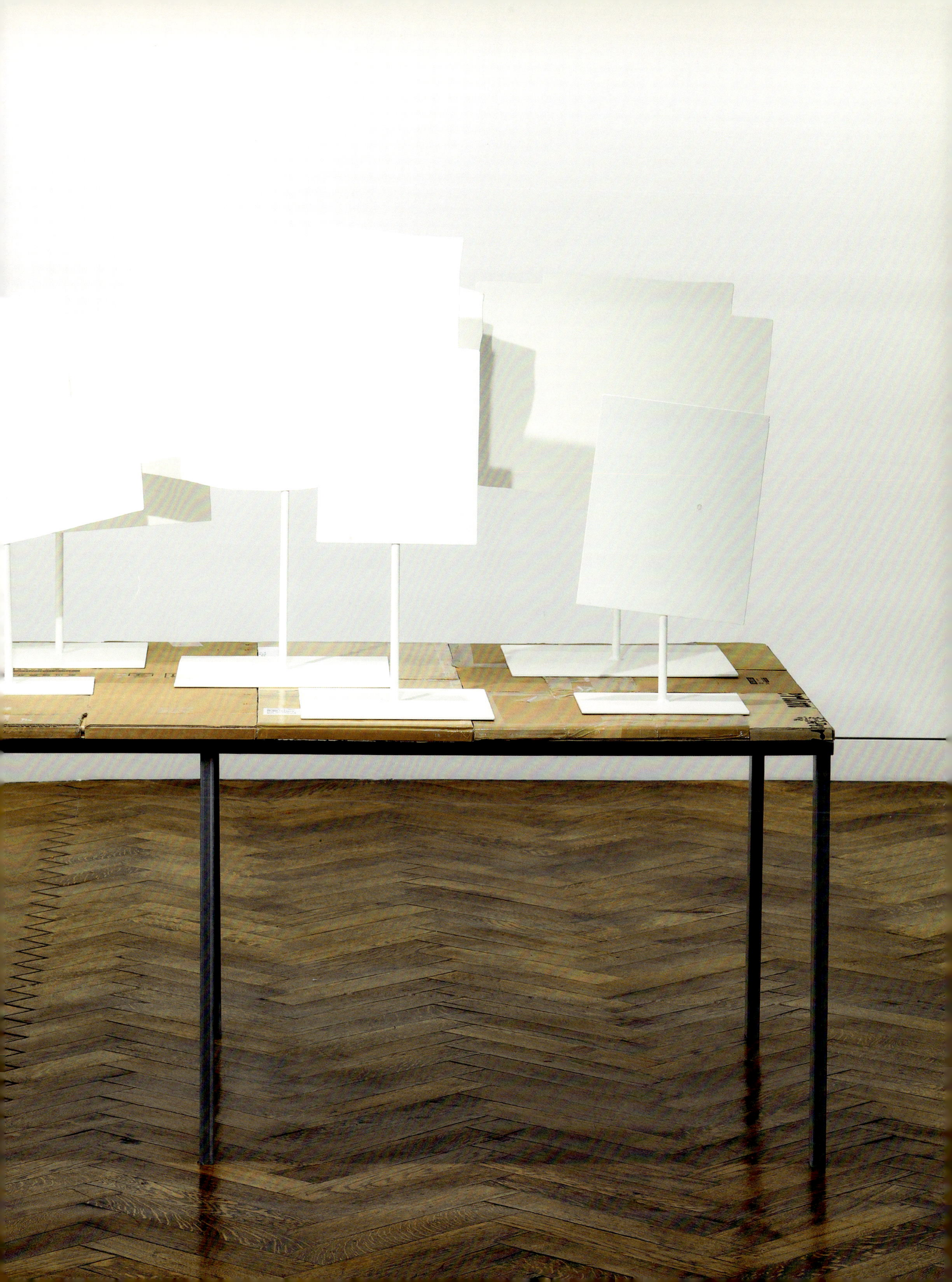

How do we come to know something? This question lies at the heart of Coley's practice and is oriented around the personal and social politics of faith and belief, control and order, and the authority of the information that is disseminated. The imperatives of his text works place the onus on the viewer to comply and be enfolded or to reject and remain outside and this provocation is often precisely located—*There Will Be No Miracles Here* (2010); *Heaven Is a Place Where Nothing Ever Happens* (2008); *We Must Cultivate Our Garden* (2010); *A Place Beyond Belief* (2012); *Burn the Village, Feel the Warmth* (2012).

The *If the Young . . .* series (2012) furthers this concern with pedagogy. Here the proverb, "If the young are not initiated into the village, they will burn it down just to feel its warmth," is embedded within a news article analyzing the cause of urban unrest. Printed above the graphite transcription of the excerpt is an apparently illustrative image: a burning building, the façade of Tate Modern at the moment the institution publicly declared its denunciation of the Chinese government in relation to its treatment of Ai Weiwei, and a picture of a quiet mangrove in the Everglades. Yet there is no direct correspondence between the two elements: the news article may or may not be specifically concerned with the London riots and the images derive from unrelated Internet searches. The viewer's instinct to read the text and image in light of one another has been manipulated by the artist rather than the historical event. The oblique nature of the series is characterized by the contrast in media between the hand-drawn text and the digital print. The unique declaration one associates with the personal signature is here at odds with its precise repetition of the excerpt, beginning mid-sentence and half cut-off like news feed. Related to this, the democratic nature of the Internet undermines its authority as a source of reliable knowledge. The searched for images in *If the Young . . .* are anonymous and unfiltered yet are presented as definitions.

Within these works, Coley explores the means by which information enters public consciousness, from the ancient tradition of passing information and a code of ethics down generations, to the daily turnover of news, to the depthless, democratic archive of the Internet. What we see and what we read complicates our understanding of the works' intent. Indeed, with its ellipsis, the title of the series, *If the Young . . .*, indicates that ambiguity rather than certainty is at the crux of the work.

— *Tom Hunt*

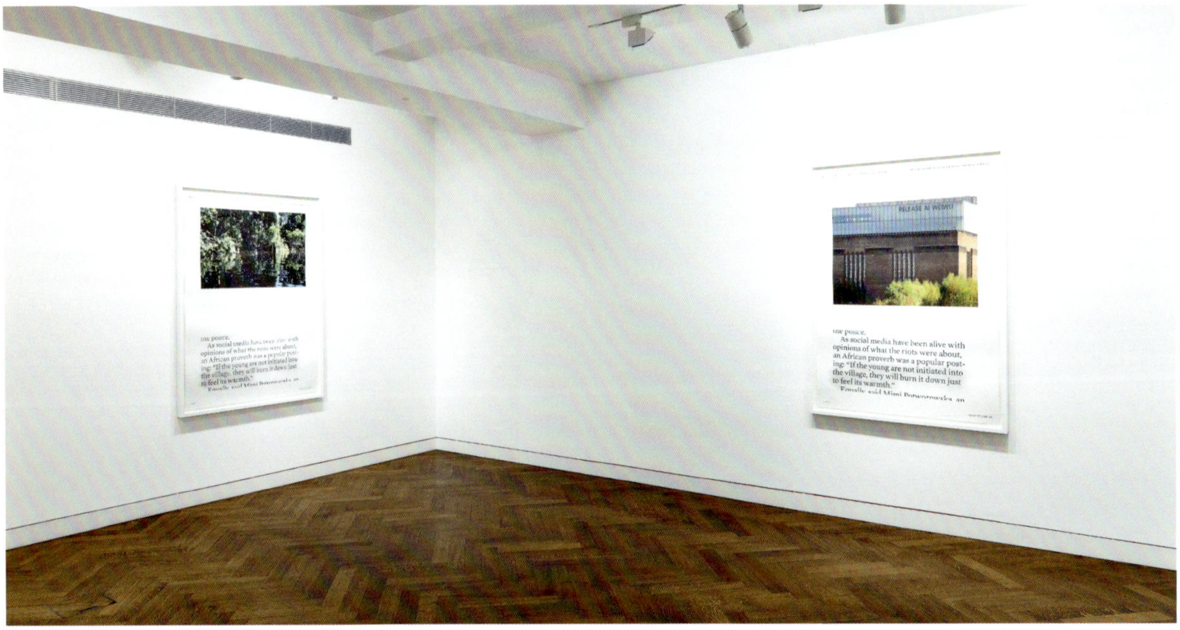

If the Young . . . (Everglade), 2012
If the Young . . . (Ai WeiWei), 2012
If the Young . . . (Riot), 2012
Giclée prints and graphite
152 × 108 cm each
Installation, Haunch of Venison, London

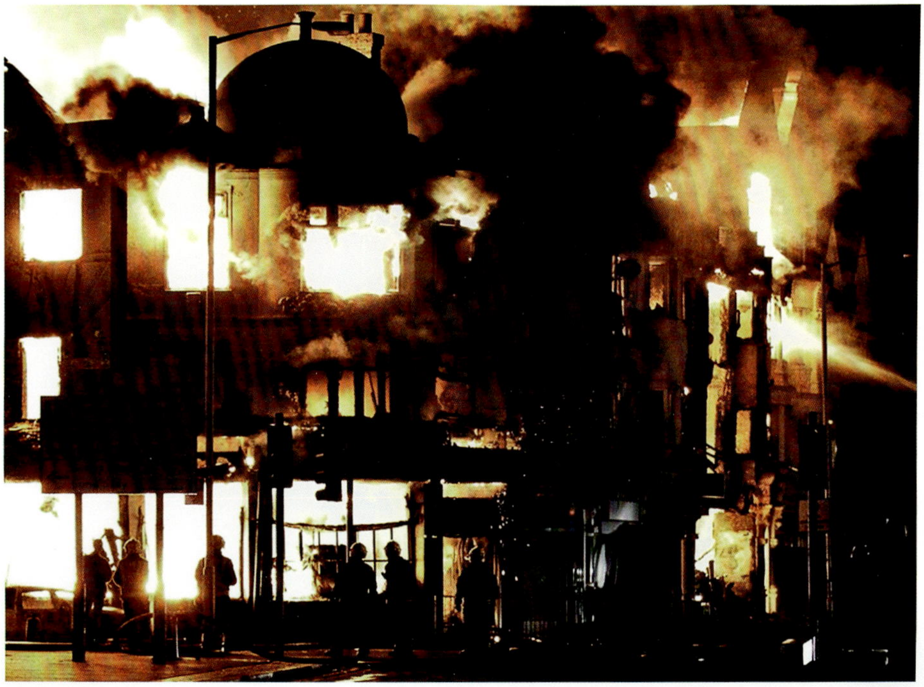

the police."

As social media have been alive with opinions of what the riots were about, an African proverb was a popular posting: "If the young are not initiated into the village, they will burn it down just to feel its warmth."

Equally, said Mimi Potworowska, an

Burn the Village, Feel the Warmth

While the condition "burn the village, feel the warmth" is logical, the proposition—comfort in return for desecration—suggests a strikingly impolitic m-anifesto. In Coley's light-box sculpture, we are given just this brief directive. The words are stacked one on top of the other, separated by a gap between the first clause, the condition, and the second, its consequence.

BURN
THE
VILLAGE

FEEL
THE
WARMTH

Each letter is formed from a sequence of circular incisions made into a lid of charcoal-colored aluminum. From these holes, as though in response to the text, shines a cool white light.

Burn the Village, Feel the Warmth (2012) extends Coley's interest in a mode of communication that holds text and object in counterpointed equilibrium. In this instance, the insistent rhythm of the words, the tablet-like form of the light box, and the incorporeal light that emerges from it, combine to stress the axiomatic potency of the argument.

As with his other work that incorporates language into its objecthood, the words Coley chooses to leave out are significant as the words he chooses to include / reveal. In this case, the apparently water-tight condition, "burn the village, feel the warmth," is shorn of a key precursing condition: "*If the young are not initiated into the village,* they will burn it down just to feel its warmth" (my italics). This African proverb makes explicit the social imperative which provides the ethical distinction / dimension to the burn cause and warmth effect.

Coley is not interested in syntactical games, per se, rather the ways in which ready-mades can be adapted for fresh meaning. As with other examples from the light-box series—*Give Up the Good Book, Pick Up a Good Gun* (2008); "All Artists Are either Cowboys or Indians" (*What Jackson Said to Andy,* 2008); *Never Trust a Loving God* (2011)—the absolute nature of their imperative is paradoxically an indication of their ambiguity as commandments. This skepticism is central to the process by which Coley adopts things that already exist in the world; by isolating them, he relieves them of a specific historical reality and returns them as representations pitched between aphorism and haiku.

— *Tom Hunt*

Burn the Village, Feel the Warmth, 2012
Powder-coated aluminium with fluorescent lamps
120 × 75 × 8 cm

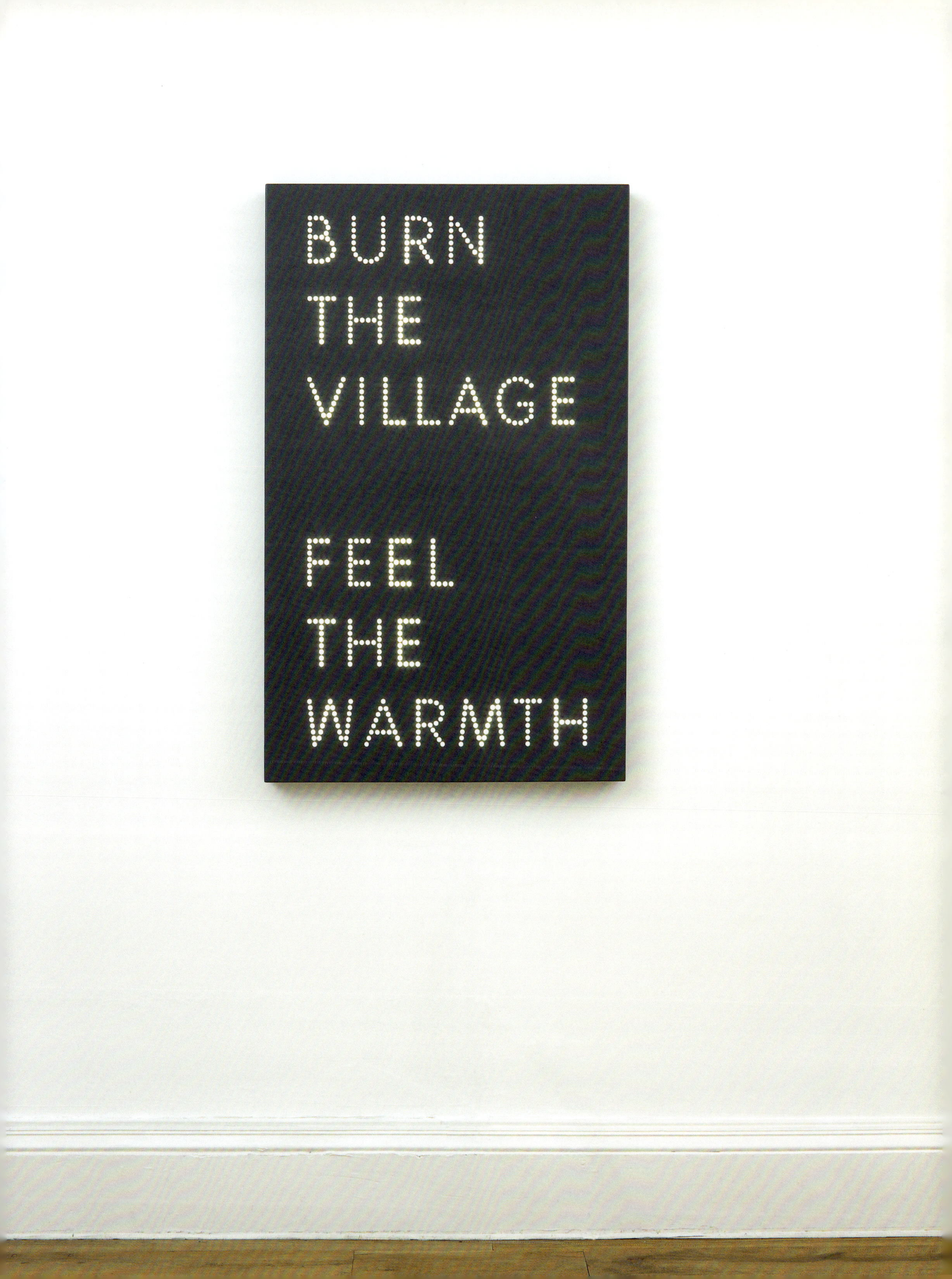
BURN
THE
VILLAGE
FEEL
THE
WARMTH

Unnamed

Unnamed (2012) is a presentation of nineteen recycled headstones. Chiseling out the names inscribed on each of the slabs, Coley draws our attention to the manner in which we invest architectural objects with personal signification. In a similar vein to his work *In Memory* (2010) at Jupiter Artland, Coley negates the specificity of each gravestone, leaving sentimental dedications and dates as the only remaining markers of the deceased's identity. This reductive strategy prompts the viewer to realize that while we may die, these objects will remain and act as reminders that we really did exist.

Arranged in seemingly casual clusters, the gravestones are raised from the floor on metal batons as if only momentarily placed or in transit to an alternative destination, serving to stress the impermanence of life's brief course. While some of the headstones rest perched against the wall like disheveled bodies, others lie horizontally on the floor as if they themselves have been laid to rest. Fundamentally, Coley begs the question: why is such importance attached to these objects? If we see the redacting of each name as a creative act, its effect is to open up a space onto which we can project our future selves or a relative of the past.
— *Jonathan Horrocks*

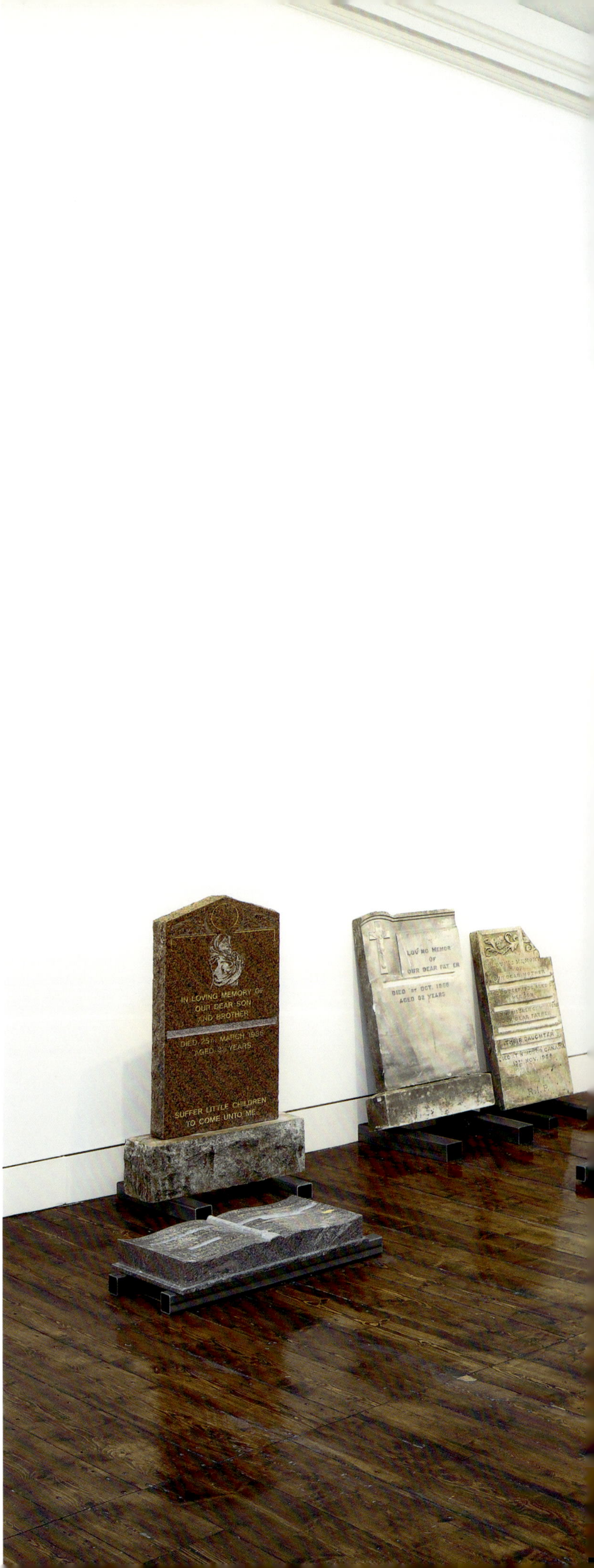

Unnamed, 2012
Re-cycled headstones and steel
Dimensions variable
Installation, Haunch of Venison, London

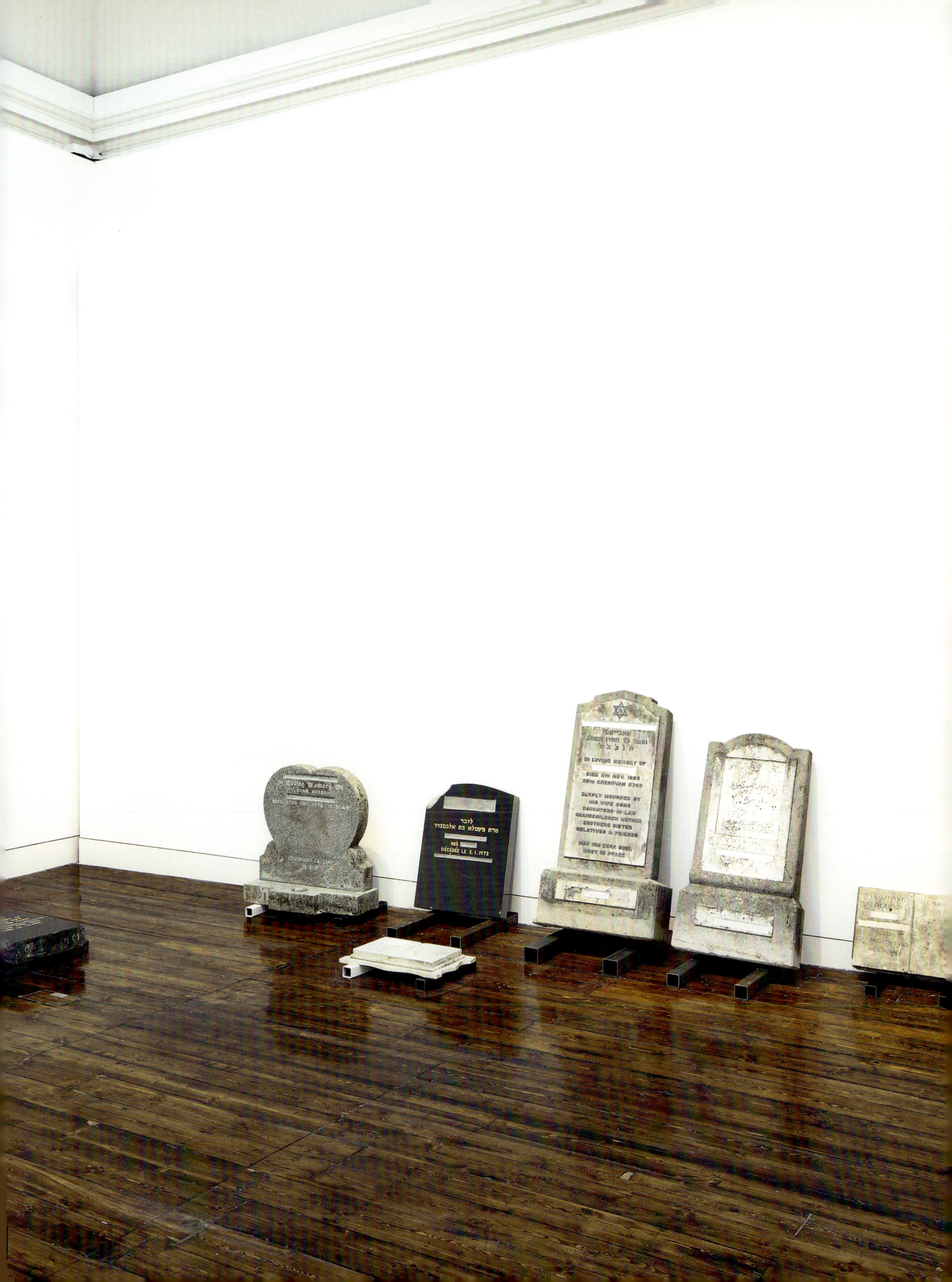

In Loving Memory Of
MY DEAR HUSBAND
DIED 25TH NOV. 1970
GOODNIGHT DARLING
R.I.P.
לזכר
מרת פעסלא בת אלכסנדר
NÉE
DÉCÉDÉE LE 2.1.1972
IN LOVING MEMORY OF
DIED 8TH NOV. 1982
26TH CHESHVAN 5743
DEEPLY MOURNED BY
HIS WIFE SONS
DAUGHTERS-IN-LAW
GRANDCHILDREN MOTHER
BROTHERS SISTER
RELATIVES & FRIENDS
MAY HIS DEAR SOUL
REST IN PEACE

Shrewd Architectonic Imperialism:
The History of a Brick, the End of an Era

The Dutch trading settlements that sprang up on foreign soil at the beginning of the seventeenth century will always stick in the mind of any world traveler. When encountered now, they trigger an unexpected jolt of recognition: they are characterized by their use of brick and typical Dutch brickwork, restrained in their Calvinistic aesthetic, with an aura of solidity. With a global Google Earth consciousness, a Dutch traveler experiences them as brick-red colored patches spread around the world, identifiable and ineradicable traces of Dutch hegemony. From India to St. Eustatius, from Old Batavia to Japan, from Suriname to Cape Town, the houses, forts, and churches function today as historic beacons. The Dutch ambition to conquer a place for themselves in the world (and its trade networks) is evident, and started somewhat over 400 years ago.

It is this history that Nathan Coley interrogates with the work that he made for Het Scheepvaartmuseum. A complex set of historical connections, running from the historic VOC East Indiamen to modern sea container shipping, lies hidden in the wall that he had built in the northern entrance hall of their new building. The work gives no answers and pronounces no judgments. Coley's concern is solely with the process of historic interpretation and experience in relation to architecture and economy.

VOC

Despite the positive gloss that still adheres to this history today—witness the admonition a couple of years ago by the then Dutch Prime Minister Jan Peter Balkenende, that the Dutch must resurrect the old "VOC mentality"—we have long known that it is a story the connotations of which are not wholly pleasant. In the mid-seventeenth century, the Dutch heavy-handedly appropriated the monopoly in cloves, mace, and cinnamon for themselves. Not only the inhabitants of the islands, but also the merchants and crews of ships belonging to competing nations like Portugal, Spain, and England, were forced to accept Dutch terms, willingly or unwillingly. Nutmeg plantations were laid out on the Banda Islands, managed and worked by colonists and slaves. The whole harvest had to be turned over to the VOC at a set price. When around 1621 it was discovered that the Banda islanders were also cutting deals with other countries, Jan Pieterszoon Coen, one of the most famous and infamous heroes of the VOC, had the vast majority of the population slaughtered. This genocide made such an impression that from that day on the whole region around the Banda Islands came under Dutch control. Holland had made a name for itself.

The brick trading settlements were the first tangible signs of a world that was moving toward an integrated, centralized economy. But this continuing presence of Dutch architecture in these other cultures is also a symbol of an ambiguous imperialism that still provokes questions. For instance, this last summer the statue of Jan Pieterszoon Coen on De Roode Steen in Hoorn was accidentally knocked off its pedestal by a hydraulic crane while a fun fair was being set up. This "accident" sparked off a fierce debate about whether the statue ought to be restored to its place at all. As their part of the protest, artists immediately appropriated the pedestal as a temporary exhibition space, because one could also do other, nicer things with such a prominent spot on a square in the middle of the city. Voices were raised, insisting that the statue should not be put back there, but go somewhere else, in a park, perhaps no longer standing upright but fallen. Emotions ran high. Presently the pedestal is used—quite appropriately—to display Dutch cheeses during the cheese market.

IJsselstein

Nathan Coley's work is about the discrepancy between the built world of architecture and the city as it is actually experienced. He raises this issue for his viewers by dismantling situations—that is to say, buildings, areas, and stories—or, on the contrary, reconstructing them in a different way. This is often not without fascinating effects, as in the work *There Will Be No Miracles Here* (2006), or his maquette—almost closer to an installation—*The Lamp of Sacrifice* (2004), of scale models of all the religious buildings in the city of Edinburgh, brought together in one vast collection. What is striking about his work is that in each situation he focuses on one detail, one word, one story, a missing link. In his work, sensitive to its context, he goes in search of that one element around which the rest of the process, and the realization of the work, is developed.

The Ballast Project, 2011
17th-century Dutch bricks
2.5 × 16 m
Permanent sculpture, Het Scheepvaartmuseum, Amsterdam

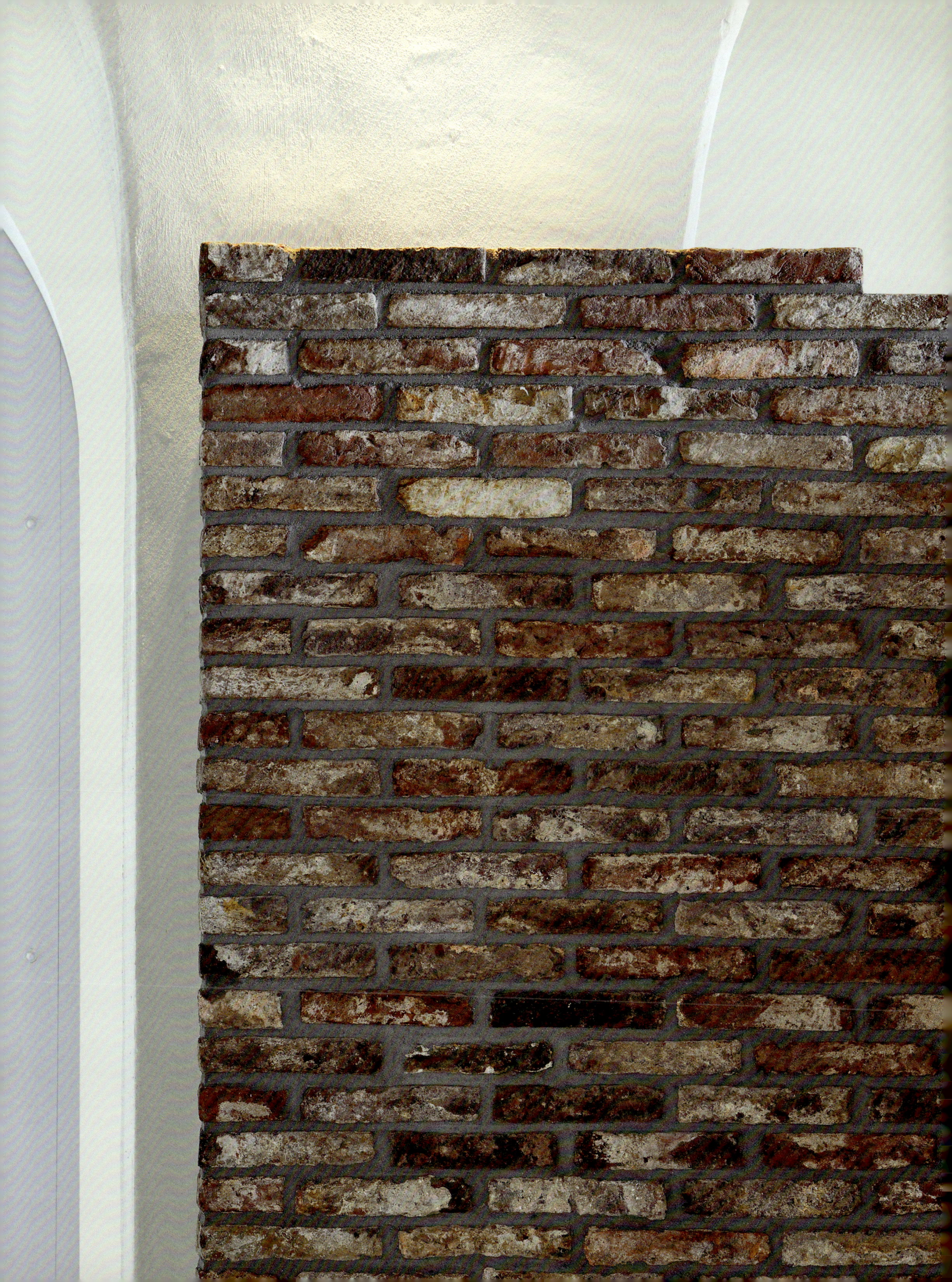

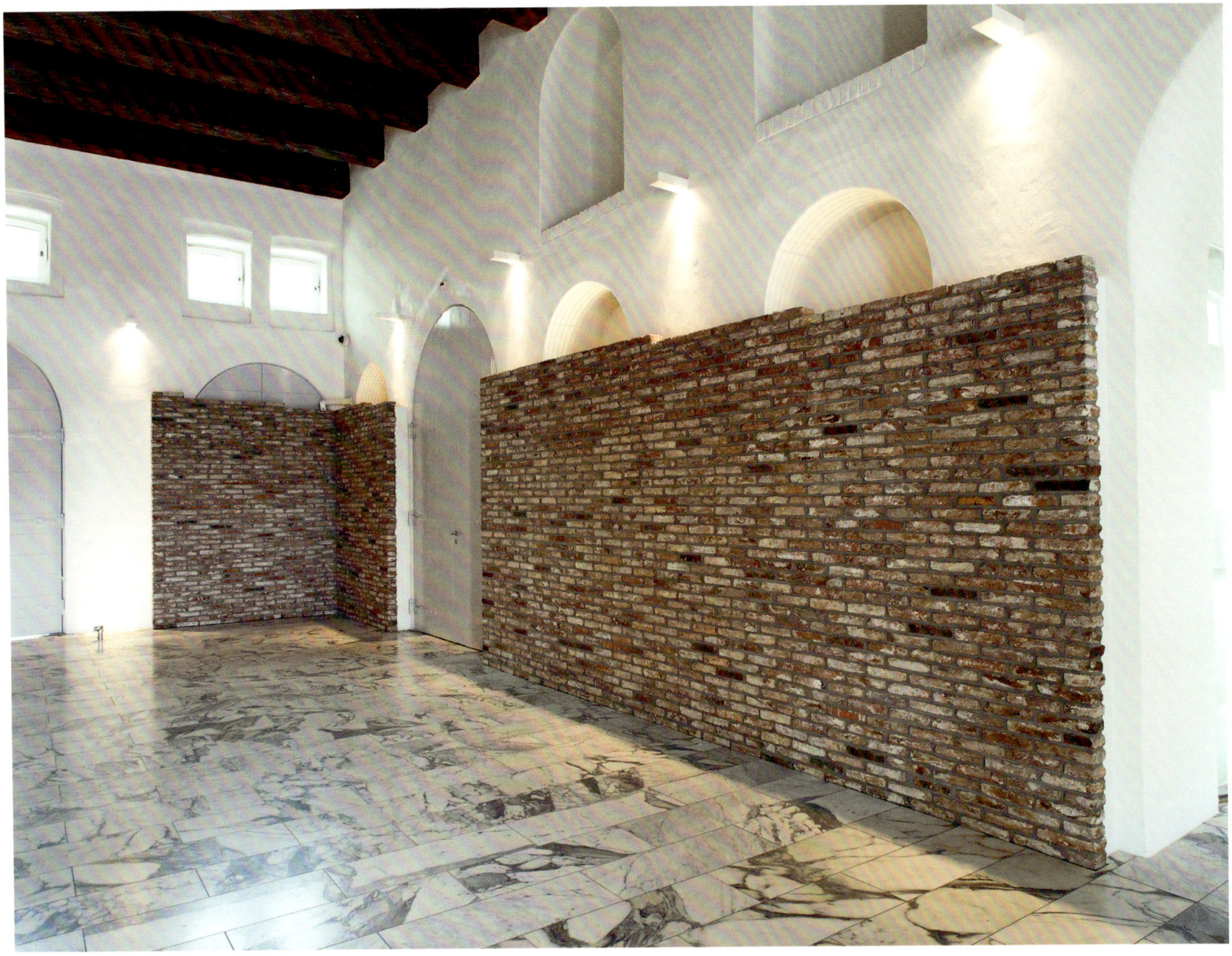

From its very inception, his response to the commission from Het Scheepvaartmuseum has focused on the logistics of goods in relation to architecture. The building on the Oosterdok itself, dating from 1656, was his point of departure: it was from this former warehouse, 's Lands Zeemagazijn, that the ships of the West and East India Companies sailed. The warehouse was the depot for goods, where the ballast (ballast is the weight necessary to stabilize a vessel, especially one not carrying the full cargo for which it was designed) was loaded before departure, and where the "booty" was unloaded on their return. The replica of the East Indiaman Amsterdam (1749) is a visual reminder of the building's original function. The dynamic of loading and unloading is a process that evokes images of distant places and possible destinations, and deeply appeals to the imagination. Amsterdam in the seventeenth century is comparable with the Rotterdam Harbor today, with its towering container storage—a contemporary variant of the 's Lands Zeemagazijn.

That, as the result of his research, Coley should have used bricks as the peg on which to hang his work is as surprising as it is obvious, and testifies to the originality of the outsider's gaze. To date, no Dutchman has ever associated the history of the VOC with bricks. What in Dutch are called *IJsselsteentjes*—unpretentious, irregular, yellowish bricks produced along the IJssel, in no way comparable with today's industrially produced bricks—were used for ballast in the VOC ships. This practical solution also proved ingenious, because once unloaded and replaced in the ship's hold by other goods, the bricks could be used for durable structures which afforded protection. In a previous interview, Coley remarks on this: "Initially the bricks were intended for building, as useful components in a larger architectonic structure. But they were carried along on the seventeenth-century voyages because of their weight. They meant nothing, were merely ballast for the ships which would have been too light without them. Out at the other end of the world this functional cargo was unloaded. In Suriname, Indonesia, people used them to build houses and Christian churches, in short, made structures with them again. The bricks went from 'something' to 'nothing,' in order to once more become 'something.' It is impossible to look at the bricks in isolation." From the beginning of his research, Coley upgraded bricks to a simple but pregnant symbol of a clever historical trade system: a triple metaphor for the ambiguity of the VOC's history, Dutch colonial architecture, and the irrepressible drive to become a major player in the world economy.

The Process

It was early in 2008. I can still see us—the members of the "NSA art team," as we were dubbed by the project leader from the Government Buildings Agency when we were formed in late 2006, to inspire us with the suggestion that we were on a mission—sitting there: the architect, the project manager, and the directors of the museum. We sat there, in equal parts disbelieving and delighted, spellbound by the rhetoric of Nathan Coley's presentation, when he laid out his plan for the first time. "We're going to ship back the *IJsselstenen* that served as ballast, enough of them to build a wall with."

That the plan created euphoria is an understatement; our thoughts were going in every direction. Is this feasible? Can we get permission? Can we get away with commissioning this, as a government agency? From a practical standpoint, how do you organize something like this? And last but not least, what are the ethical implications of an action like this? Wasn't this terribly arrogant, and didn't the plan have at least a whiff of a new imperialism about it, to think that we could turn back the clock of history all by ourselves, even if only symbolically? Might we not end up unnecessarily stirring up a lot of emotions, and not just bricks?

It took Coley two years of planning, in close cooperation with Joost ten Bruggencate of Mothership, in Rotterdam, to sketch out the logistics of acquiring and shipping the bricks. Appeals were put up on the Internet, discussions held with embassies, long-term loan agreements drawn up. Letters of support from the burgomaster of Amsterdam, the director of the Het Scheepvaartmuseum, and the Government Architect's advisor on monuments were needed to tip the scales. Then there were discussions with potential shippers. For a long time we cherished the dream that somewhere there must still be a desolate, unclaimed ruin, the removal of which would pass unnoticed.

In the meantime, in a parallel course with the development of the logistics, Nathan Coley moved forward with conversations with the architect of the new building, Liesbeth van der Pol, who, during the building process, also succeeded Mels Crouwel as Government Architect. Earlier, in 1997, she had already designed the depot for the museum a bit farther up on the same site. Broadly, the design that Van der Pol did for the alterations to the 's Lands Zeemagazijn involved roofing over the inner courtyard, a new routing through the museum, and a new climate control system. The original robust character of the building had to be preserved as much as possible.

The relation between architecture and art in Coley's work is obvious. His background as an artist shows through as he explores the boundaries of what is possible. He plays the game for all it's worth, and enters into discussion with the architect. What is at stake is the dilemma of functionality. In the discussions with Liesbeth van der Pol he sought a formulation for the point at which architecture can go no farther. Unhindered by limiting conditions, lists of requirements, and functionality, he had the baton passed to him precisely at the point where architecture stops, resulting in a functionless wall which connects to nothing, bears nothing, and is unfinished—or, as he himself put it, "a stubborn wall." A pure statement. How impudent can you be? He went as far as the architect permitted.

In June 2009, Coley and Mothership presented the results to the art team. There were three promises of a minimal number of bricks from each location, and there were still more clandestine offers that we couldn't get involved with. We didn't have enough bricks to build a wall. This necessarily led to a radical change in the process, and in the thinking about the work: this practical disappointment also refined the question about its legitimacy. In the final plan the dilemma of historical imperialism resulted in the actual return trip with the promised bricks becoming part of a "reenactment" of the sea journey: containers full of original Vecht bricks, which are still available in abundance here in the Netherlands, would call in at four locations, sailing to Australia, Singapore, Suriname, and St. Eustatius—places where the chance of being able to bring back some of the original "booty" too would be greatest. Coley had previously already done a reenactment in Belém, Brazil with the work *The Land Marked* (2001), by building a historic tower anew, on the basis of a temporary projection. The shipping of the bricks and travelling the routes once again was a monumental gesture of almost unimaginable magnitude.

On March 22, 2010, a special container designed by Studio Leon & Loes in a typically Dutch makeover departed from Rotterdam, accompanied by a briefing with information about the project, in the eventuality that the shippers would receive questions about it. With several detours and delays for storm season, then making up time, it covered the following itinerary: Rotterdam-Singapore-Freemantle (Australia)-Rotterdam-Paramaribo (Suriname)-St. Eustatius-Paramaribo-Rotterdam. Because there is no direct ocean-going freight service from Australia to the Caribbean, the container first had to return to Rotterdam before it could go on through to St. Eustatius. Thus the container followed the current navigation routes. On December 16, the container ship with the Vecht bricks was again back in Rotterdam. All told, on the way it had picked up another thirty bricks that had made the sea journey over 300 years earlier.

The Wall

In March 2011, the wall was built in the northern entrance hall according to the plans. The difference in the origin of the bricks is invisible to the layman, but precise records were kept of which are which. The wall is a modest yet very prominent part of the northern entrance, which the visitor literally and figuratively can't get around. At first sight it appears to be a part of its context, a remnant of the original building, but on further inspection you see that the wall relates to the new building rather than the other way around. Parts of the new plastered walls are incomplete behind the wall. What's going on here? It is precisely this carelessness that focuses attention on the new construction as something new. The wall poses questions to the building, to its architecture, its history, and the future in relation to Amsterdam, the Netherlands, the world.

In its lack of function we see the wall as a basic architectonic element. A wall is a limit, a boundary, an end. Just as the bricks represent the history of the VOC, for those who can see its significance, the wall refers to the limits of a world economy that began with historic imperialism. It is a proclamation of the end of an era of faith in economic growth, and of the exploitation of people and resources that has made that growth possible.

It is precisely this interweaving of social and economic forces, the ways in which we have constructed the world, and the way in which we subsequently experience that architecture, that is the subject of Nathan Coley's work. His work reveals the influence that architecture has on us, the way in which it directs our thinking, in a vicious circle of influencing and being influenced. It is an attempt to disentangle that process. He moves the viewer with minimal means, with consequences that reach as far as you can and will think.

— *Tanja Karreman*

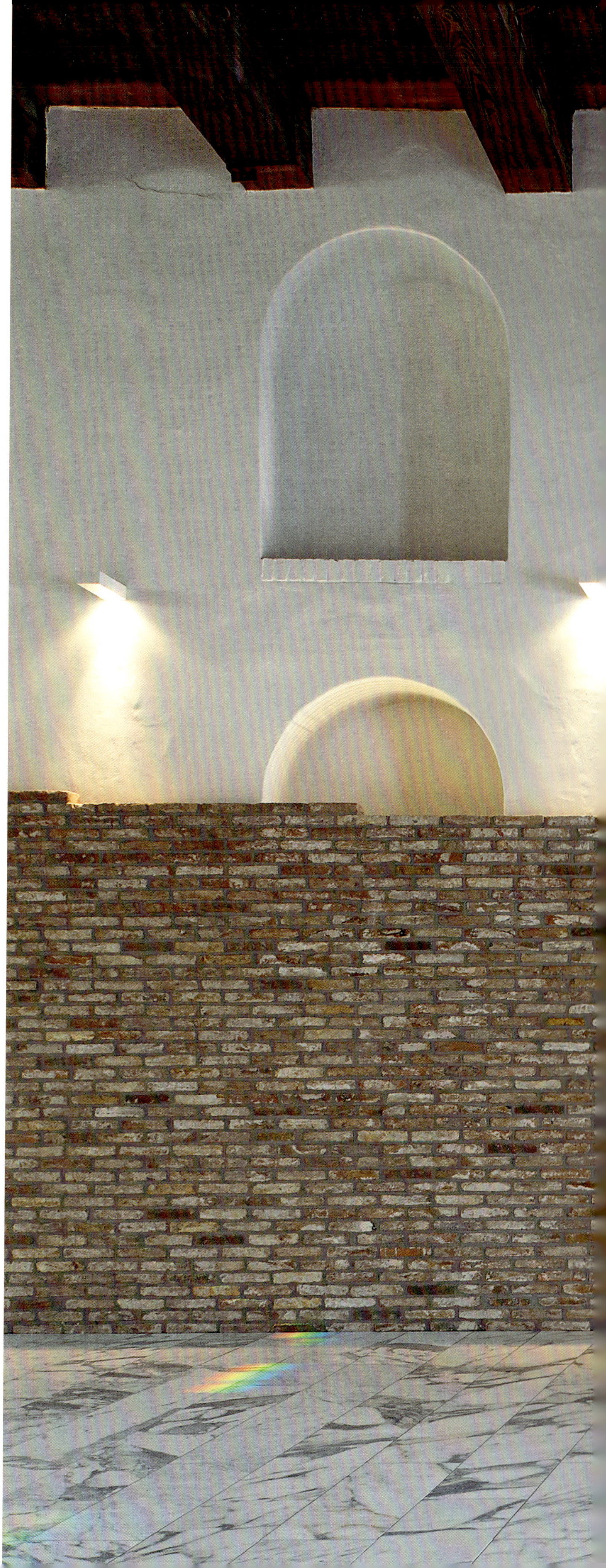

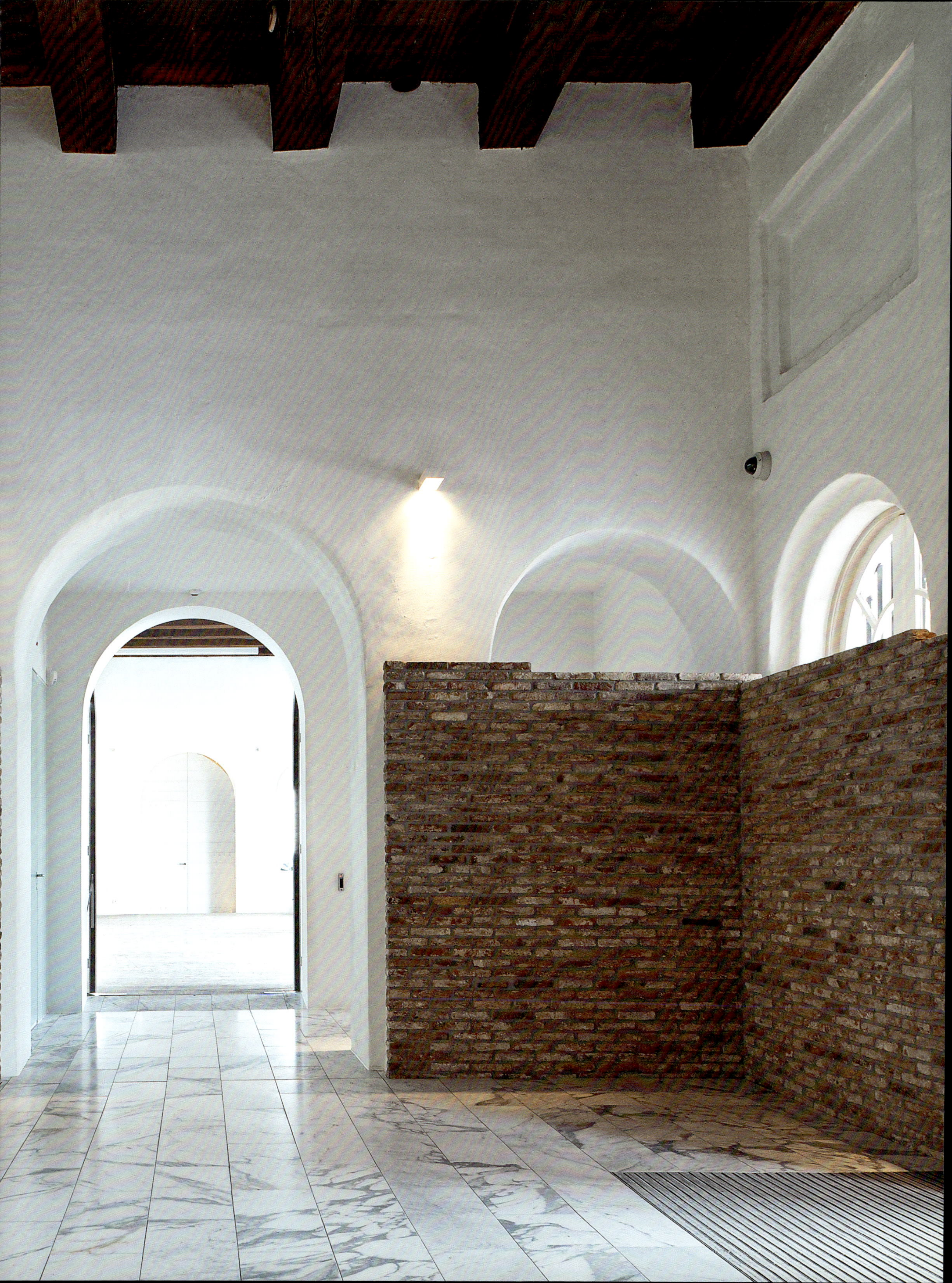

The Square of the Three Powers / Landings

Out on the Platform

"By placing the cemeteries at the ends of the residential highway axis, funeral processions will not need to cross the urban center. These cemeteries will be landscaped with lawns and suitable trees, the tombs to be smooth and the headstones simple—in the English tradition—the whole to be completely unostentatious."
—Lúcio Costa, Report on a pilot plan for Brasília, 1957

Some years ago Nathan Coley took a series of photographs in the Square of the Three Powers (Praça dos Três Poderes) in Brasília. He pinned them up in his studio, where they became the objects of a certain fascination: "I kept going back to the images, not knowing why." The square in question, and its attendant administrative buildings, was among the first public spaces completed for the inauguration of the new Brazilian capital on April 21, 1960. To the west stand the twin towers of the National Congress, to the north the Palácio do Planalto, the administrative seat of the republic's president, with its glass walls, expansive flat roof, and sail-like white supports. To the south, 400 meters away across a vast open square interrupted only by a statue of the blind figure of Justice, sits a building of similar design, on a smaller scale: the Supreme Court. The square, around which Brasília was originally conceived, is both a meaningful expanse—symbolic of both the state powers that flank it and of the immense flat plain on which the city is built—and a public space for the use and enjoyment of citizens and tourists. (It is also, lest one forget, the civic and national function of the place, home to the largest continuously flown national flag in the world.)

Aerial photographs of the Square of the Three Powers suggest (because this writer has not been there) that the space is uninterrupted apart from flagpoles and sculpture. But Coley's photographs reveal that a structure—perhaps mundane, maybe extraordinary—rises at its southern side and complicates the flatness or platitude of this utopian precinct. The images depict in a monochrome that looks as if it might date from the square's completion (but for the clothes of the few people that appear there and the trees behind the court building), a low, stained-concrete platform, rectangular in shape and several meters in horizontal extent. It seems to hover above the rougher paving of the square. A dark void subtends the floating upper surface, and two perpendicular sides are interrupted by shallow flights of four steps each, which may bring visiting tourists or native flaneurs up onto the platform. Nobody has ventured onto this surface itself, but in Coley's photographs five figures sit at the edges of the structure—at least one lounges relaxed, one foot raised onto the concrete. Behind them, the Supreme Court mirrors distortedly the government buildings at the other side of the square; from another vantage, a vast, curving, glass-fronted building (a much later addition to this space, conceived with a clear unity of purpose, design, and significance in mind) reflects a lower, gray cloudscape. The court itself contributes both rectilinear and curving, organic forms to the scene, but almost all else is starkly perpendicular. A thin vertical of concrete—perhaps a sculpture, an observation or bell tower—divides one photograph in two, and off to the right a pair of low and unpeopled concrete benches rhyme modestly with the central platform.

It is unclear what function this laconic object performs in the square, beyond the apparent and perhaps unofficial one of a place of rest. It is patently of a piece, design-wise, with the contemporary building and the other minimal furnishings that surround it. The thing might, as the artist suggests, be a kind of stage or bandstand designed for carrying out official functions or ceremonies, less formal celebrations, or spontaneous entertainments, even demonstrations, on the part of the citizenry. It is both oddly self-involved and mysterious, and a type of invitation to the performance of state-sanctioned or unofficial rituals. As Coley notes, it looks distinctly unfinished, as if another building were meant to rise at the southern extremity of the square but has remained incomplete; it is perhaps a vacant space in which to dream of another building on a more human or intimate scale than those that flank the square. Most strikingly, it adds another level, another stratum, to a portion of the city that already rises above the surrounding plain: one ascends by steps to the Square of the Three Powers and looks down on the city that it is meant to govern and control, and has, to some degree, famously failed. Looking at the artist's photographs of the platform—and perhaps this is what Coley himself began to discern—one begins to imagine Brasília as a stratified city, a series of layers somehow at odds with the concept essential to

The Square of the Three Powers, 2011
Gold leaf on Giclée prints
Two parts, 50 × 70 cm each

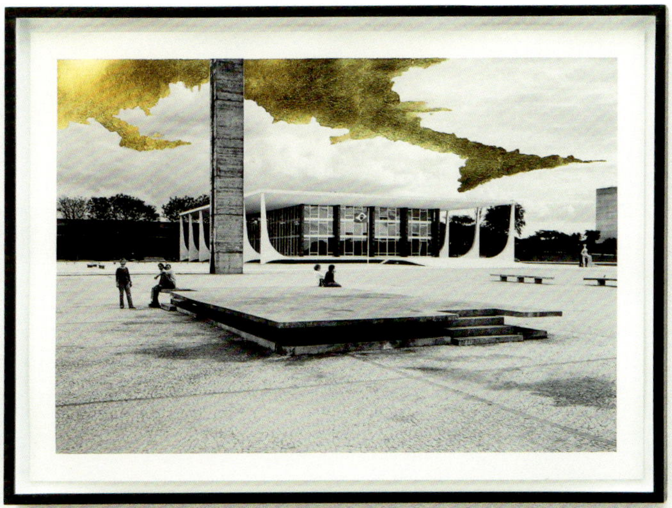

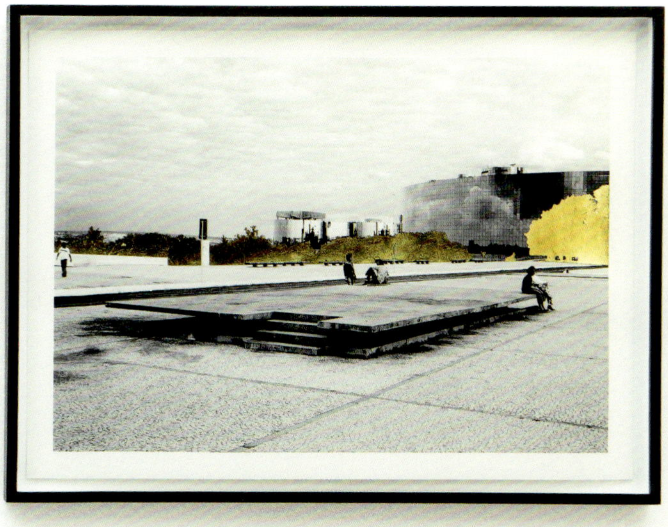

its original vision of a city radiating horizontally, along cross-wise axes, from its administrative center. This enigmatic structure seems to suggest, especially as one tries to plumb the blackness under it, unknowable depths beneath the public façade.

A type of elevated flatness or horizontality has, in fact, long been intrinsic to the vision of Brasília as an administrative, political, and urban center. Central to its legendary origins is a vision that Dom Bosco, subsequently patron saint of the capital, claimed to have had on August 30, 1883, while traversing Brazil's great central plain. He dreamed that while travelling across the Andes he was joined by a celestial guide:

> I saw the bowels of the mountains and the depths of the plains. I had before my eyes the incomprehensible riches . . . which would one day be discovered. I saw numerous mines of precious metals and fossil coals, and deposits of oil of such abundance as had never before been seen in other places. But that was not all. Between the fifteenth and the twentieth degrees of latitude, there was a long and wide stretch of land which arose at a point where a lake was forming. Then a voice said repeatedly: when people come to excavate the mines hidden in the middle of these mountains, there will appear in this place the Promised Land, flowing with milk and honey. It will be of incomprehensible richness.

Bosco's vision was officially sanctioned in the Old Republic Constitution of 1891. It was not a wholly visionary plan: the 14,000 square meters of the central plain envisaged for the city constituted, among other things, a safe haven from naval attack—always a danger in the then capital of Rio de Janeiro—but languished unfulfilled until the mid nineteen-fifties, when President Juscelino Kubitschek made it state policy to build the city by 1960.

The city's subsequent history is well known. Urban planner Lúcio Costa drew up a scheme and his chief architect, Oscar Niemeyer, designed much of the fabric of the city in a style that consciously combined the modernism of Le Corbusier with the organic forms of native architecture. Brasília stands today as both a monument to the progressive, even utopian, ambition of modernism and a notorious lesson in its limitations; the socially and physically zoned "horizontal" city soon stratified itself in precisely the terms it was planned to avoid. Class distinctions asserted themselves in the ostensibly communal and open city center, a vast hinterland of the poor grew up to service that center, and the city's inhabitants began to speak of suffering from brasilite, or Brasília-itis, an urban disorder brought on by the starkness and inhuman scale of the place.

What does it mean today to remake, obliquely, such a structure as the concrete platform that Coley discovered in Brasília? In part, the gesture is in keeping with a certain archaeology of modernism that has been undertaken by many artists in the last decade or so. It seems that the

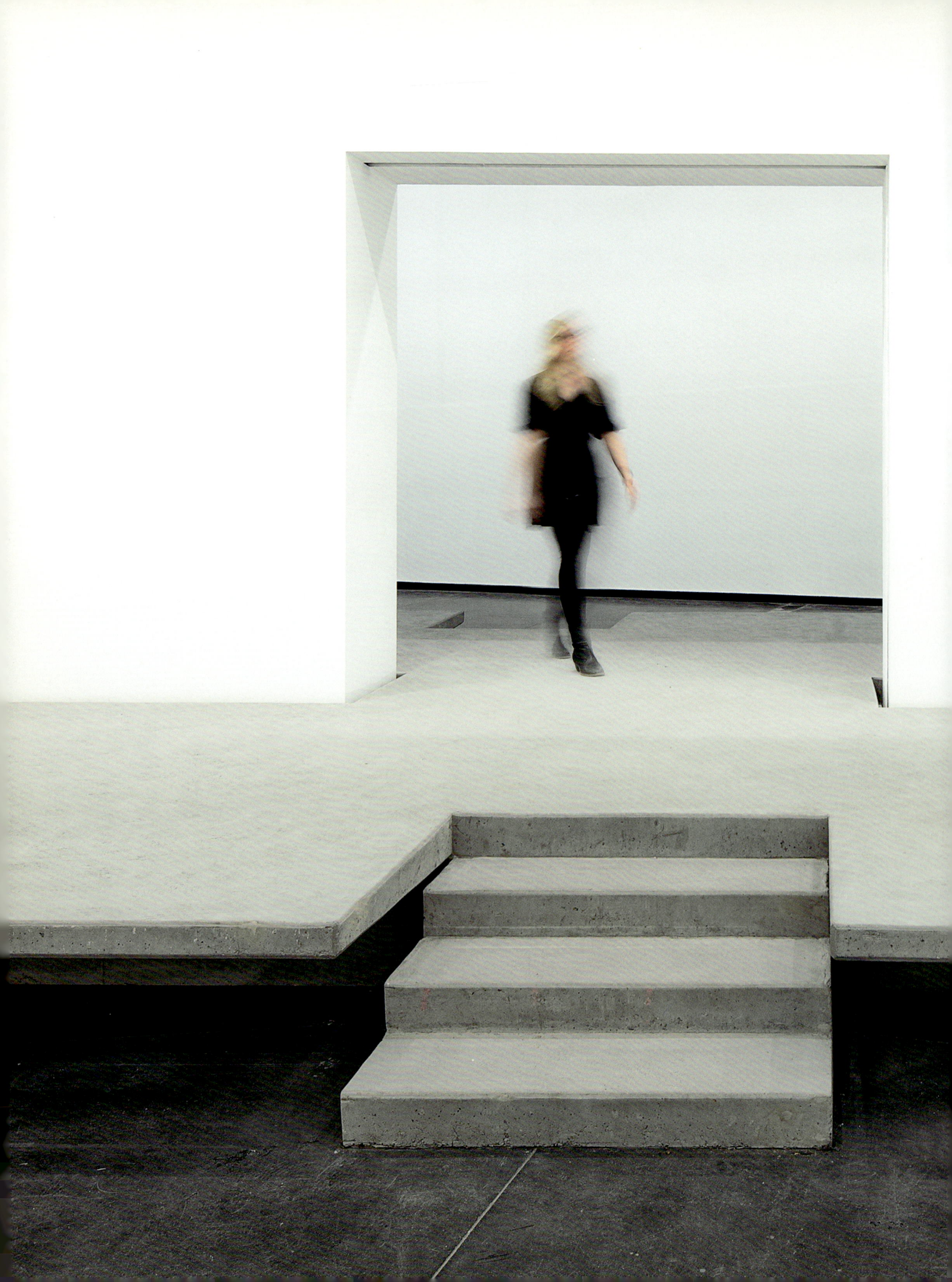

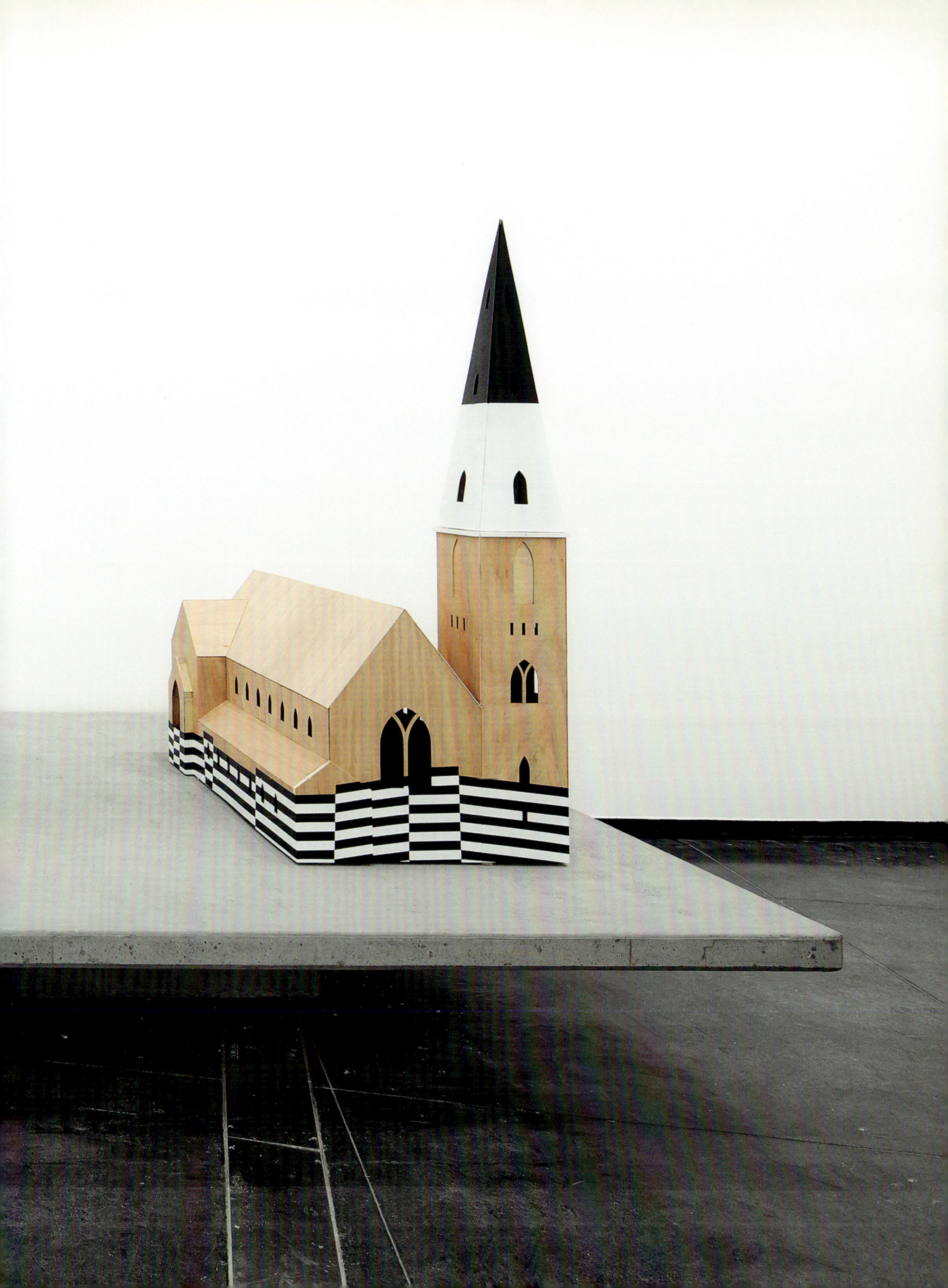

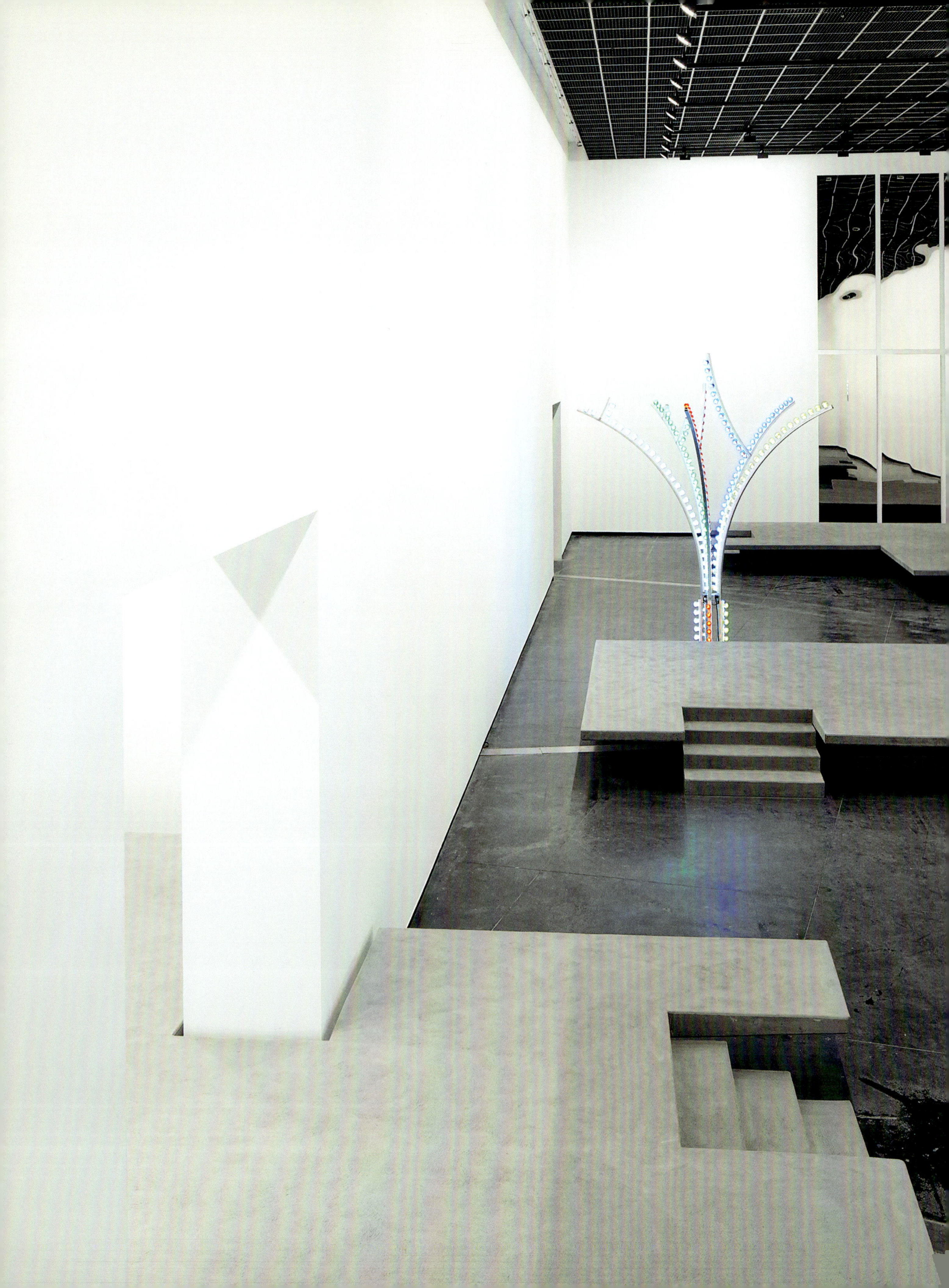

forms and the ideologies of modernist architecture, in particular, have returned to haunt a present that lacks both the aesthetic vision and the progressive political ambition of the mid twentieth century. Inevitably, much of the work made in this vein engages the past in a melancholic fashion; the modernist ruin has become a familiar motif in contemporary art, so much so that it is possible to speak of the architecture of last century as having attained, in a prodigious acceleration of decay and regret, the status that classical ruins had for the ruin enthusiasts of the Romantic period. There were artists who knew this in the immediate wake of modernism. Robert Smithson is the prime example, with his concept of "ruins in reverse": those structures and sites that seem to fall into ruin at the same time as they are being built or rebuilt. The concrete ruins of the recent past, on this reading, are dialectical entities, facing past and future at the same time.

Brasília, of course, is not a literal ruin, though it is certainly a relic. The functioning city—its serenely or thrillingly open spaces now considerably complicated by further construction, traffic, and the messiness of actual urban life—is also a repository of utopian memories of a possible future. Coley's vacant platform is a tabula rasa on which the hopes of the mid-century and their subsequent protracted dashing may be written. It is not exactly a melancholy object, and nor do its avatars in the gallery simply recall, in a nostalgic or ironic fashion, the futurism it once embodied. Coley's sculptural response to the platform is a series of varied iterations of the original, their concrete poured in the gallery itself. The moment of their solidification in that space is an inauguration of sorts, an invitation to slightly elevate oneself above the gallery floor, thereby entering into a subtly different ritual or performative space and state. One of the platforms intrudes between two rooms of the gallery, becoming both an obstacle and a means of passage. There are reminders, too, of the site of the original platform itself—mirrored steel panels on the gallery wall reflect the spectator who has mounted a platform, recalling the glass architecture of the Square of the Three Powers. They open the gallery up to another place and time in which transparency and spatial openness were intended to foster something similar at the level of political and social interaction. At the same time, the work makes clear references to the minimalist sculpture of the nineteen-sixties, and Robert Morris's notorious assertion that sculpture had simply declined (spatially speaking) from the vertical to the horizontal.

This material becoming and spatial alteration has a ritual or sacred aspect, quite coterminous with Coley's longstanding critical interest in spaces of worship and the alternative cartography they describe around a city. We may recall his installation *The Lamp of Sacrifice (286 Places of Worship, Edinburgh)* (2004), with its massed cardboard scale models of every church in the city. Or more materially his *In Memory* (2010), a modestly sized family graveyard constructed at the Jupiter Artland sculpture garden in Edinburgh, in which the headstones lack names and the whole is surrounded protectively by a blank concrete wall. The very enclosure and discretion of the work become the condition by which it opens itself to the memory and imagination of the visitor. It is not so much a work of mourning or melancholia as a space and substance in which certain possibilities, and a fluid relation with time and memory, are broached. The Brasília platform maintains something of this unostentatious openness. Its very self-sameness (the fluid concrete hardening to a uniform solid) is once more a sort of invitation, not merely to ascend the steps but to reflect on the stubborn survival of the original object and the continued uncertainty of its status in such an ordered and "cold" environment.

Many photographs exist of the Brazilian capital under construction in the late nineteen-fifties, and they include black-and-white and color views of the southern side of the Square of the Three Powers. One depicts the area as a scratted and apparently unruly building site, with the plain on which the city was constructed stretching in the distance. The impression is of an emptiness or flatness from which Bosco's dream of 1883 is about to emerge. A shallow ramp of earth delivers materials to the site of the Supreme Court, a single structure rising from the mass of crosshatched scaffolding: the thin white curve of the first support for the building's roof. The support is massive but frail-looking from a distance, a tentative assertion of utopian ambition on the empty and hostile plain. It is exactly this intrusion of the lonely and hopeful vertical into the vacant landscape that Coley's art asks us to consider, with its fragile, garish remnant of fairground architecture interrupting tree-like between the concrete plateaux hovering just above the gallery floor. It is an image of solitary presence—like the model of Scots' Church perched on an adjacent platform—that holds promises at the same time that it holds the possibility of collective being and the persistence of a sense that here on the platform anything might happen.
— *Brian Dillon*

Landings, 2011
Poured concrete
63 cm high
Installation, Australian Centre for Contemporary Art, Melbourne

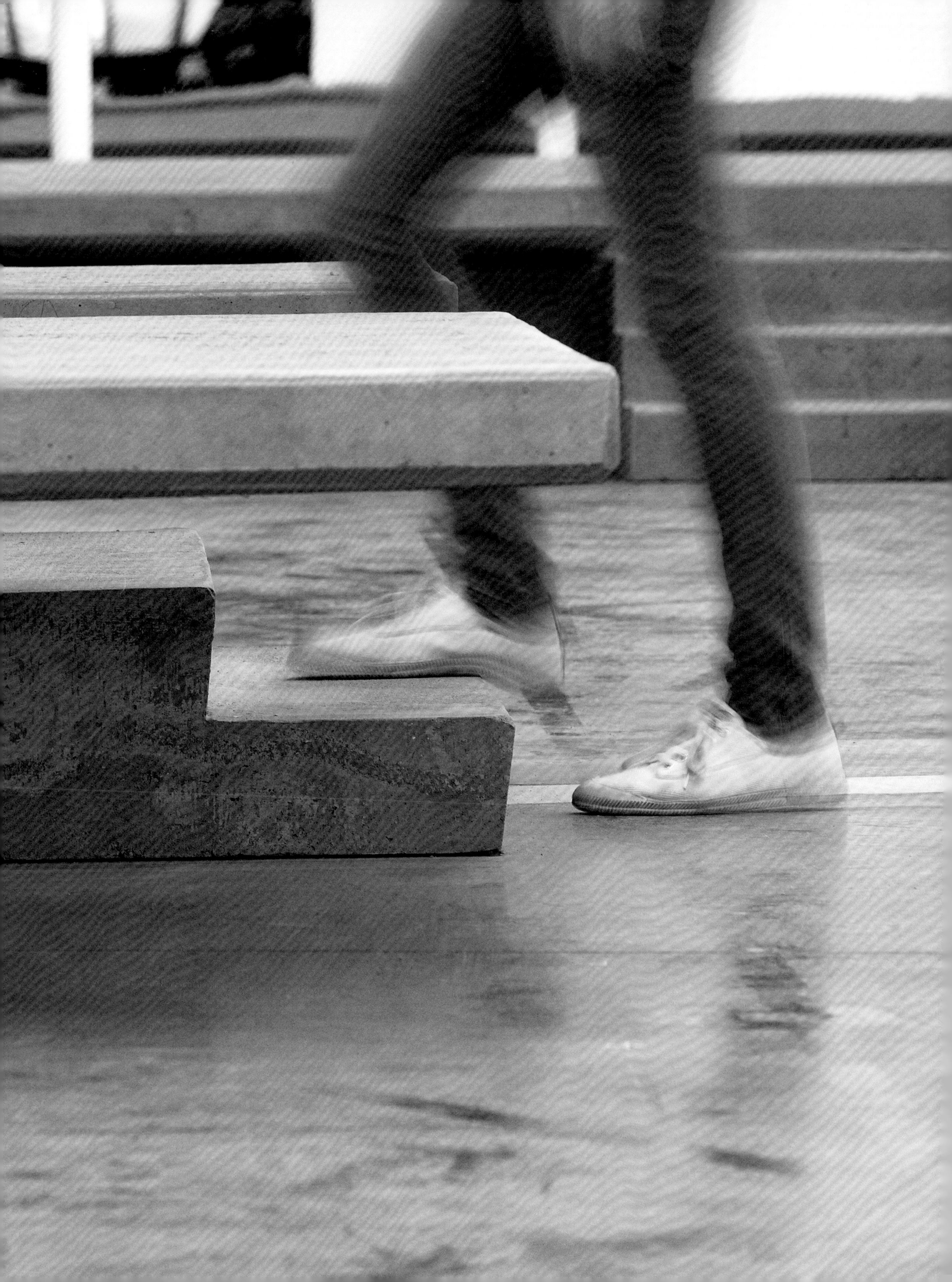

Luna Tree

For his solo show at the Australian Centre for Contemporary Art in 2011, Coley transformed the main exhibition space into a vast, civic square consisting of a series of poured concrete platforms. Inspired by Oscar Niemeyer's architectural designs for Brazil's capital city, Brasília, Coley fabricated an urban environment within the gallery. Merging the organic with the artificial, *Luna Tree* burgeons from the center of the space and rises above the surrounding landings, staging a dichotomy between the brutal, permanent quality of the concrete and the fragility of the illuminated bulbs. Echoing Coley's text works, the artist refashioned an architectural structure from an amusement park he visited in St. Kilda, near Melbourne. Punctuated with fluorescent bulbs / leaves, each branch burgeons upward in a sweeping motion, recalling the speed and dynamism of the fairground rides from which the form was originally appropriated. *Luna Tree* also harks back to the carnival culture of Brazil and enlivens an otherwise dour, gray environment. As Coley explains, the work "adds a degree of color, of glamour and celebration, into what could have been a rather monotone controlled proposition. Perhaps it takes us back to Brazil in an unexpected way."[1]
— *Jonathan Horrocks*

---

[1] Excerpt from an interview with Charlotte Day, first published in the exhibition catalogue to coincide with the solo exhibition *Appearances* at the Australian Centre for Contemporary Art (Melbourne, 2011).

Luna Tree, 2011
Illuminated sculpture
3.3 × 2.5 × 2.5 m
Installation, Australian Centre for Contemporary Art, Melbourne

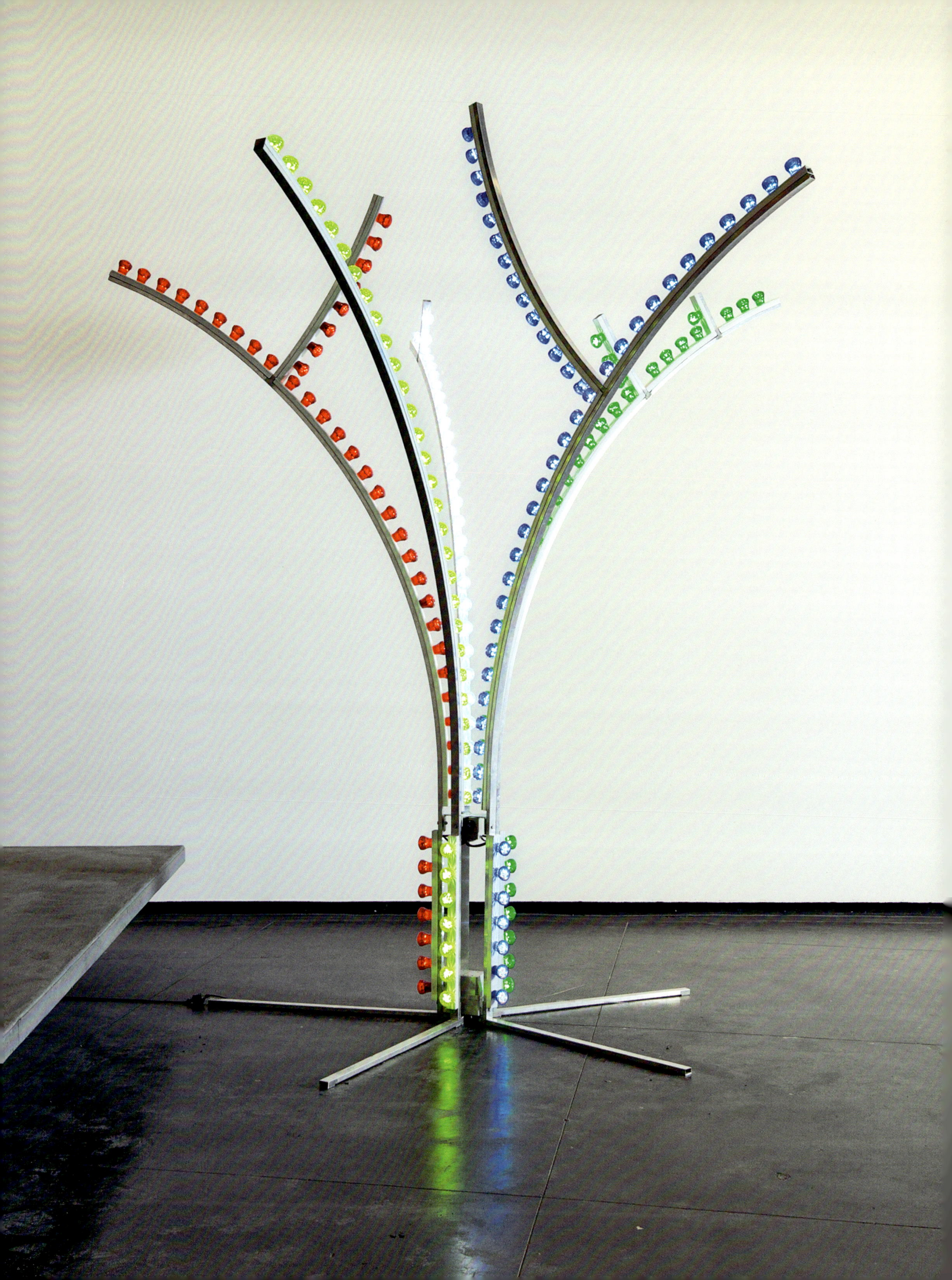

Tattooed Church

Produced for his solo exhibition at the Australian Centre for Contemporary Art in 2011, Nathan Coley's *Tattooed Church* sits upon a ledge which forms part of the central, concrete platform which traverses the main gallery space. Hand-made from raw plywood, with joins visible and pencil marks evident, the little neo-Gothic church, its spire reaching 1.8 meters high, is like a curio, a newly made relic from an era preceding secular modernism. Its smallness implies its undemonstrative demeanor. It is like a doll's house that we tower over. We can command it, practice our faith without long-term commitment.

Coley's concrete plinth becomes an island for his model church. He conforms to and confirms the necessity of the utopian, sequestered, uncontaminated private space for this Lilliputian item, so that we may look down upon the perfection of the miniature, which we cherish, like a child, because of our opportunity to oversee its proportions and balance in totality.

Coley's little church is the antithesis of modern standardization of mass-produced structures and things. His hand-crafted model is unique—an item that excites our nostalgia for craft and for pre-industrial, authentic labor. In miniaturization, the church seems a perfect gem, a charismatically charming thing.

To emphasize its seductive lure, Coley has added a decorative "razzle dazzle" to the external walls of the church. Black-and-white striations rise around the structure in jaunty fashion, like a happy zebra herd. The dazzle is a riff on the camouflage painted on battleships during World War I: an optical illusion intended to confuse the enemy by disguising the direction of the boat. The dazzle was first tested on models by its instigator, Norman Wilkinson, and his team, who bunkered down in the basement of the Royal Academy workshop in London. With its modern, bold patterned design, it is perhaps one of the first examples of non-figurative painting in British art.

Perhaps the "razzle dazzle" is also a tilt to Orchestral Manoeuvres in the Dark's *Dazzle Ships* album (1983), the band's less successful successor to its *Architecture and Morality* of 1981. Coley is, after all, drawn to examine unspoken things contained within structures: morality, faith, fear, and arrogance. The dazzle lends a certain jewel-like quality to the church, but the decorative origins, nevertheless, are about deceit and trickery, a kind of mirage.

The viewer is drawn to peer inside the church's hyper-enclosed interior, which emphasizes the phenomenological and psychological difference between the private and public space that has just been crossed. But it also confirms the perfection of its sanctuary for the select who might inhabit its nostalgic meaning.

Appearances can be deceiving, and so we might assume Coley's dazzle also suggests a metaphor about the seductions of the religion, or, more sympathetically, that it acknowledges that religions are now embattled and have become targets in the newly drawn religio-geopolitical landscape. In this sense, Coley's church is the every-church, a symbol under siege.

— *Juliana Engberg*

Excerpt from the essay "Razzle Dazzle, the Situation Now," 2011

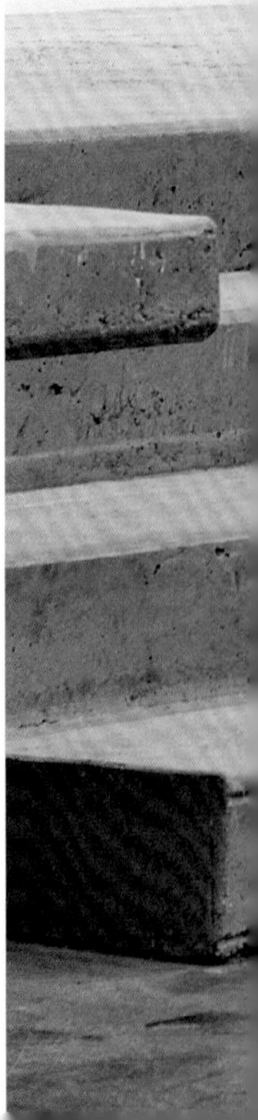

Tattooed Church, 2011
Painted plywood
130 × 45 × 146 cm
Installation, Australian Centre for Contemporary Art, Melbourne

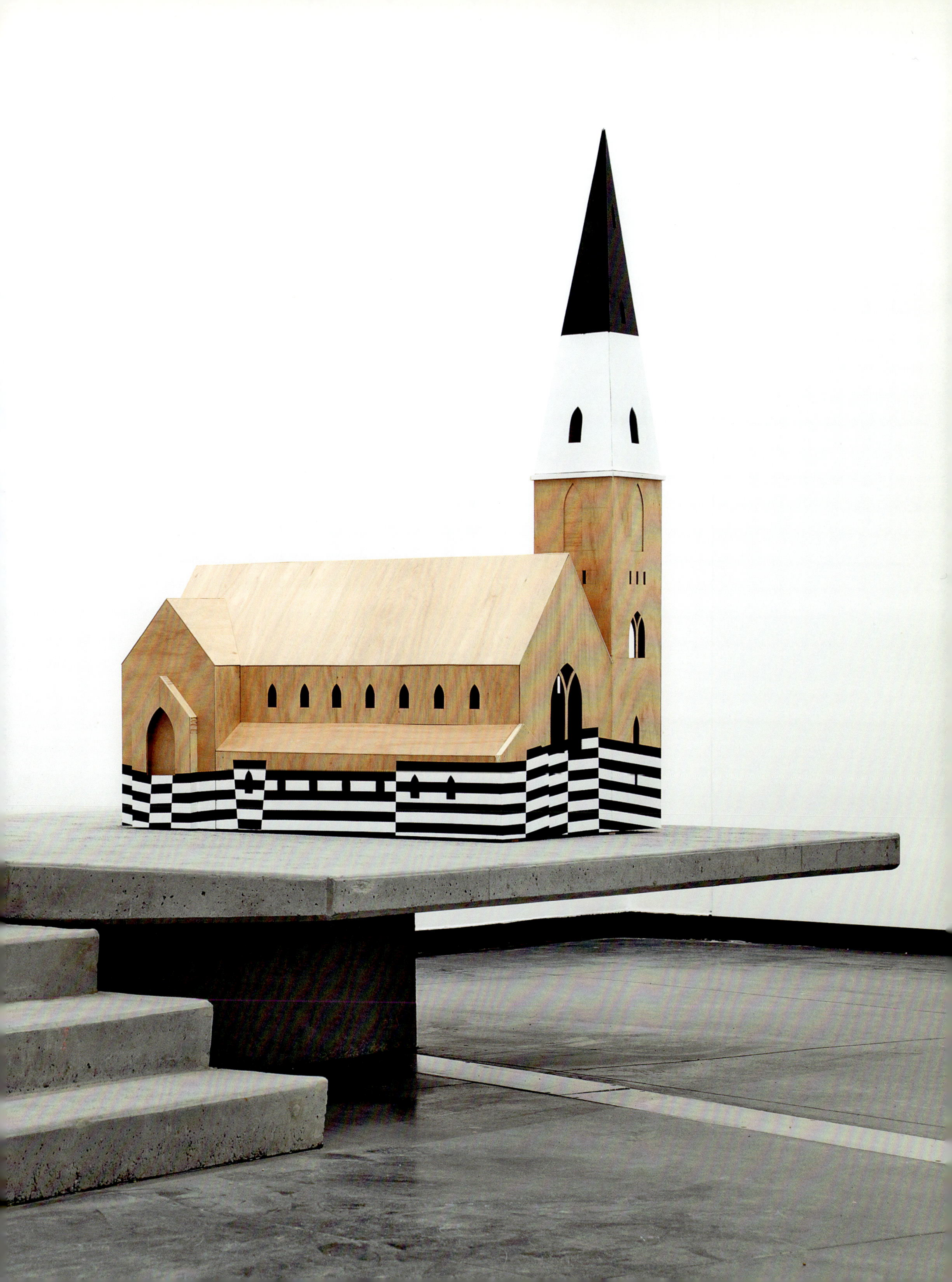

Camouflage Room

Coley provides an antechamber into which we might retreat to contemplate the utopian environment constructed in the main space. It is a sanctuary of sorts, decorated with large striations of blue and white. In the middle gallery of the Australian Centre for Contemporary Art, it is enclosed at one end of its non-Euclidian shape. Such retreat is to no avail. The bands of color accentuate the warp of the space to make it disorienting and discombobulating. The only refuge against this derangement appears in the form of three smaller framed abstractions, each a pattern of colored bands: blue and white, gold and white, black and white. Coley says these represent, to his way of thinking, the Christian, Muslim, and Jewish faiths. Each, in its own way, provides a secure resting point in this larger space, which remains unstable and distracting. They are the same but different, separated and distinguished by their frame of reference. To me, the room represents the interior, exterior, and phenomenological space in-between.
— *Juliana Engberg*

Excerpt from the essay "Razzle Dazzle, the Situation Now," 2011

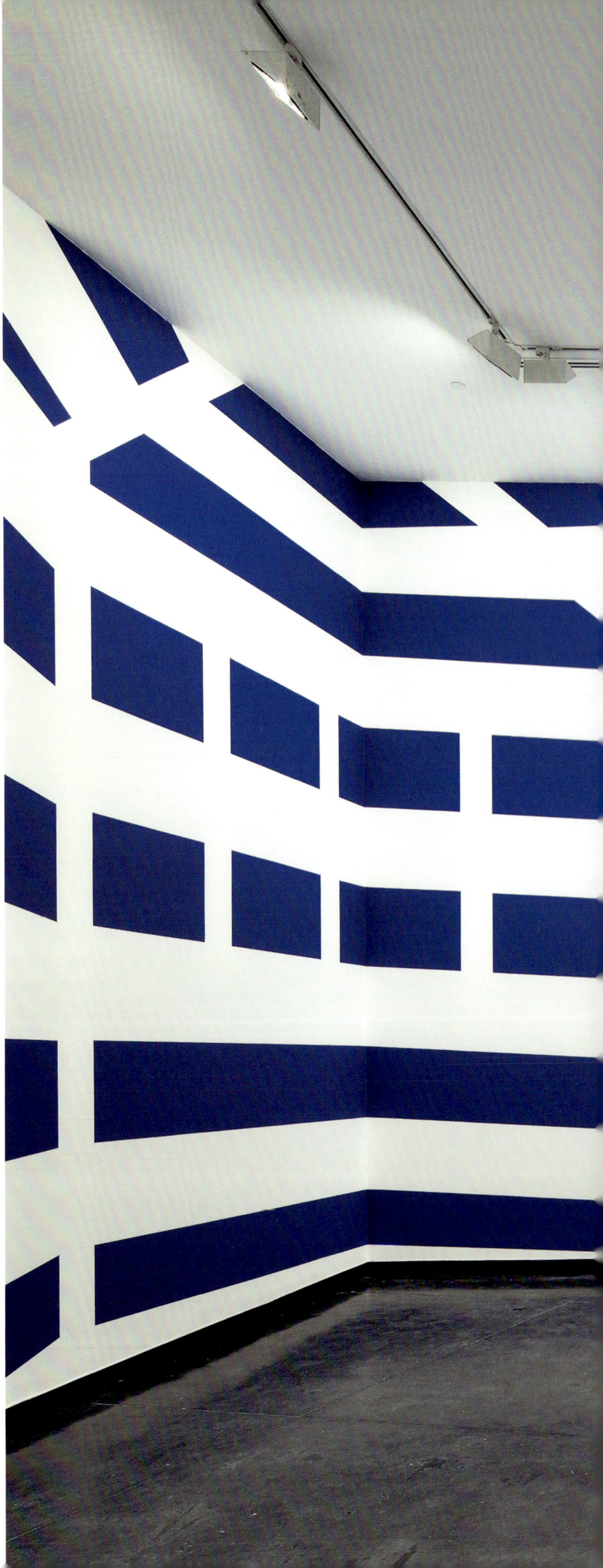

Camouflage Room with *Untitled (Black), Untitled (Gold), Untitled (Blue)*, 2011
Wall painting with 3 enamel paintings on board
84 × 63 cm each
Installation, Australian Centre for Contemporary Art, Melbourne

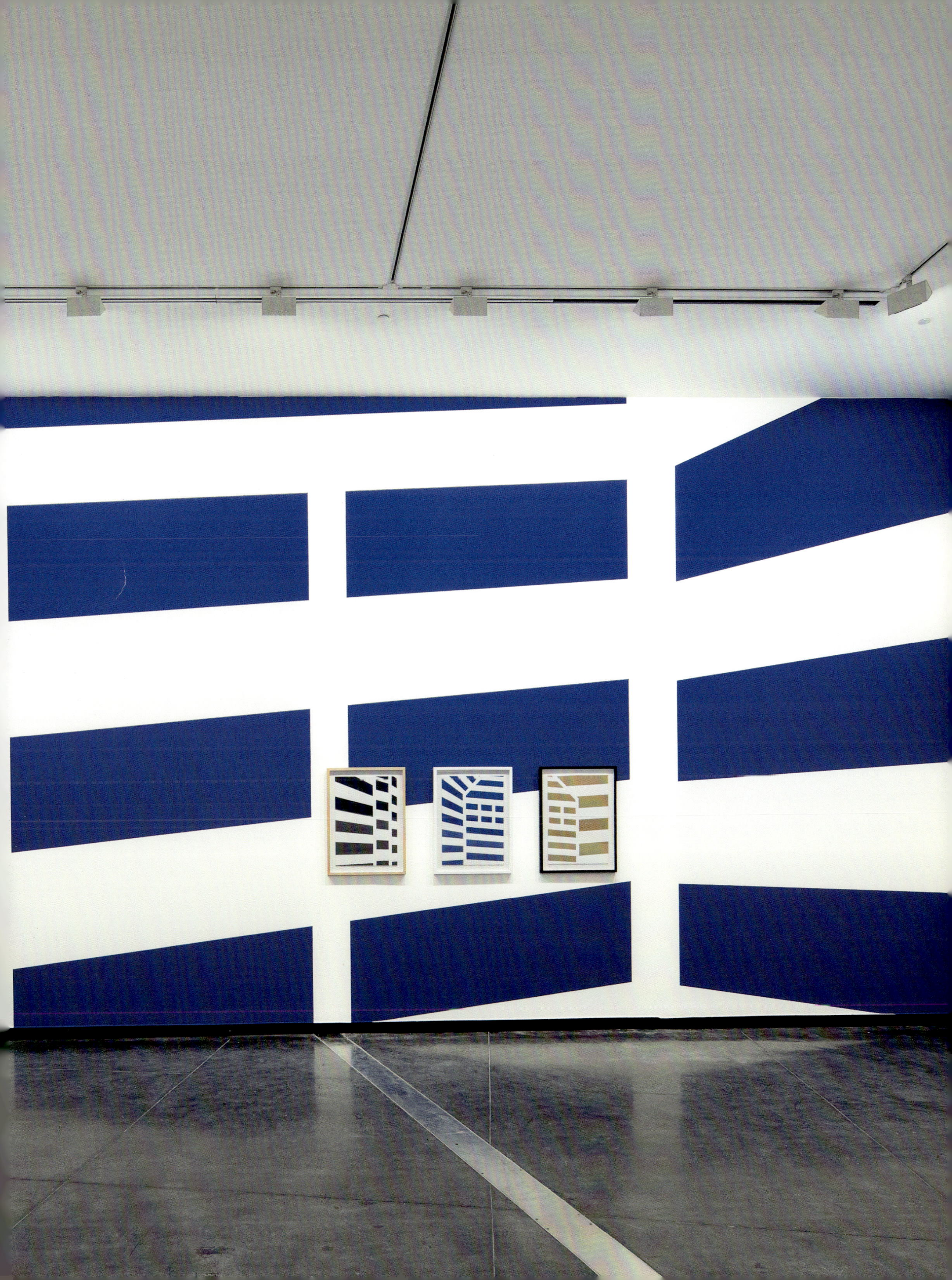

Another Lecture

Recreating a dimly lit lecture theater, Nathan Coley's *Another Lecture* (2011) takes the form of a satirical PowerPoint presentation. Recalling lecture-based works produced by the artist in the nineteen-nineties, the work establishes a dialogue between the urban environments of Glasgow and Melbourne. Officious in tone, the female voiceover discusses the motives behind recent, fictional interventions that her architectural firm has purportedly instigated in both cities.

Meandering through the urban landscape, the slide-show captures glimpses of overlooked spaces within Glasgow and Melbourne left unnoticed by the cities' inhabitants; stills of derelict sites, rubbish-strewn lots, and dilapidated buildings are discussed with pride as if part of the firm's portfolio. At one instance, the voiceover, narrated by actress Cate Blanchett, dryly asserts that a graffiti signature on the door of a run-down Cash & Carry was an addition implemented by the company in order to "make it clear where to enter the building." On the one hand, the video's underlying irony makes a mockery of the aloof nature of architectural discourse, while on the other it celebrates the discovery of insignificant structures and spaces often overlooked in everyday life.
— *Jonathan Horrocks*

Another Lecture, 2011
Single-screen video projection
13-min durational loop

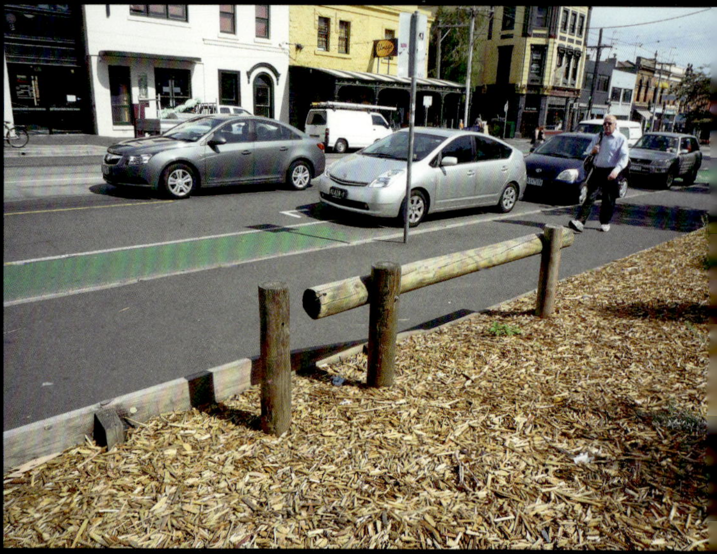

Sometimes we introduce a really rigid set of rules, only allowing ourselves one material or one color.

We came up with a very simple solution here with these three timber uprights, punctuating the space, and a single linear element connecting the three.

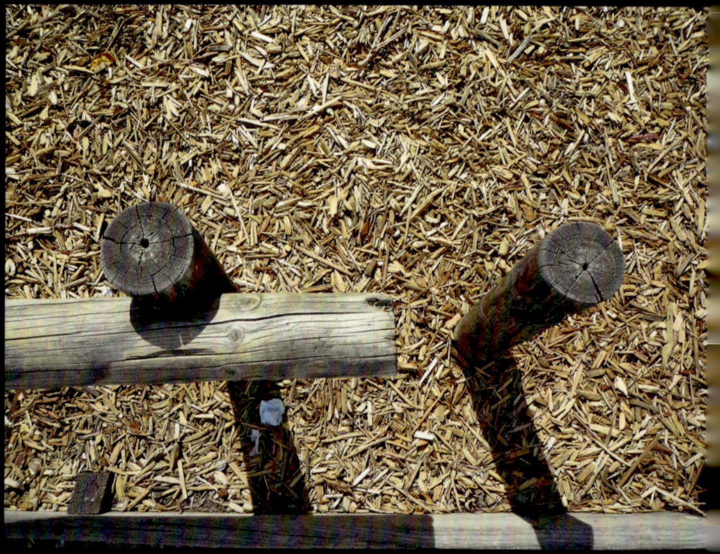

This is another shot.

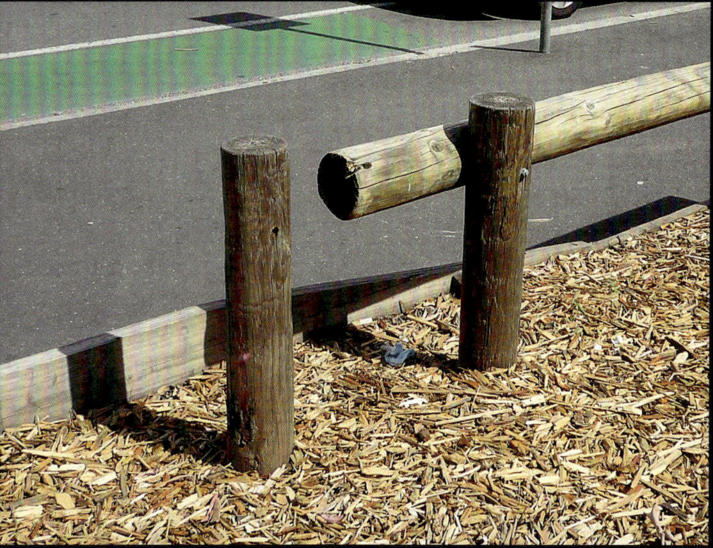

We let the horizontal element finish just before the join, almost touching, but not quite.

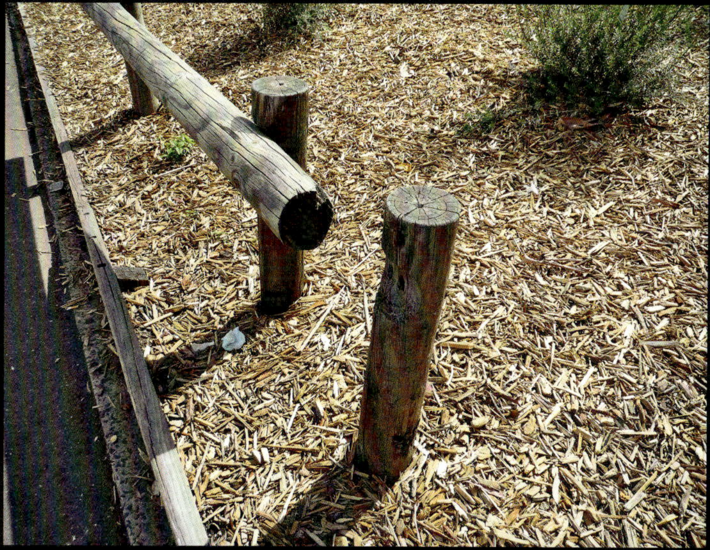

The detail of that circular cut, ready to accept the timber, I think is . . . really exciting.

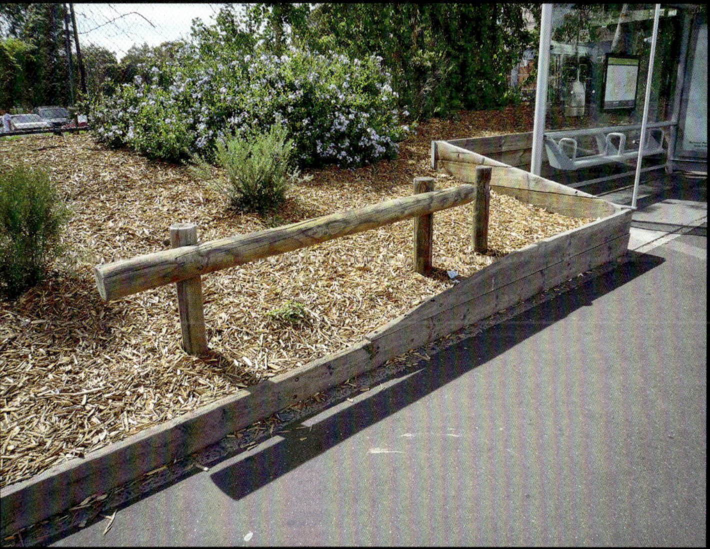

Quite a brave addition to a difficult site.

I like the way it echoes the seat in the bus stop.

In Memory

In the gently rolling, wooded grounds of Jupiter Artland, on the outskirts of Edinburgh, *In Memory* (2010) is a permanent installation comprising a concrete enclosure, which contains what appears to be a small, private graveyard, not dissimilar to those family burial sites to be found within many a private estate. The enclosure is a stark square, open to the elements and entered through a single, narrow aperture, the width of which is defined by the width of the artist's shoulders. It is encroached by a single tree, a large branch of which rests on the upper edge of one side of the enclosure, but the tree itself is long dead, offering some pleasing form but no foliage.

Within the enclosure stand a number of headstones. They are quite clearly real headstones, rather than facsimiles, retrieved from burial sites. Yet, for one reason or another, they have been removed from the places for which they were made. The stones are clearly aged, preexisting, in effect "ready-made" objects retrieved from where they have been discarded. They appear here with one small but significant alteration: the name of the deceased has been excised from each stone, leaving only a blank: a negative space exposing fresh, unpolished stone. Surrounded by neat grass, some leafy planting, and accompanied by steel sculptural elements that combine the form of a headstone with a more industrial aesthetic, the lives marked are here anonymous. These very physical, material markers of lives

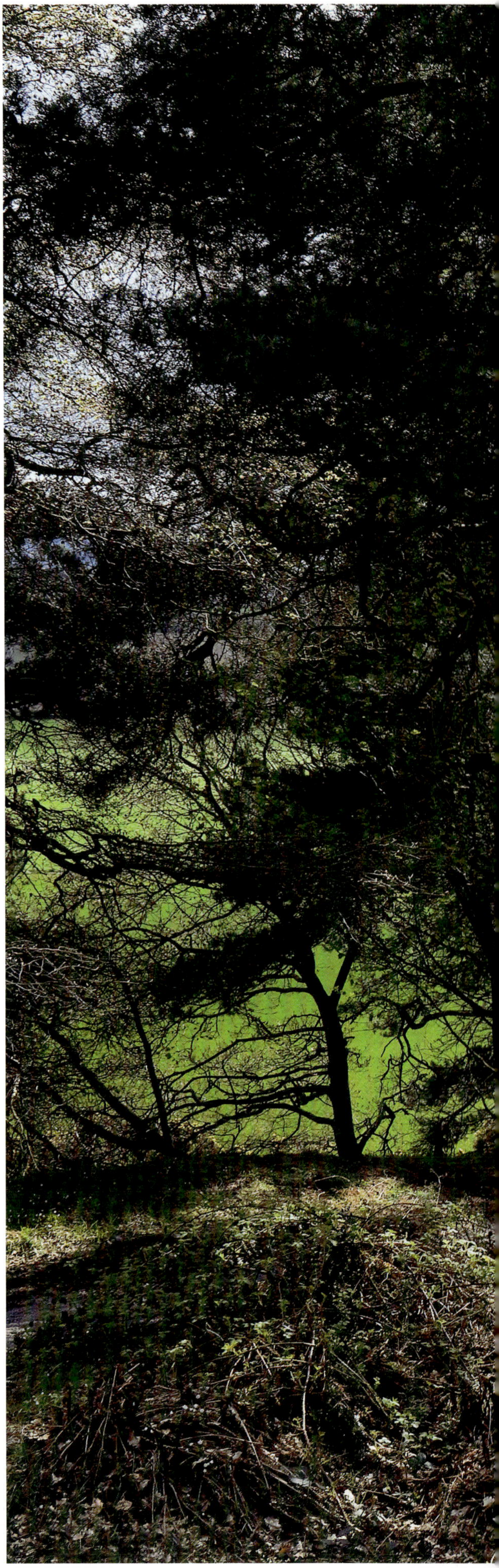

In Memory, 2010
Poured concrete, grass, gravel, dead tree, re-cycled headstones
2.4 × 7.5 × 7.5 m
Permanent sculpture, Jupiter Artland, Edinburgh

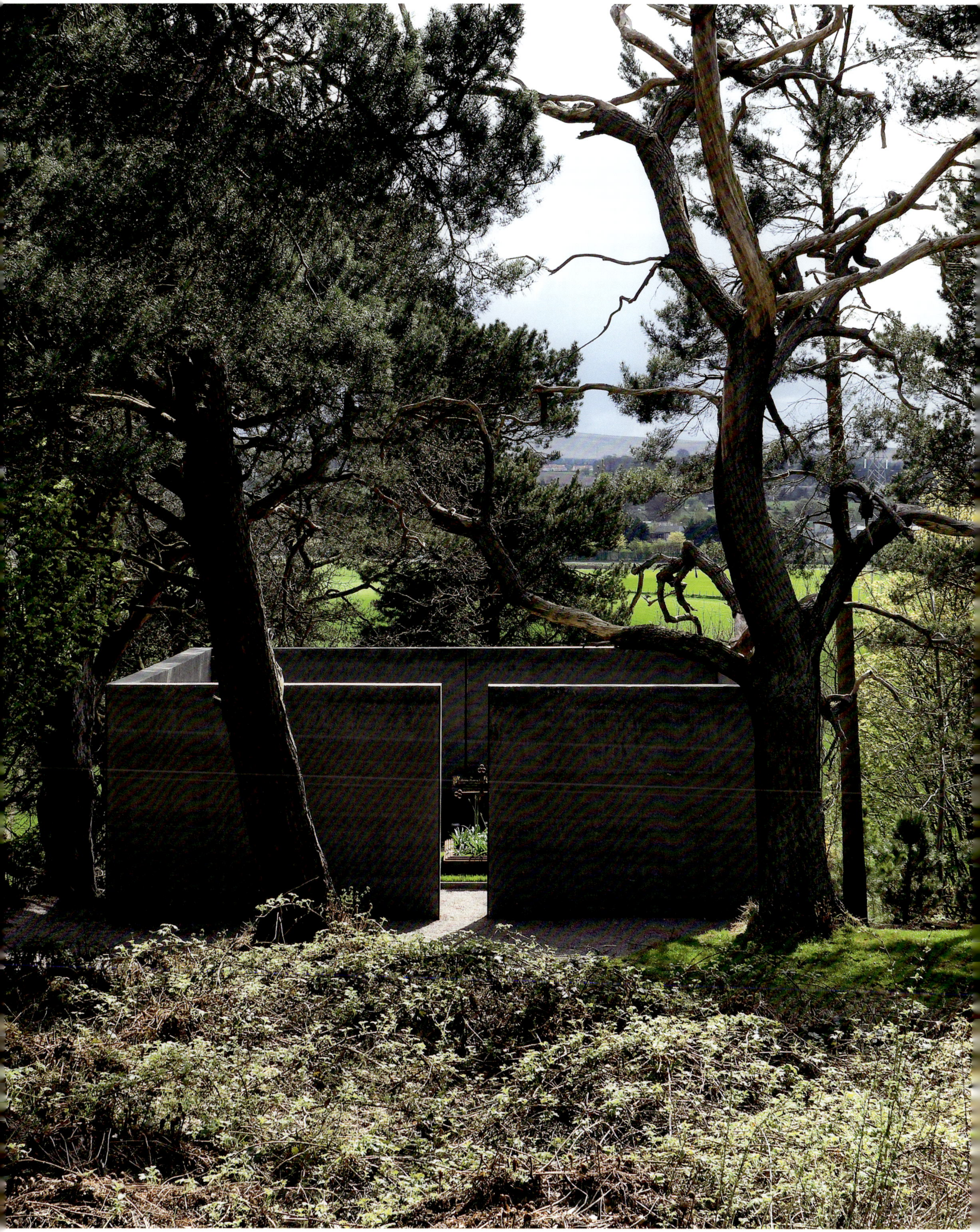

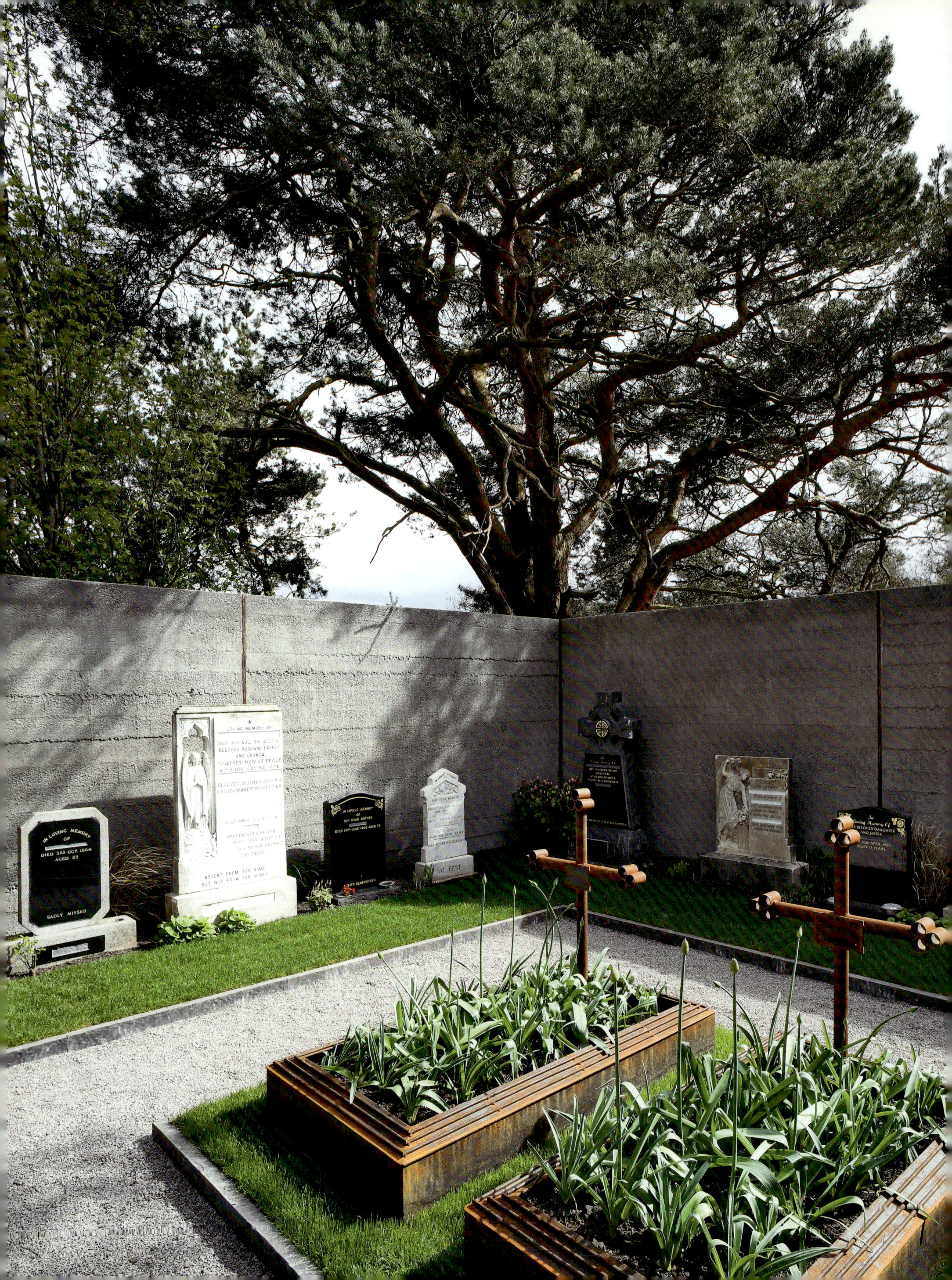
IN LOVING MEMORY
OF
DIED 3RD OCT 1984
AGED 62
SADLY MISSED

lost have in their own way become lost, only to be gathered here. All that remains is the stone and the apparent labor of their making.

Though devoid of name, each stone retains its individuality through the remaining wording and imagery carved into its surface. Only meager, bald facts remain: dates, relationships. Words proclaim enduring memory, at odds here now with the stones' reality as salvage. The removal of the names of course reminds us now of nothing more so than many an official, confidential document, contents edited, key details obliterated for "security reasons," released to enquiries and investigative journalists. In so doing it introduces the idea of privacy and protection in the public realm, the sense of public space amplified through the planting—and the one included bench—being decidedly municipal in appearance.

Just as Coley's earlier works, *The Lamp of Sacrifice* (Birmingham, 2000, and Edinburgh, 2004) looked at the physical manifestation of faith in a city, or rather organized religion, through a gathering of cardboard models of every place of worship listed in a phone directory, *In Memory* creates a different gathering, a place of coming together. It contrasts the immutable physical existence of the stones with the most immaterial and transient of concepts.
— *Katrina Brown*

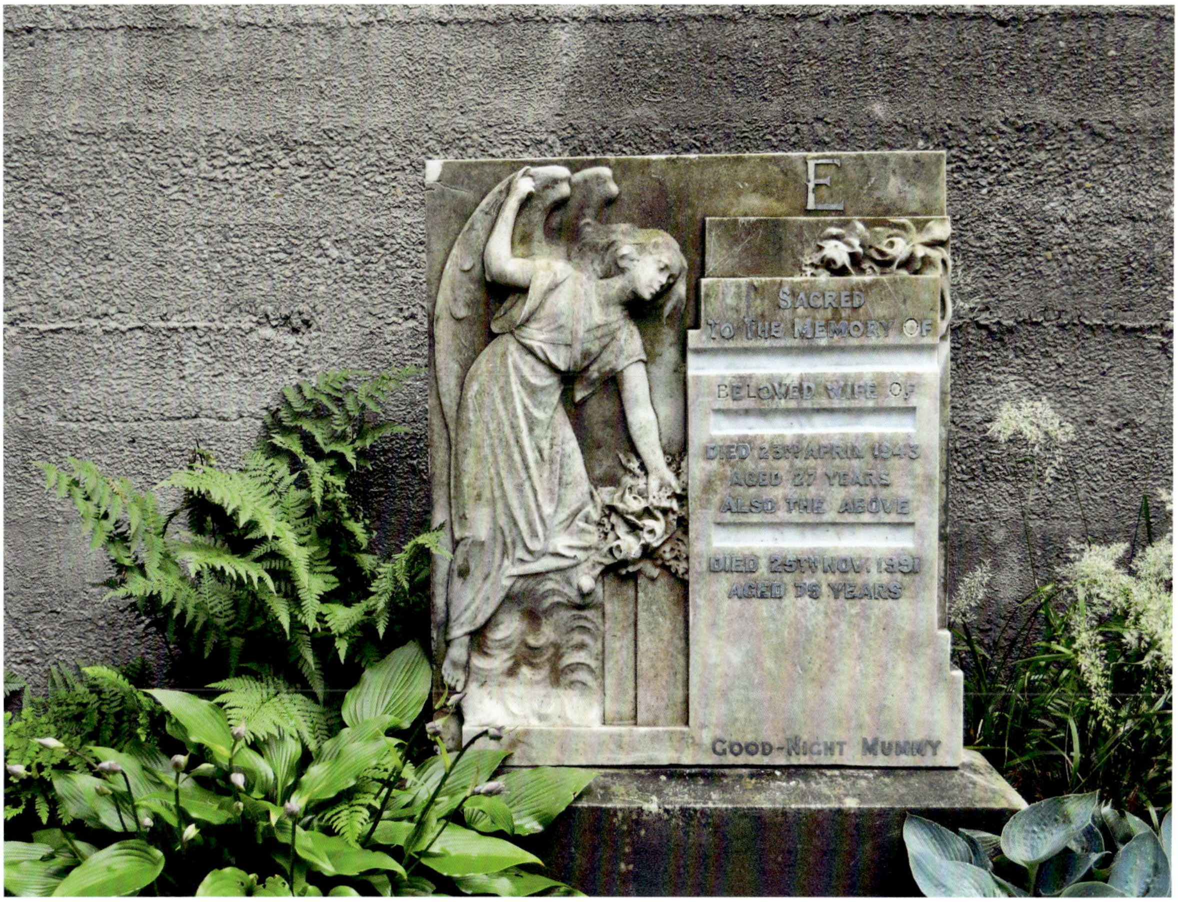

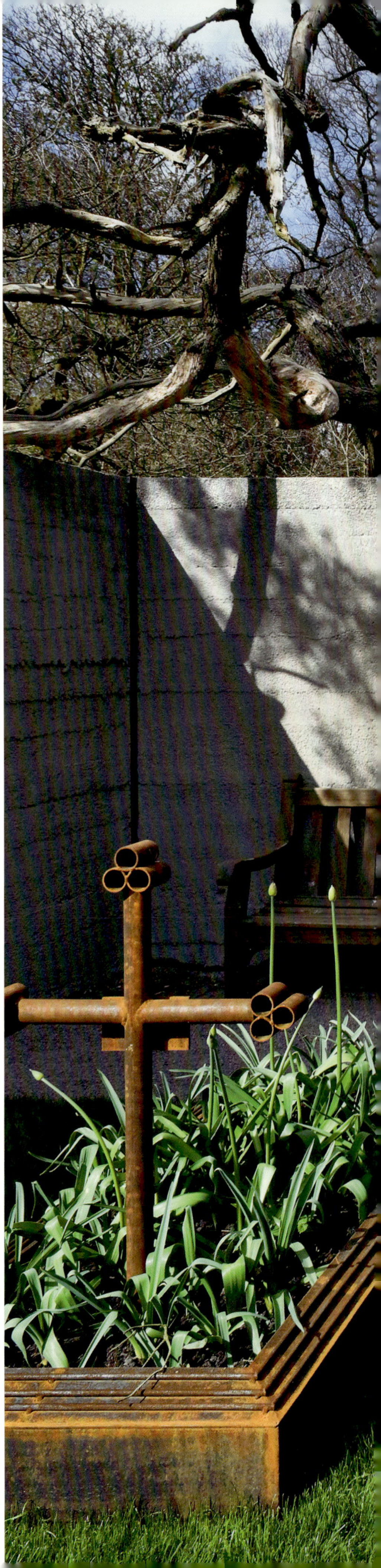

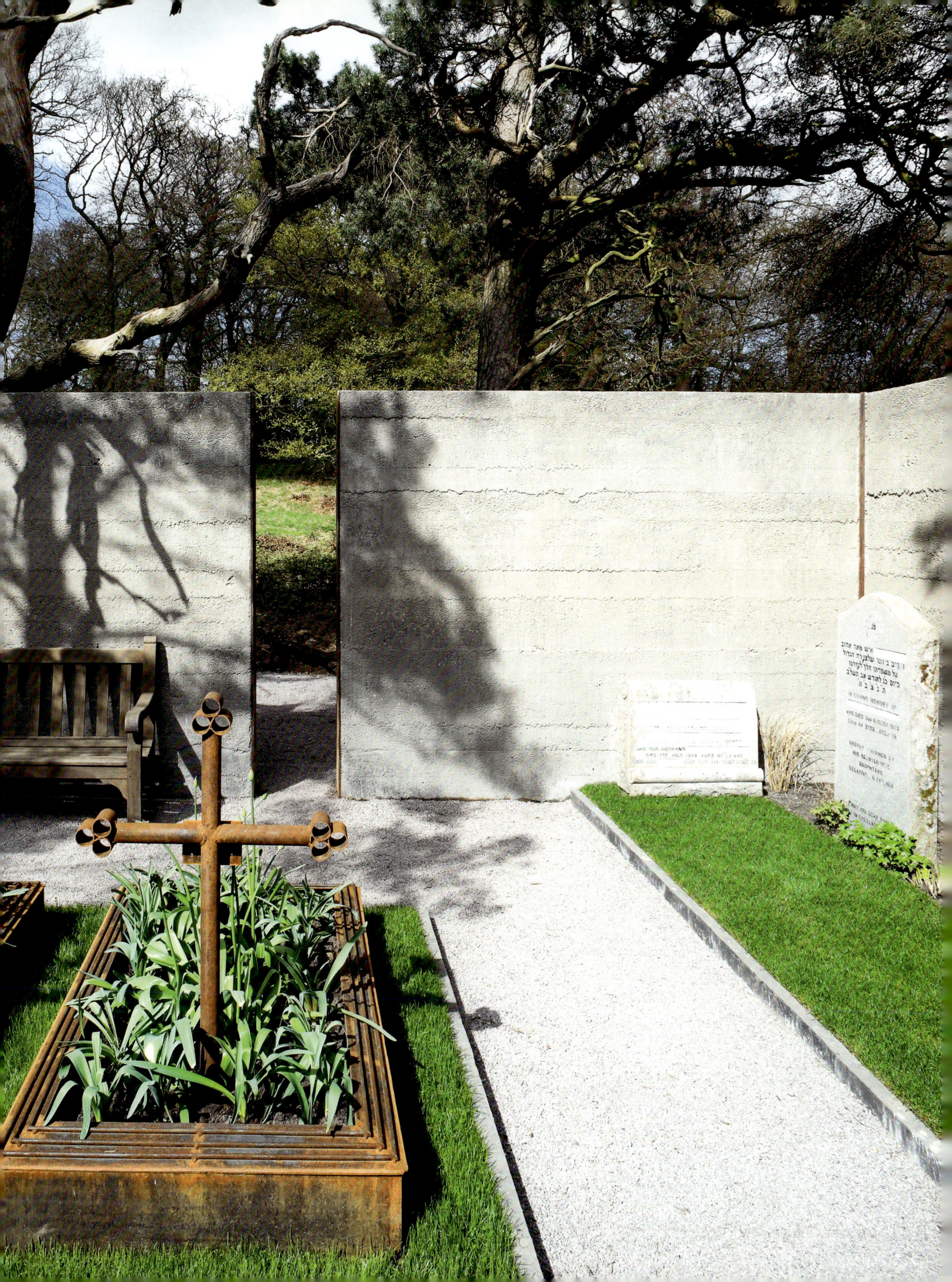

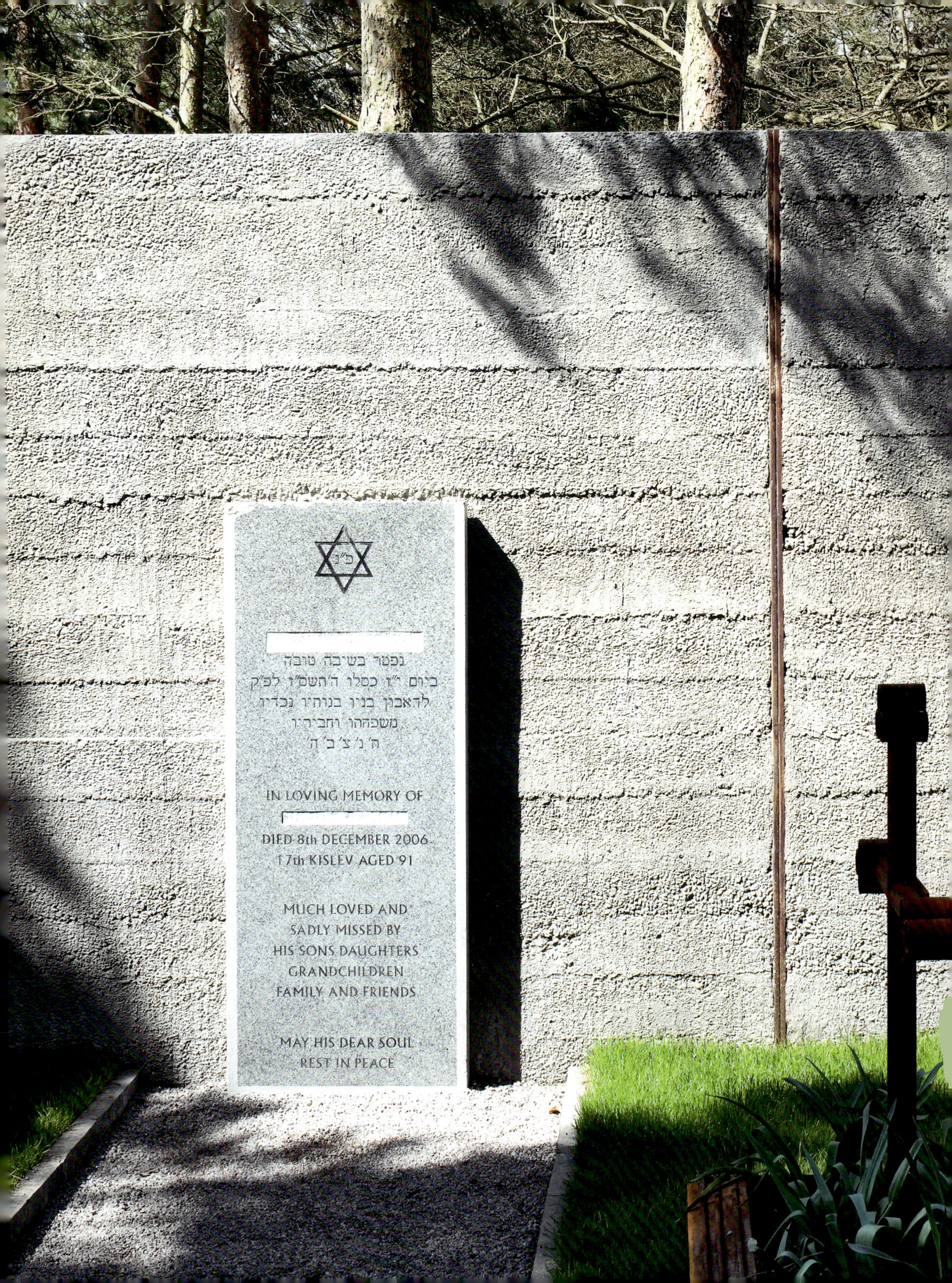

פ״נ
[redacted]
נפטר בשיבה טובה
ביום י״ז כסלו ה׳תשס״ז לפ״ק
לדאבון בניו בנותיו נכדיו
משפחתו וחביריו
ת׳נ׳צ׳ב׳ה׳
IN LOVING MEMORY OF
[redacted]
DIED 8th DECEMBER 2006
17th KISLEV AGED 91
MUCH LOVED AND
SADLY MISSED BY
HIS SONS DAUGHTERS
GRANDCHILDREN
FAMILY AND FRIENDS
MAY HIS DEAR SOUL
REST IN PEACE

Fear of Death

Interested in the relationship between religion, ceremony, and the unknown, the series, *Why I'm Not a Christian* (2009), is inspired by a famous lecture given by Bertrand Russell in 1927:

> Religion is based, I think, primarily and mainly on fear. It is partly the terror of the unknown, and partly, as I have said, the wish to feel you have a kind of elder brother who will stand by you in all your troubles and disputes. Fear is the basis of the whole thing—fear of the mysterious, fear of defeat, fear of death.

Coley takes staples of atheist criticism—"Fear of Death," "Fear of Defeat," and "Fear of the Mysterious"—and converts these into text slogans which he wraps around tree trunks commonly found at headstones on graves. The scripts provide suggestive alternatives to the epitaphs the dead have written as summa for their lives, and as quasi-totemic sentinels these works suggest a telling disjunction between the dignified silence of death and the indoctrinated underpinnings of Christian ritual.
— *Rory Mitchell*

Fear of Death, 2009
Painted wood and mixed media
242 × 50 × 50 cm each
Installation, Haunch of Venison, London
Collection of the Artist Pension Trust, London

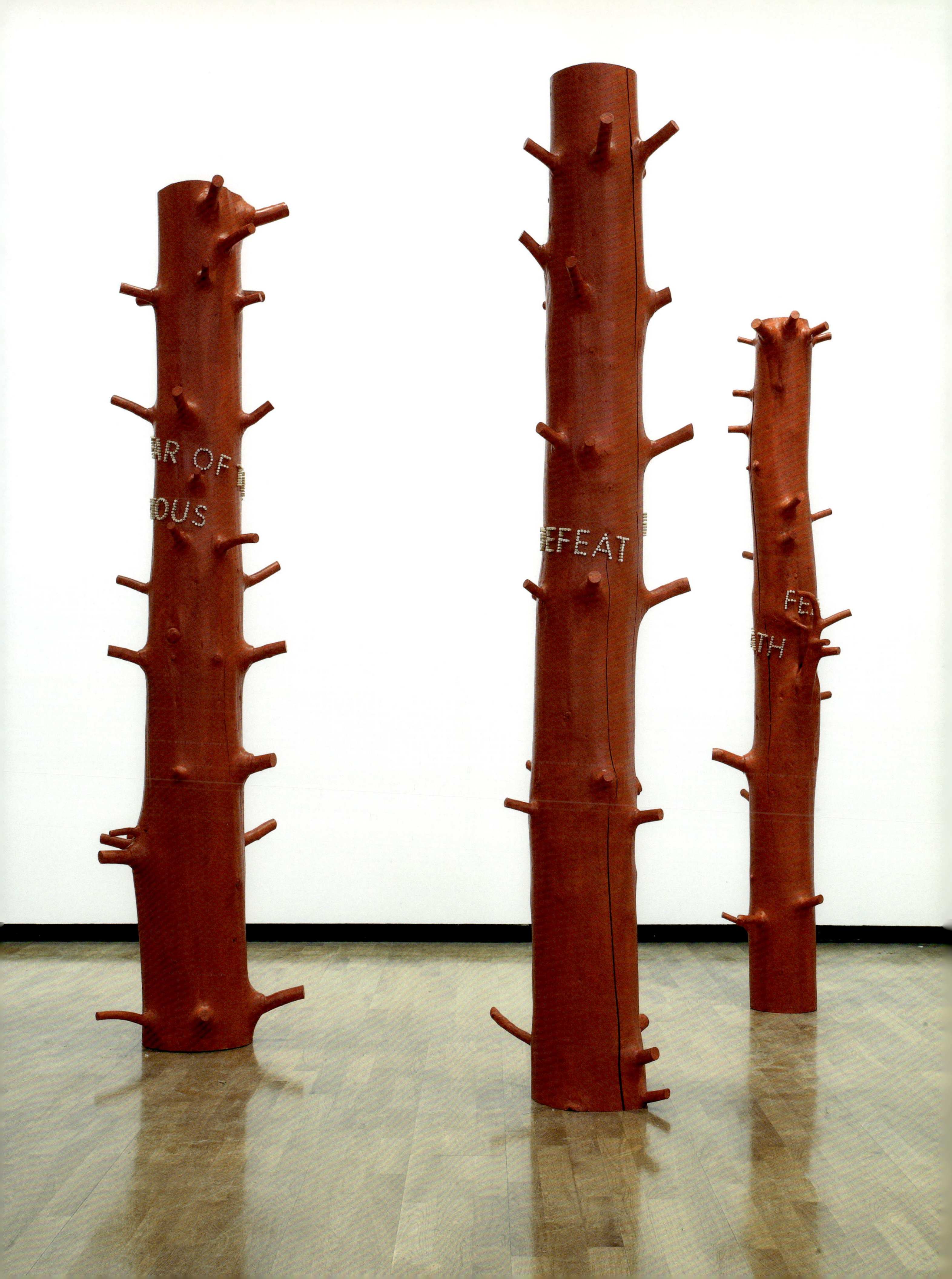
AR OF
OUS
EFEAT
FE
TH

46 Brooklands Gardens

Jaywick was established in the nineteen-thirties by the property tycoon Frank Stedman as a place where east enders could escape polluted London air and enjoy a holiday by the sea. A pioneering individualistic spirit developed through the sale of low-cost freehold plots and self-build chalets, many of which have since evolved into homes which are inhabited throughout the year.

46 Brooklands Gardens (2008) was installed on an empty plot in one of the small residential roads in the area of Jaywick known as Brooklands. The sculpture took as its starting point the footprint of the original house, which had been recently demolished. Its paired down aesthetic (plywood slats bolted onto a rusting steel frame) reflected the simplicity and inventiveness of the surrounding houses. The language of opposition, as expressed in the dazzle pattern created by the wooden slats, created a barricade-like form which played on the perception of Jaywick as a run-down town. From the outside, the sculpture appeared ghostly and abstract, but its multi-colored interior opened up a vista through which expectations could be reappraised and faith, temporarily, restored.

During its three-month life span, *46 Brooklands Gardens* fuelled ongoing debate both locally and nationally on issues relating to the future of Jaywick and the value of contemporary art in the public realm. It was the focus of intense media coverage on local radio and television as well as national broadsheets and art and architecture magazines. While the sculpture was primarily made for the residents of Jaywick and installed over the winter months, it was visited by a large number of people from across the UK and abroad. These groups included a number of representatives from the United Reform Church, who set up a nativity scene in the adjacent garage over Christmas, as well as members of the Jaywick diaspora who were looking for the ghosts of their past.

Coley's response to Jaywick was immediate; he found its unique architectural expression, extraordinary history, and anarchic atmosphere a rich context in which to develop his long-term exploration into society's relationship with the built environment and the nature of faith.

— *Jes Fernie*

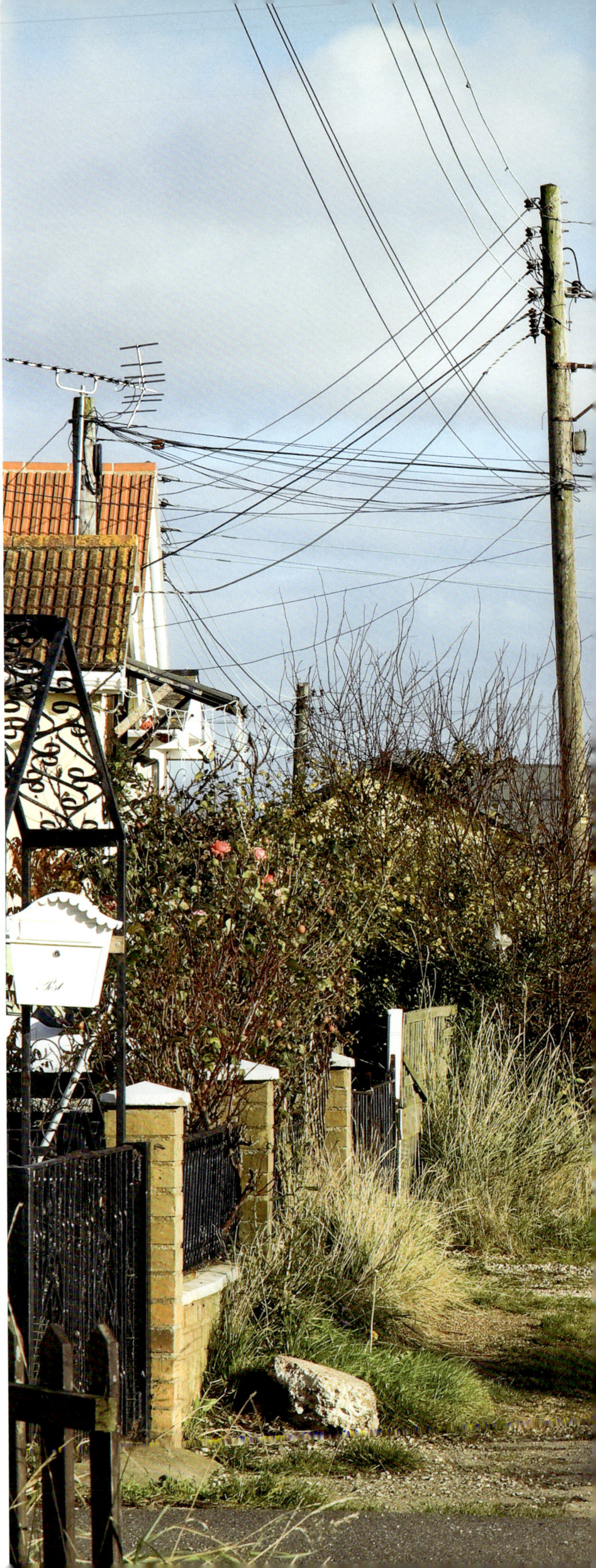

46 Brooklands Gardens, 2008
Welded steel, painted plywood
10 × 6.2 × 5.3 m
Installation, Jaywick, Essex
Realized by firstsite, Colchester

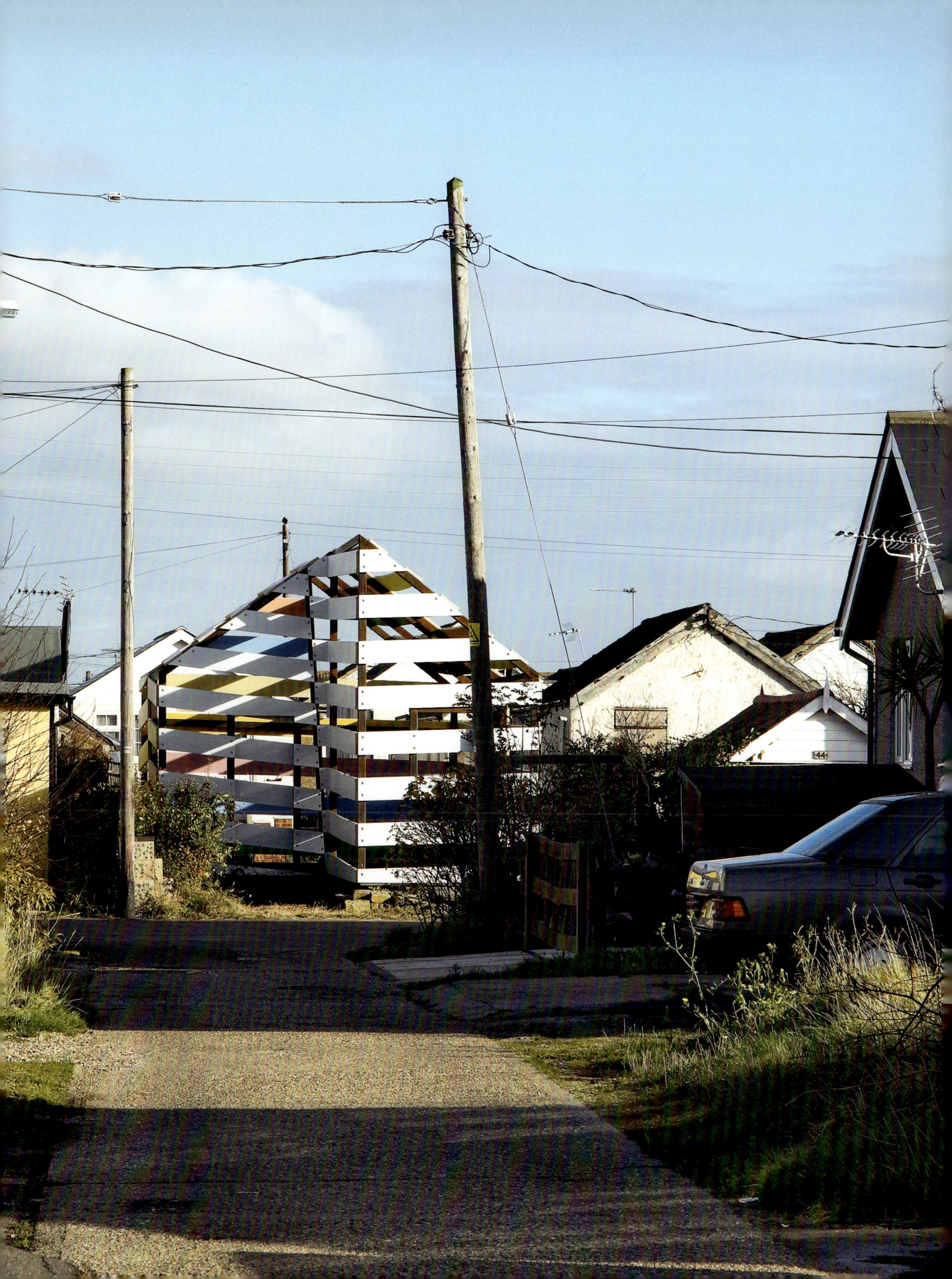

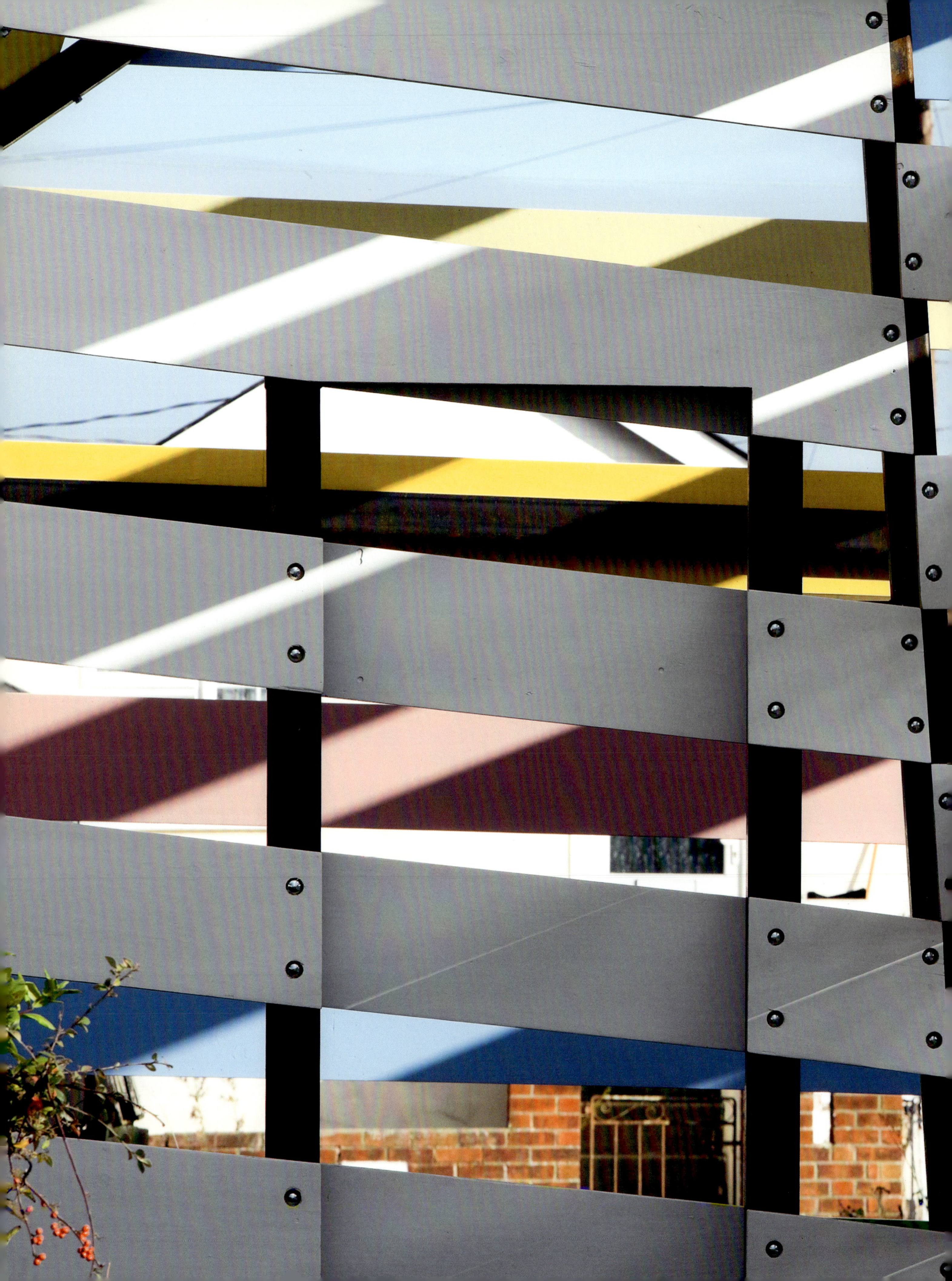

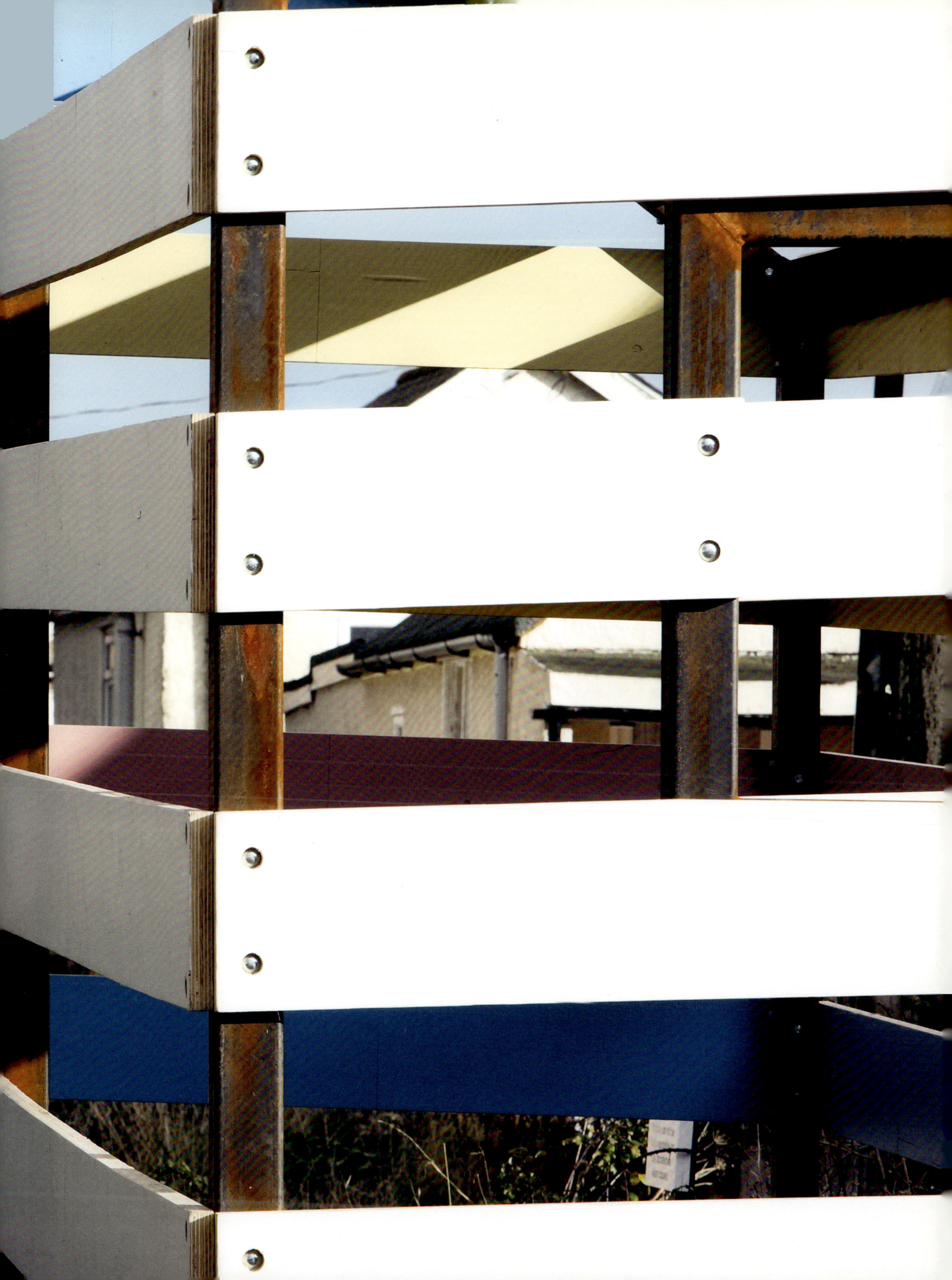

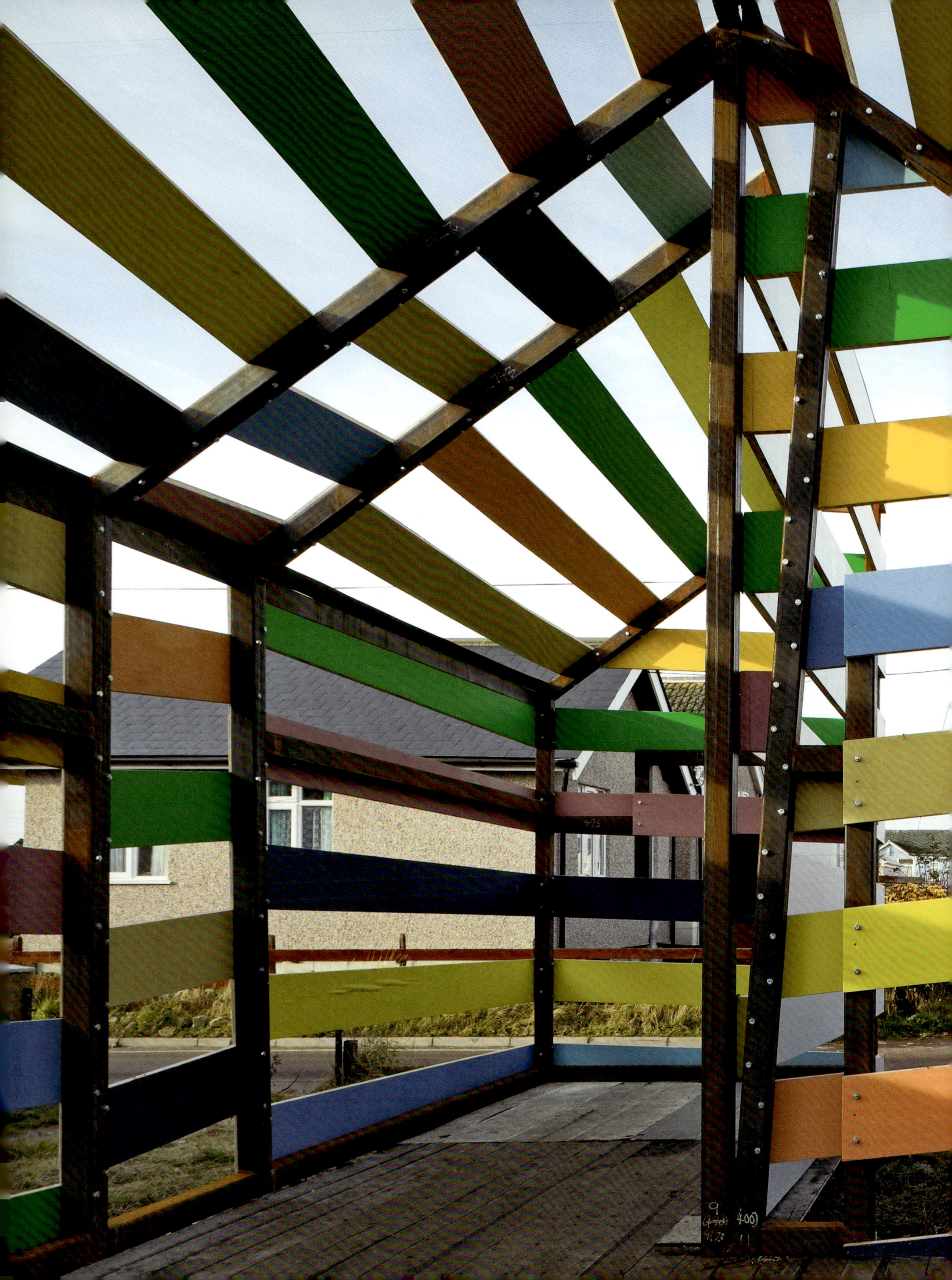

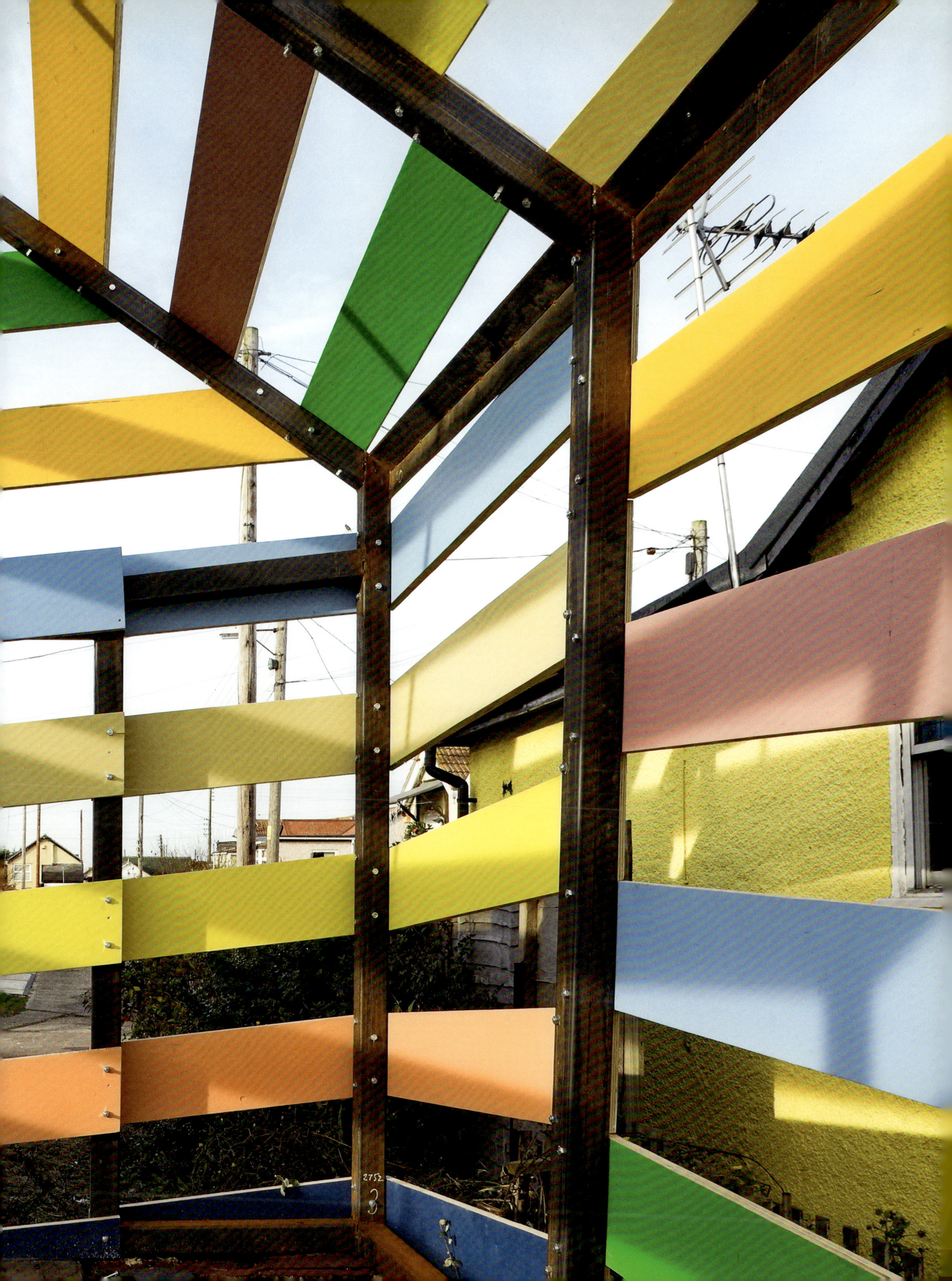

Heaven (\'he-van\)

n (Sometimes cap.) Christianity. 1. The abode of God, the angels, and the spirits of the righteous after death; the place or state of existence of the blessed after the mortal life. 2. (Initial capital letter.) Often, Heavens. The celestial powers; God. 3. A metonym for God (used in expressions of emphasis, surprise, etc.): For heaven's sake! 4. Heavens (used interjectionally to express emphasis, surprise, etc.): Heavens, what a cold room. 5. Usually, heavens. The sky, firmament, or expanse of space surrounding the earth. 6. A place or state of supreme happiness: She made his life a heaven on earth.

"Stairway to Heaven" is a song by the British rock band Led Zeppelin composed by guitarist Jimmy Page and vocalist Robert Plant and recorded on their fourth studio album, *Led Zeppelin IV*. It is the most requested and most played song on FM radio stations in the United States, despite never having been released as a single there. In November 2007, through download sales promoting their recent *Mothership* release, the song hit # 37 on the UK Singles Chart and # 13 on the New Zealand Singles Chart. In 1982, a prominent US Baptist claimed that the song (when played in reverse) contains Satanic references. This so-called "backmasking" was discussed at a hearing of the Consumer Protection and Toxic Materials Committee of the California State Assembly into popular music where the song was played as evidence. Led Zeppelin for the most part have ignored such claims; for years the only comment came from Swan Song Records which issued the statement: "Our turntables only play in one direction—forwards."

Heaven is a wooden roof or canopy over the outer stage of an Elizabethan theater.

Heaven is a film directed by Tom Tykwer, starring Cate Blanchett and Giovanni Ribisi. A woman takes the law into her own hands after police ignore her pleas to arrest the man responsible for her husband's death, and finds herself not only under arrest for murder but falling in love with an officer. At roughly an hour and a half, *Heaven* is a cinematic triumph that nudges open the gates to the philosophy and psychology of the lone man or woman along with those of society on the whole. It takes place in Italy, but Tykwer himself stated in an interview that really it could have been shot in any number of places with the message remaining the same. *Heaven* is a thinly-scripted, in-depth commentary on issues prevailing throughout the modern world. Drugs, sex, sexuality, identity and the fibers that make up humans as a race are what this film revolves around: it is not a film for tourists or spectators. First released in 2002, duration 97 mins.

Heaven is famous gay nightclub in Villiers Street in London. It first opened its doors in the mid nineteen-eighties. Club nights include "Popcorn," "Porn Idol," and "Camp Attack." "London is fortunate to have all its options, but nothing quite matches Heaven's endurance, size or variety." Getting into Heaven is best accomplished by buying tickets online in advance: www.heaven-london.com/london.

Heaven is a farm in the heart of Sussex Weald where time stood still. It celebrates 170 years of farming life throughout the year, catering for all visitors including groups and coach parties: www.heavenfarm.co.uk.

Heaven is a place where nothing ever happens.

Heaven Is a Place Where Nothing Ever Happens

Standing six meters high, Nathan Coley's illuminated text sculpture overlooks the seaside resort of Folkestone in Kent. Originally commissioned as part of the first Folkestone Triennial, the sculpture's glitzy typeface spells out the words: "Heaven Is a Place Where Nothing Ever Happens." Adorned with 480 illuminated globes, the phrase is taken from a famous Talking Heads song composed in 1979.

Like his other text pieces, the work acts as a proclamation. Investigating the dynamic between the rational and the spiritual, Coley proposes a theological question: once transcendence is achieved, what else is there left to do? Despite the rigidity of the work's scaffolding, Coley's sculpture destabilizes the spiritual foundations upon which religion is built by suggesting that the afterlife can only guarantee boredom.

This melancholy outlook is also mirrored by the sculpture's seaside location, encapsulating the ennui which has ravaged Folkestone and similar seaside towns across Britain in recent years. Evoking the outdated, seaside glamor of the nineteen-sixties and seventies, the lightbulbs lend the work a tacky elegance which offsets the foreboding message prophesied within the text.

However, one could interpret the message in an alternative way. Coley explains "that which is invisible (heaven) when thought about (or got to) is not 'boredom' but 'safe.' A place where events don't change, where everyone knows you, where you are secure and your knowledge is fixed."[1] In this sense, the work reassures rather than warns; heaven becomes a place which is dependable and constant rather than something which merely promises monotony.

— *Jonathan Horrocks*

[1] Author in conversation with the artist.

Heaven Is a Place Where Nothing Ever Happens, 2008
Illuminated text on scaffolding
6 × 6 × 4 m
Installation, Folkestone Triennial

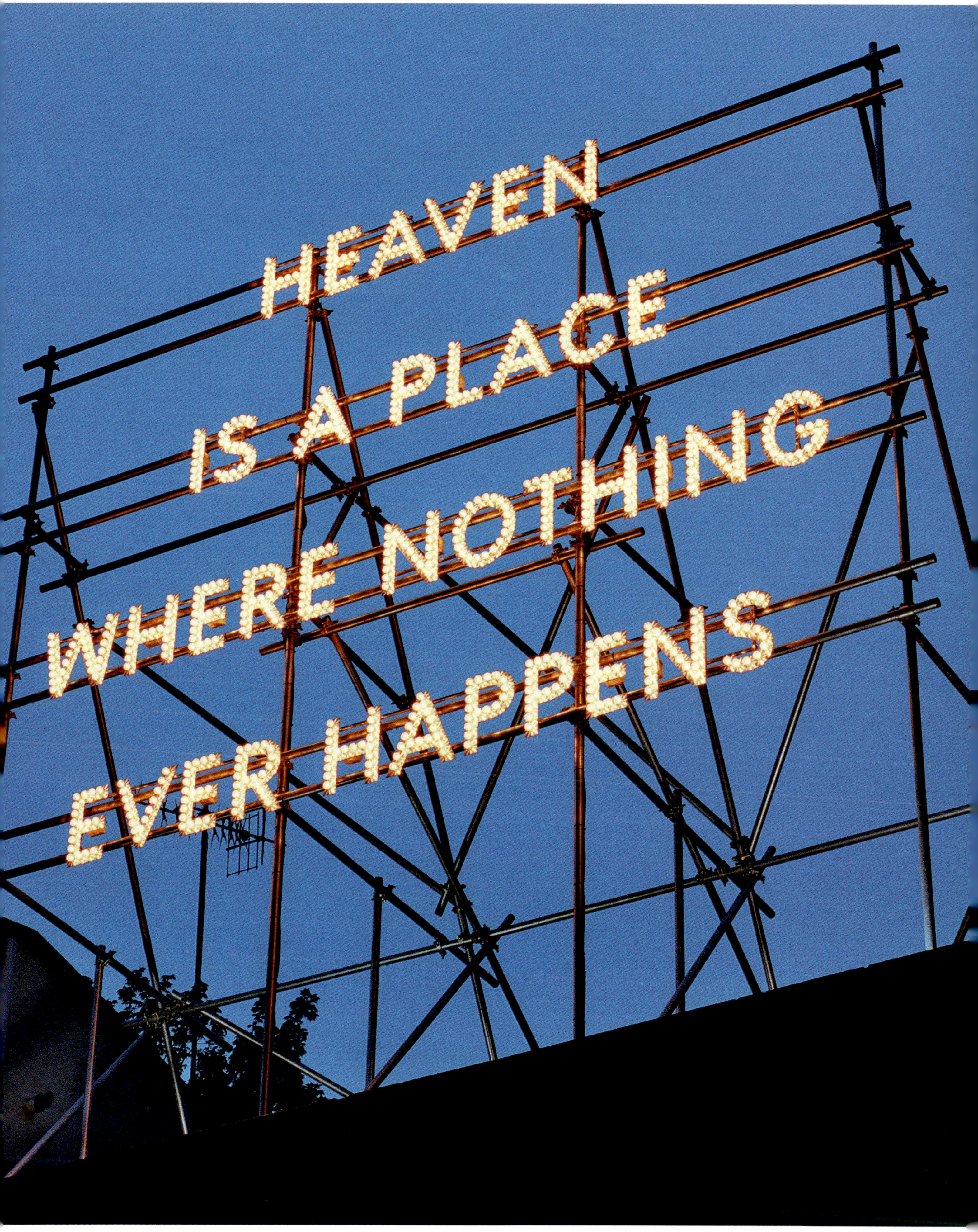
HEAVEN
IS A PLACE
WHERE NOTHING
EVER HAPPENS

Palace

The first impression of Nathan Coley's *Palace* (2008) is of a dark silhouette against the white walls of the gallery. The blackness implies heaviness; its entire surface, every detail, is blackened. The black might be read as an indication of the sacred: like the black of the Ka'ba, a sixteen-meter-high shrine located in the courtyard of the Great Mosque at Mecca, the holiest place in Islam. All Muslims, wherever their location on earth, turn toward the Ka'ba during prayer; it is draped entirely in black silk cloth, with Arabic calligraphy spelling out selected verses of the Qur'an. Or perhaps the black here has mythical associations, as it did for the Abstract Expressionists in America in the nineteen-fifties. Or maybe this is a minimalist, "secular" black that draws the viewer in, to focus, free from distraction or further invention. The black of *Palace* is not jet, gloss, or velvet black, but a matt black, redolent of charcoal. Utilitarian timber buildings can be tarred black as a method of preservation. Or is this the charred remains of a burnt-out building, destroyed by fire. This could be the melancholic black, familiar in Western art and culture, signifying a sad, abandoned, and isolated object.

Beyond its overwhelming blackness, the form of *Palace* emerges: a nineteenth-century saloon façade. Constructed with timber, it is nearly six meters tall and ten meters wide. It is made with minimal details and features—just enough to convey the idea and no more. Shallow steps, integral to the structure, lead up to a porch and saloon door, but given the gallery context, the viewer is unlikely to enter; it feels forbidding. At ground level, the carpentry articulates empty window frames and three doors (each are notably in a different style), while at first-floor level there are more empty window frames with a pediment roughly center. Behind the façade, the structural supports are evident; but curiously, the space here feels habitable; there are niches to stand in, to get closer to touch the rough finish and to gaze back through the empty window frames. At the center of the back of the structure there are more shallow steps up to the wooden platform on which the structure rests. The work invites people to walk on this and those that do can hear the sound of themselves walking on the work: the hollow sound of a suspended wooden floor. The action makes them a visible part of the façade; others can hear and see them, they are on display, acting out a routine. The saloon doors can be pushed, to allow the viewer to walk through from front to back and vice versa; the saloon doors slap back behind them.

The façade is familiar, plucked straight out of the main street of an American Western movie. Its language is taken directly from the film set, at eighty percent of its actual size; it is deliberately scenographic in presentation. Like a stage set, it invites occupation and interaction between the work and the viewer. The thin slits of white light shining through the planks of wood make it clear that it is shallow, hollow, a thin slice of something. The function of a façade on a film set is to convince only when viewed through the camera lens and then on the movie screen; an object to be looked at. It does not need to be truthful in itself, but this structure reveals itself for what it is. It does not demand that you suspend disbelief, it invites you to think.

The Western

Coley is interested in the mythology of the Western produced in America during the nineteen-fifties and sixties, a notion of which was upheld by Europeans as much as Americans. Hollywood film directors, influenced by the prevailing political climate and, more specifically, presidential policy at this time, purposefully set out to grapple with issues of morality in an age of political and social unease in postwar America; political paranoia with the McCarthy era (nineteen-forties / fifties), the US civil rights movement (1955–68), Vietnam (1956–75), the emergence of the Cold War (nineteen-fifties to sixties) reaching a hiatus with the Cuban missile crisis (1962)—the closest the world has been, to date, to nuclear war. The Western was a populist vehicle "about America rewriting and re-interpreting her own past, however honestly or dishonestly it may be done."[1]

The Western was largely set in a reimagined America of the eighteen-seventies, in the aftermath of the US Civil War (1861–65). It points to a period in history when cowboys were migrating out into the American desert, pushing forward frontiers, creating new towns, and seeking their fortune in gold while displacing the North American Indians. The movies played out epic adventures in widescreen that dealt with law and order, good versus evil, the individual versus the state, and revenge: ". . . movies shown and re-shown in the mind could grow and take on enlarged and distorted forms. Or in the case of Westerns, merge into one gigantic frontier picture."[2]

Palace, 2008
Painted timber
9.5 × 4.1 × 5.6 m
Installation, Haunch of Venison, Berlin

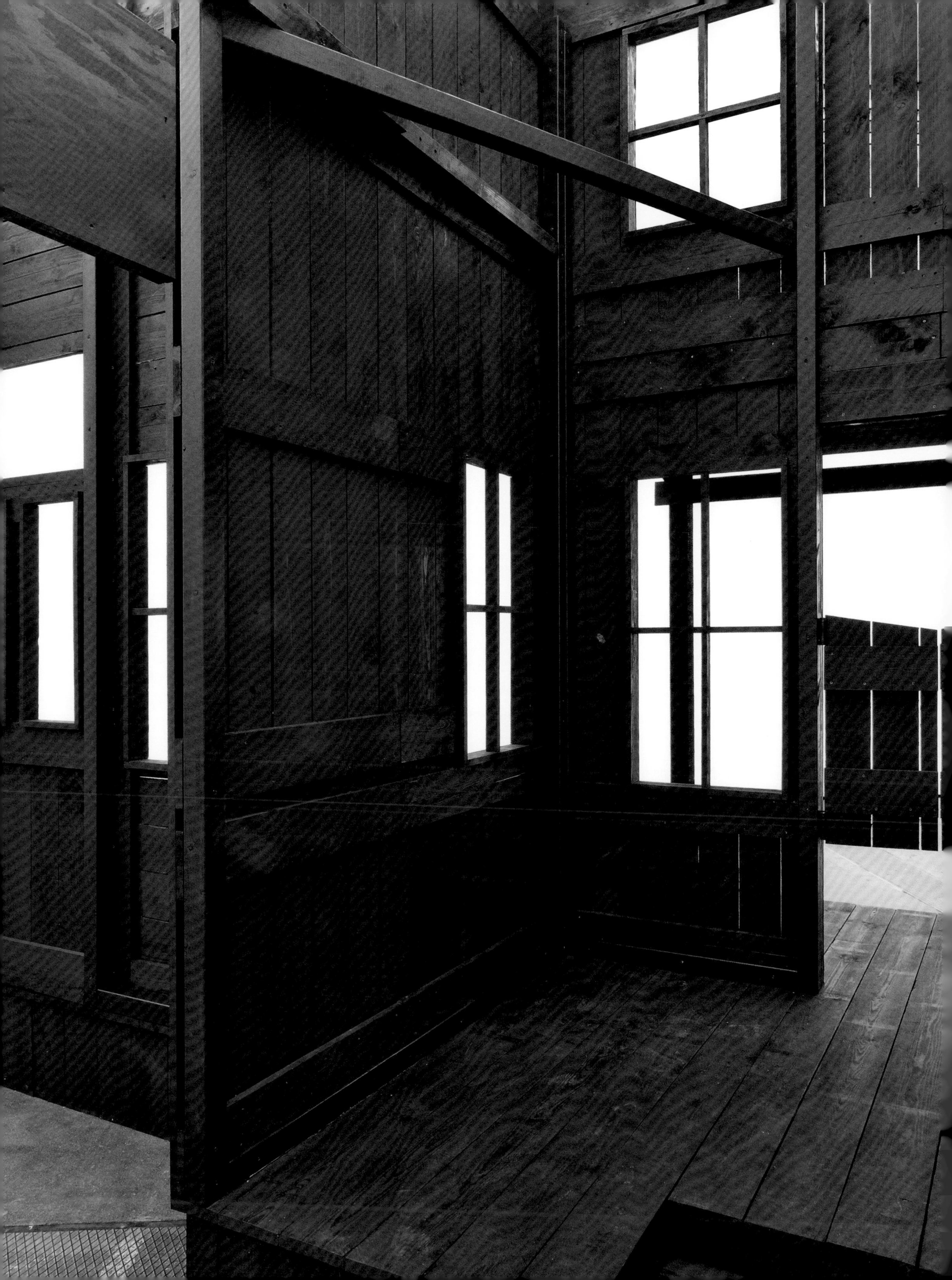

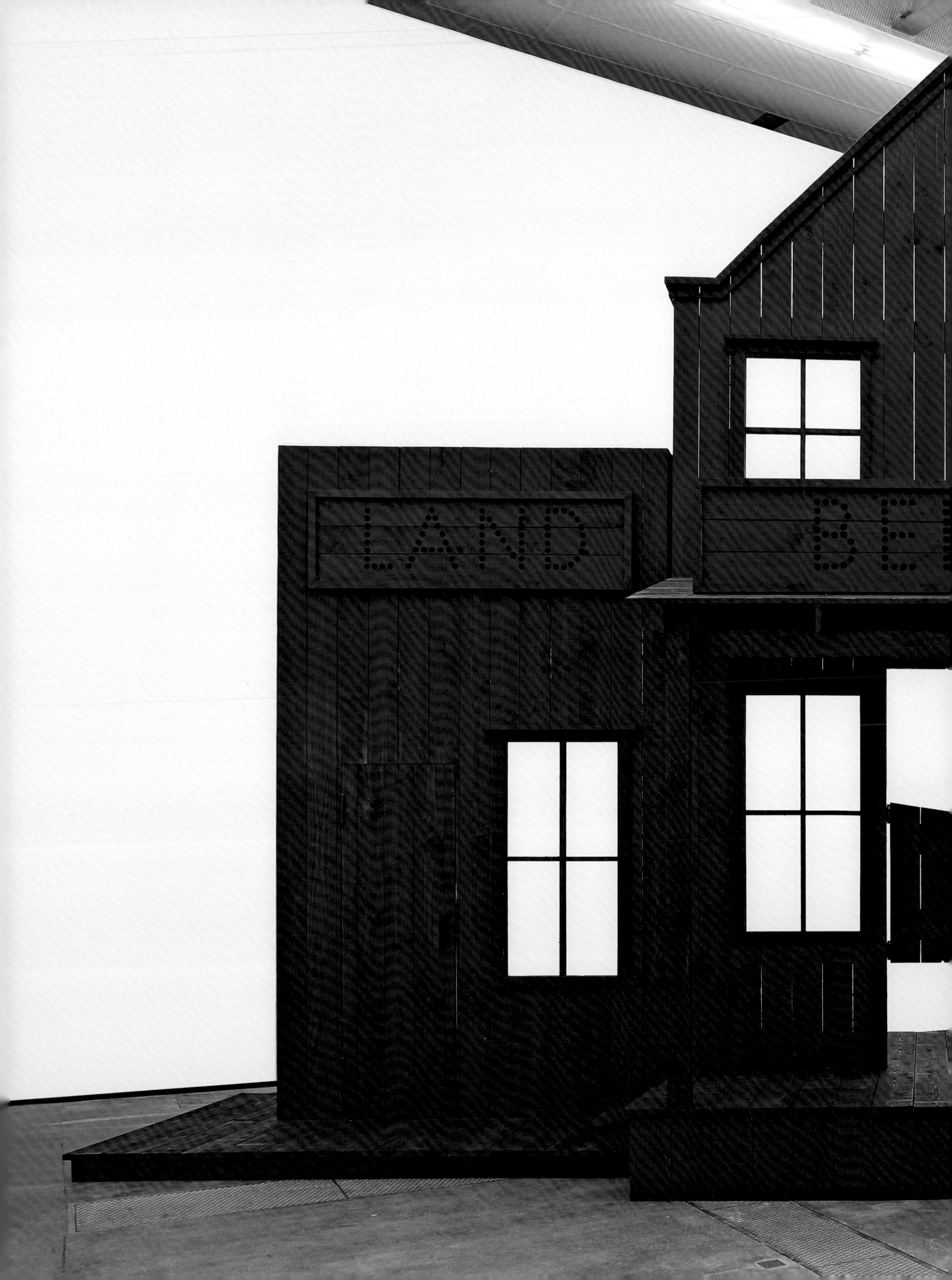
LAND

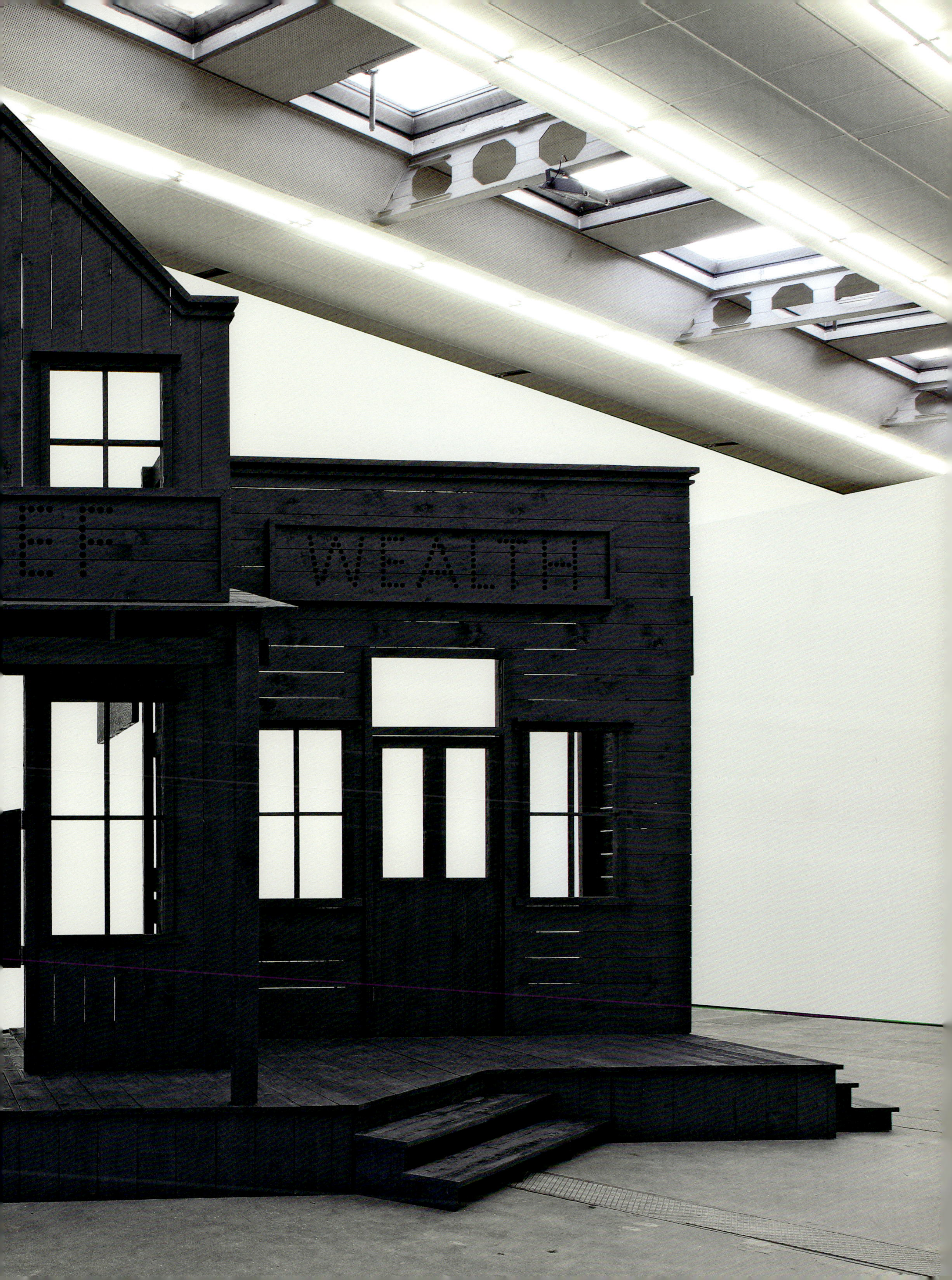
WEALTH

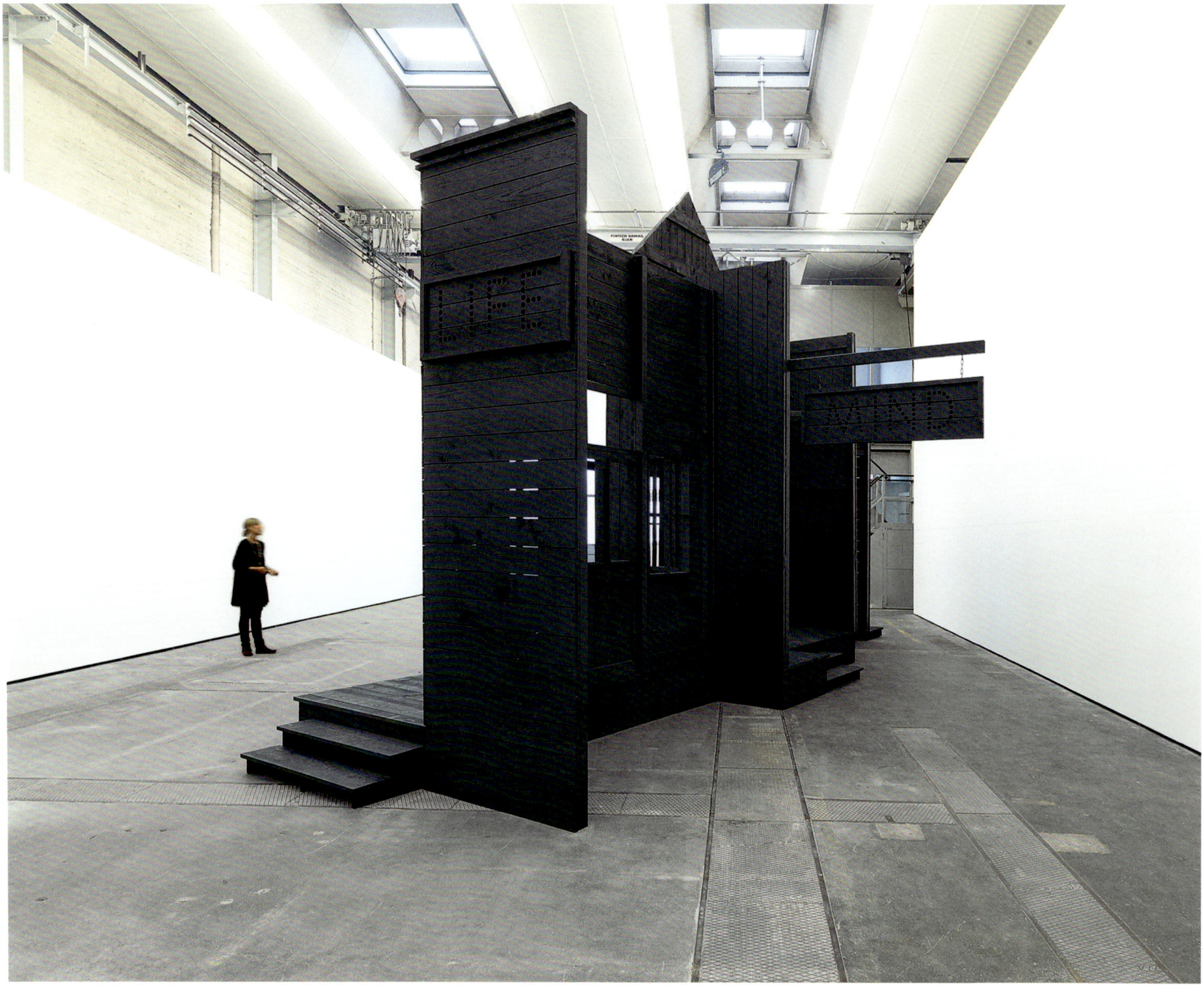

Legend and fact often entwined in the Western, as it was a means by which Americans invented and reinvented their history. The farcical Western *The Life and Times of Judge Roy Bean* (1972) is based on the real-life outlaw and self-appointed Justice of the Peace known as Hanging Judge Roy Bean (1825–1903). Story has it that armed with an outmoded Texan law book he held court in his saloon dispensing liquor and unpredictable justice, driven by prejudice and greed. He reportedly had signs over his saloon saying, "Ice-Cold Beer" and "Law West of the Pecos."

The saloon was the social center of the main street and was often the first and most prominent building to be built in new settlements by frontiersmen. Frequented by outlaws, gamblers, and deserters from the Civil War, the saloon was unwelcoming territory for soldiers or foreigners. A notoriously violent establishment, the saloon was the site of a drunken brawl and shoot-out. The Western saloon represents the lawless and vigilante activity of the Wild West in microcosm: in Coley's work it is a metaphor for an age of increasing moral uncertainty.

The Palace

The etymology of "palace" is *Palatium,* the Palatine Hill in Rome, where the house of the Roman emperor was situated. The word originally referred to a royal residence, seat of state, sovereign or religious order. Most often palaces were built in important urban settings to symbolize power in a homeland but also to lay claim to land in new frontiers. In their original form they represent the awakening of a society's civil culture. The architectural extensions and amendments to palaces over time epitomize the shifting political, religious, and social values of the society that built them.

In America, colonial governor's palaces were renamed "executive mansions." The most prominent executive mansion in the world is the White House. Today a symbol of the US as a super power, in 1814 it was almost completely destroyed by British forces during the Burning of Washington. The British Empire troops hoped that burning the capital of the American nation would have a psychological impact on the will of the Americans to continue to defend their land. Only the burned-out shell of the building remained; it was torn down and reconstructed.

More generally, the word "palace" has been used to infer wealth and status or enjoyable experience: gin palace, crystal palace, movie palace. Perhaps the most well-known palace in North America is Caesar's Palace, a luxury hotel and casino on the Las Vegas strip in Paradise, Nevada, the city of façades and wealth. Taking the Ancient Roman Empire as its theme, it is currently owned by the largest gaming company in the world, Harrah's Entertainment, Inc. Coley's work is preoccupied with the languages of both commercial signage and architecture, and *Palace* can be seen as a fragment of nineteenth-century American main-street architecture: "decorated sheds" in Robert Venturi and Denise Scott Brown's terms[3]: three buildings in a row, each with their own decorative nuances and signs. But in *Palace,* the clarity of this sort of architecture is denied. The architectural character of the façades and the words on the signboards borrow from familiar languages, but there are strange details that undermine the familiarity: words are formed from letters; they are decorative but also reminiscent of bullet holes on a building; there is a choice of three doors into what look like three buildings, but only one can be easily accessed. Familiar elements are combined and recontextualized in an unfamiliar way creating a conceptual space for you to enter into the work. The signs on *Palace* do not say "saloon" but rather, "land," "belief," "wealth," "life," and "mind." Initially looking as if to make a direct historical connection with the frontier spirit of North America, these words may be read as "badges" of the western frontier, "tattoos" of the cowboy. However, these words were sourced by the artist as being the five rights that every man is granted under Islam.[4] *Palace* as a structure is understood to be deliberately false, and here Coley brings together two ideologies from different corners of the globe. They invite us to speculate on whether these words share a commonality across seemingly opposed ideologies.

All words on buildings present themselves as positive; often they are rhetoric for the religious or political power that the building represents. Coley is aware of the potential mulitvalency of the words written upon the structure of *Palace*. This can lead us to consider how this work might be read in the prevailing political / cultural climate in different locations: Washington, Berlin, or Baghdad. Are these words shot into the structure in protest, or are they propaganda? In *Nineteen Eighty-Four* (1949) George Orwell explored the political use of language and deliberate ambiguity to distort meaning, with "doublethink" and "doubletalk" used to control attitudes and belief. Can these words be trusted? Are they any more reliable than this piece of stage scenery?

Five words are partially drilled out of the timber structure of *Palace.* On the left-hand side of the front façade is the word "land." This section of the façade is utilitarian: its door "hidden" within the boards. In the center section the word "belief" sits prominently on the porch roof, below the central pediment and cornice and above the saloon doors. To the right is "wealth." Here there is a simpler roofline with a cornice. The door (now a feature) and windows are symmetrical. On the side of the structure is "life." The fifth word, "mind," is on a sign which swings from a chain like a shop sign on the back of the structure: the otherwise purely functional support for the scenery on the front. This is unexpected and invites us to read this word differently from the other four.

Palace is a work of borrowed ideologies, exaggerated stories, and beliefs taken from both fact and fiction. It simultaneously offers a familiar illusion as its most prominent visual characteristic and denies its believability through the choice of means used to achieve it. Deliberately allegorical and ambiguous, our understanding of *Palace* depends on our position. A provocative work, it has the potential to make more myths.

— *Celia Davies*

---

[1] Philip French, *Westerns: Aspects of a Movie Genre* (Manchester, 2005), p. 13.

[2] Ibid., preface, p. xii.

[3] In *Learning from Las Vegas* (Cambridge, Massachusetts, 1972), American architect and theorist Robert Venturi explored and analyzed American main-street commercial buildings. He coined the term "decorated shed" to describe these simple functional buildings with exteriors embellished to operate as signs conveying the meaning and purpose of the buildings.

[4] Nathan Coley sourced the words from Hassan Butt, "My Plea to Fellow Muslims: You Must Renounce Terror," *The Guardian,* July 1, 2007, www.guardian.co.uk/commentisfree/2007/jul/01/comment.religion1 (accessed December 10, 2013).

Give Up the Good Book, Pick Up a Good Gun

"Give Up the Good Book, Pick Up a Good Gun" is a mantra rooted in the Western tradition and Dime Novels of the nineteenth and early twentieth century. The Dime Novel format focused on stories about the Wild West and quickly became popular with the soldiers on both sides during the American Civil War (1861-65). They were cheap, widely available, Western adventure narratives, written and read at a point when the American Wild West was being developed. The text illuminates through drilled out holes of gun-metal gray aluminum (evocative of bullet holes), imploring you to escape the church and the state, and make your own way and your own laws, with the help of a trusted firearm.
— *Nathan Coley*

Give Up the Good Book, Pick Up a Good Gun, 2008
Powder-coated aluminium with fluorescent lamps
160 × 74 × 8 cm

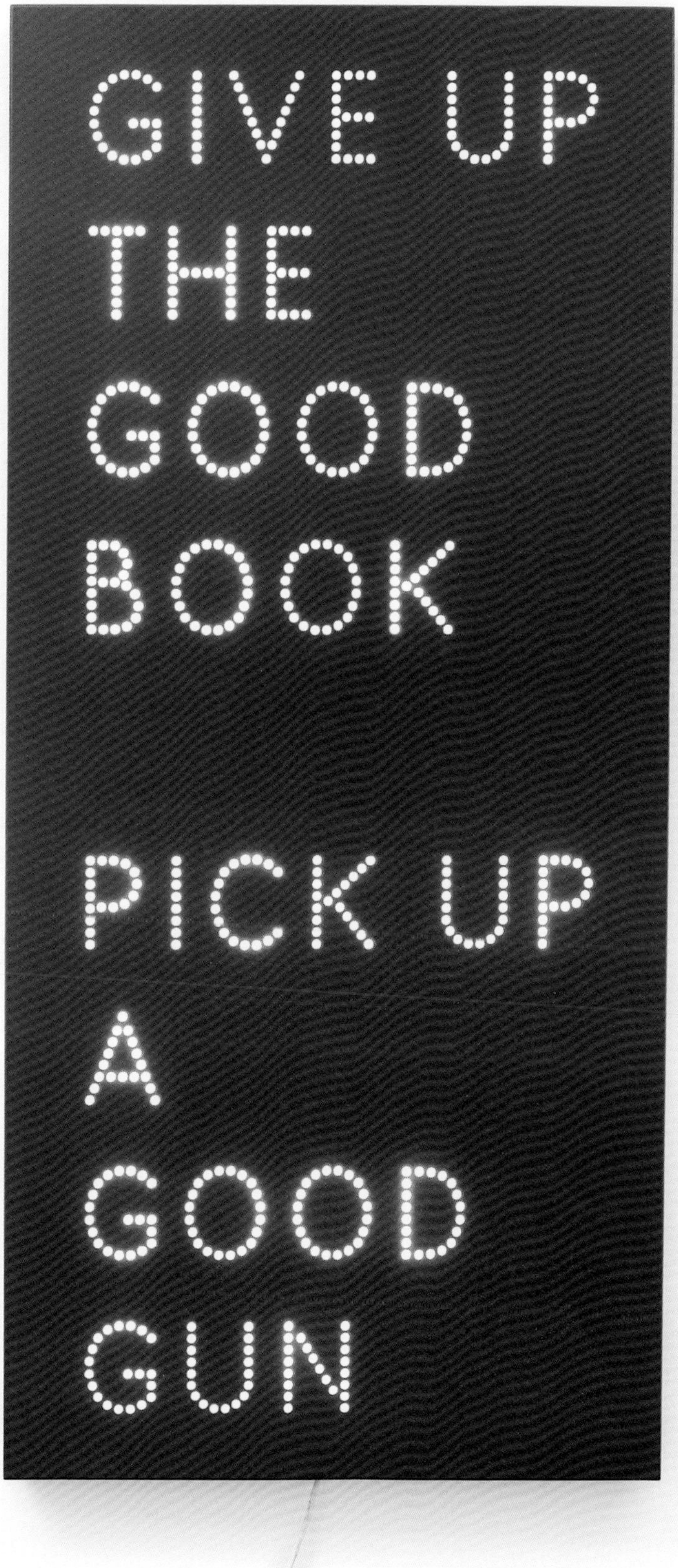
GIVE UP
THE
GOOD
BOOK
PICK UP
A
GOOD
GUN

Untitled (Threshold Sculptures)

The threshold sculpture is a simple eight-centimeter-high plank of wood on the floor, which you have to step over to enter the gallery space. Very simple and a bit annoying—I think of them as being a frame for the space. Critics hate them, as they think I am trying to trip them up, which of course is exactly what I am doing.
— *Nathan Coley*

Excerpt from an interview with Charlotte Day for the solo exhibition *Appearances*, 2011.

Untitled (Threshold Sculptures), 2007
Cherry, 7 × 5 × 99 cm
Oak, 10 × 8 × 196 cm
Installation, doggerfisher, Edinburgh

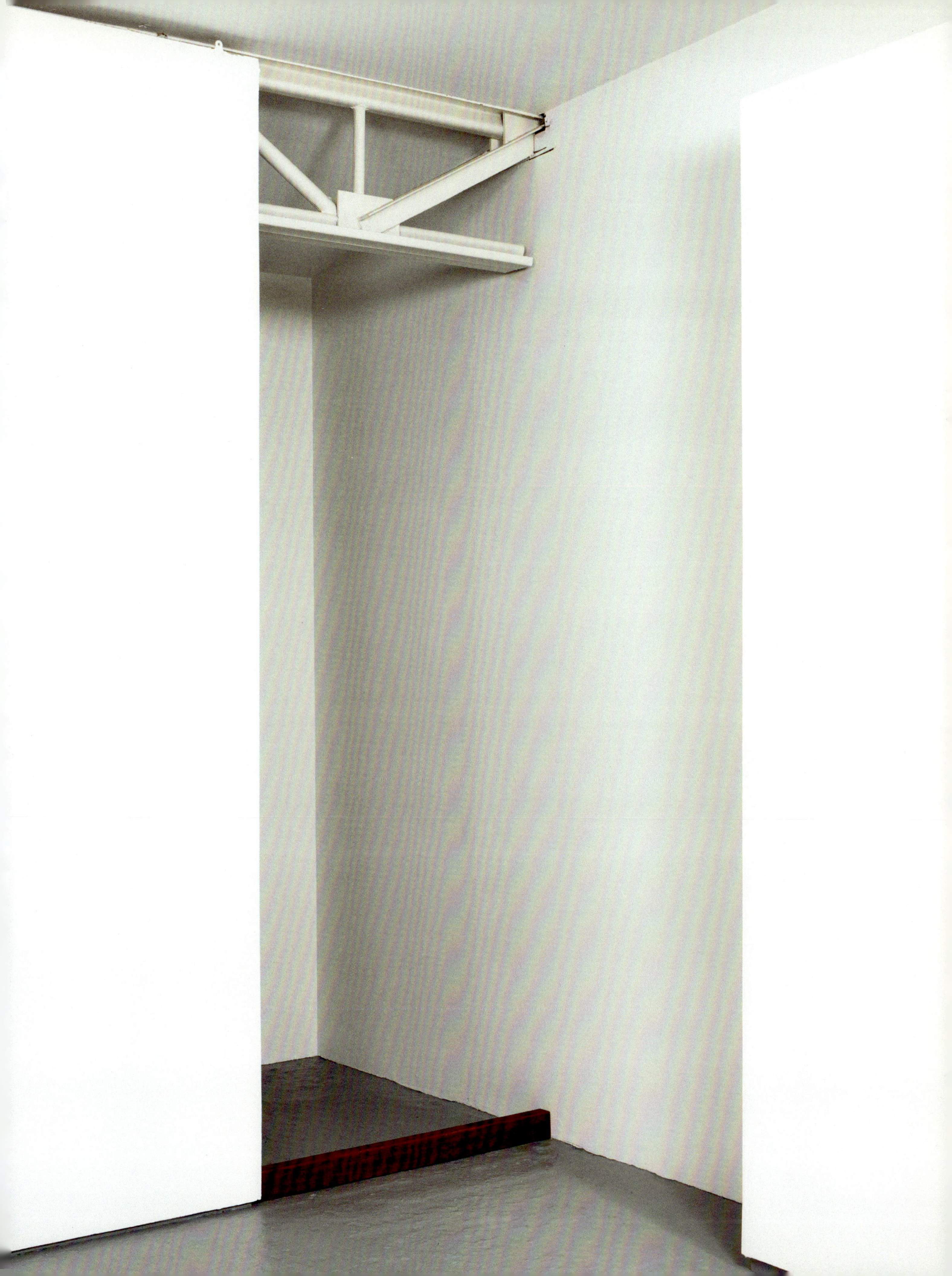

Annihilated Confessions

Within the space, we are faced with three works, each entitled *Annihilated Confessions* (2007). Exquisite and immediately seductive, the framed black-and-white photographs of ornate confession boxes are obliterated by a rectangle of black spray-paint administered to the surface of the glass, which floats in front of the image. Although concealed, we are able to partially glimpse the photograph beneath the surface, providing a tension in which we are offered and simultaneously denied access to the image. Wealth and ascendancy are implied by the lavishly ornamental nature of the confession boxes, whose symbolic weight and functioning is premised on absolution being made in private before an assumed power not, in fact, visible during the correspondence. In an age in which apologies are often played out in view of the media and motivated by a desire to maintain public image rather than genuine atonement, the works raise questions about the role of the confession box in modern society.

The pristine yet ultimately neutral beauty of the works' surface brings to mind the reductive strategies deployed in Ad Reinhardt's black monochrome works, which were motivated by the idea that painting should express nothing but the very essence of art. Furthermore, by using spray-paint as a medium, Coley references street graffiti, a visceral means by which the marginal and the transient assert their identity. The obliteration of the image might also be seen to metaphorically register the politics of censorship as well as the desecration of holy monuments and icons, triggered by the conflict between religious beliefs and the instability of territorial boundaries. The *Annihilated Confessions* ask us to consider whether spaces exist beyond the reach of state jurisdiction or religious doctrine, and continue the artist's interest in fostering an expansive freedom of thought and expression within what he regards as an oppressed world.
— *Darren Pih*

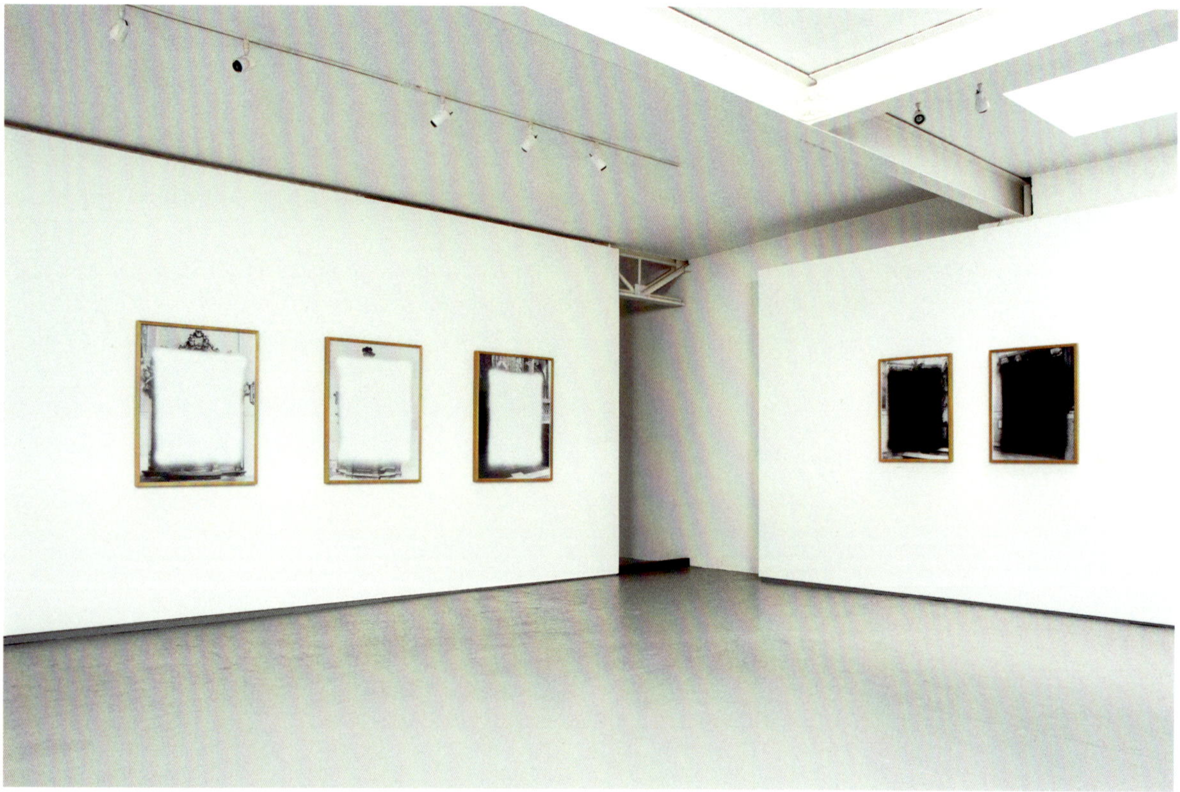

Annihilated Confessions (Black and White), 2007
Black-and-white photograph, framed behind glass, over-sprayed with enamel paint
105 × 80 cm
Installation, doggerfisher, Edinburgh

Islamic Safe House

Islamic Safe House (2007) makes an association in form to the Renfrewshire council house rented by two terrorists who attacked Glasgow Airport with a car bomb in 2007.

The work's title, alluding to a sort of haven, belies the structure's precarious placement on top of a tall, spindle-legged table.

Fabricated in a "boy's bedroom" manner, the sculpture is labeled with the words "life," "mind," "wealth," "land," and "belief"—the five rights of man under Islam.
— *Nathan Coley*

Islamic Safe House, 2007
Hardboard and timber
146 × 65 × 40 cm
Installation, doggerfisher, Edinburgh

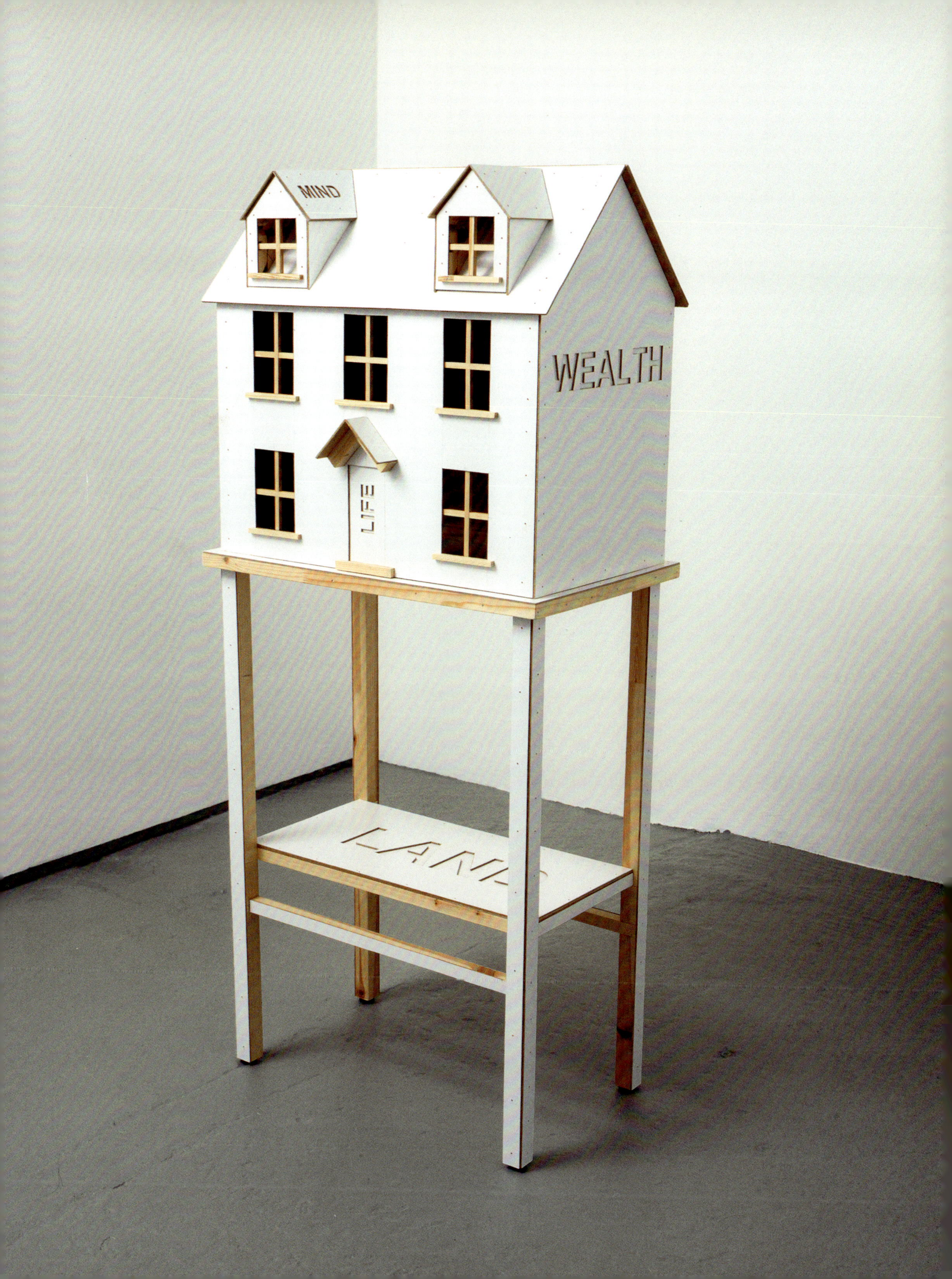
MIND
WEALTH
LIFE

Aristotle had the idea that for any major town to be a "true city," there needed to be a broad diversity within its population. People with different histories, beliefs, incomes, and knowledge are the foundation for any successful urban environment. It is what makes us dissimilar that holds the city together. He felt that for any city to be successful, it had to embrace the gathering of strangers.

Gathering of Strangers

Coley's text piece *Gathering of Strangers* (2007) oddly advertises the uncomfortable circumstances of an assembly of unrelated, unfamiliar people, implying a condition of contemporary global nomadicism. The multicolored, fairground lightbulbs evoke an amusement park attraction, yet the phrase they spell is a common idiom for Christian congregations or the Church itself, presenting a modern-day conflict between carnival and Lent. Like Coley's camouflage churches, *Gathering of Strangers* questions how our environment is invested with meaning, how meaning shifts from one social context to the next, and how the values to which we aspire are reflected in the way we describe ourselves and the associations we make.
— *Michael Rooks*

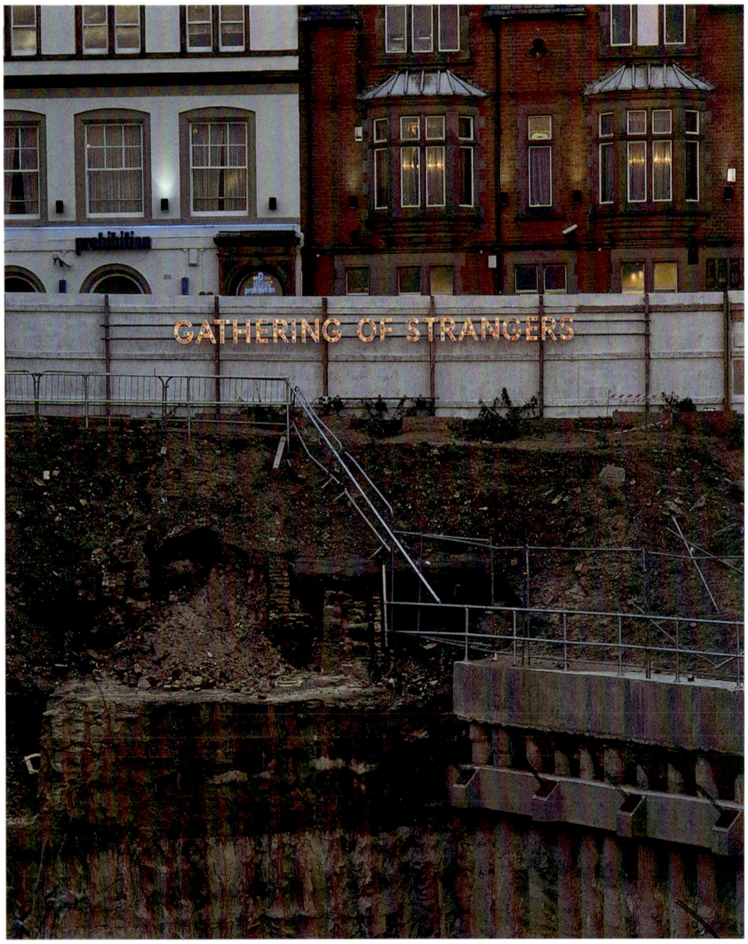

Gathering of Strangers, 2007
Illuminated text on scaffolding
0.45 × 8.25 m
Installation on the site of Nottingham Contemporary
Collection of the Whitworth Art Gallery, University of Manchester

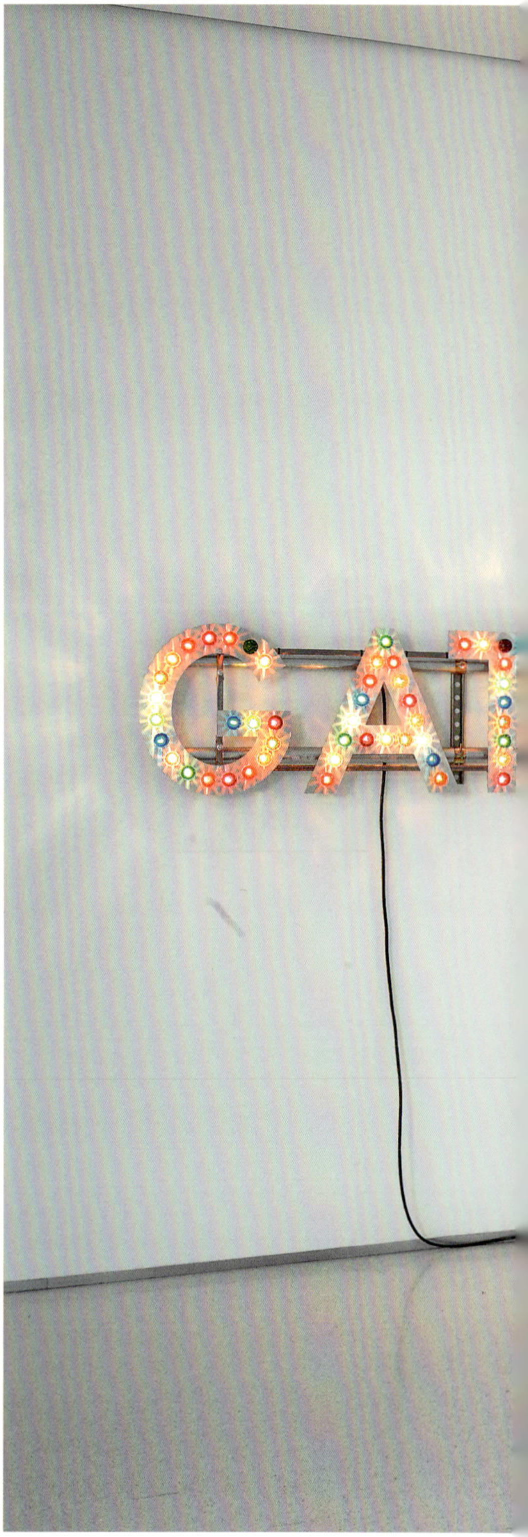

Gathering of Strangers, 2007
Installation, Haunch of Venison, New York

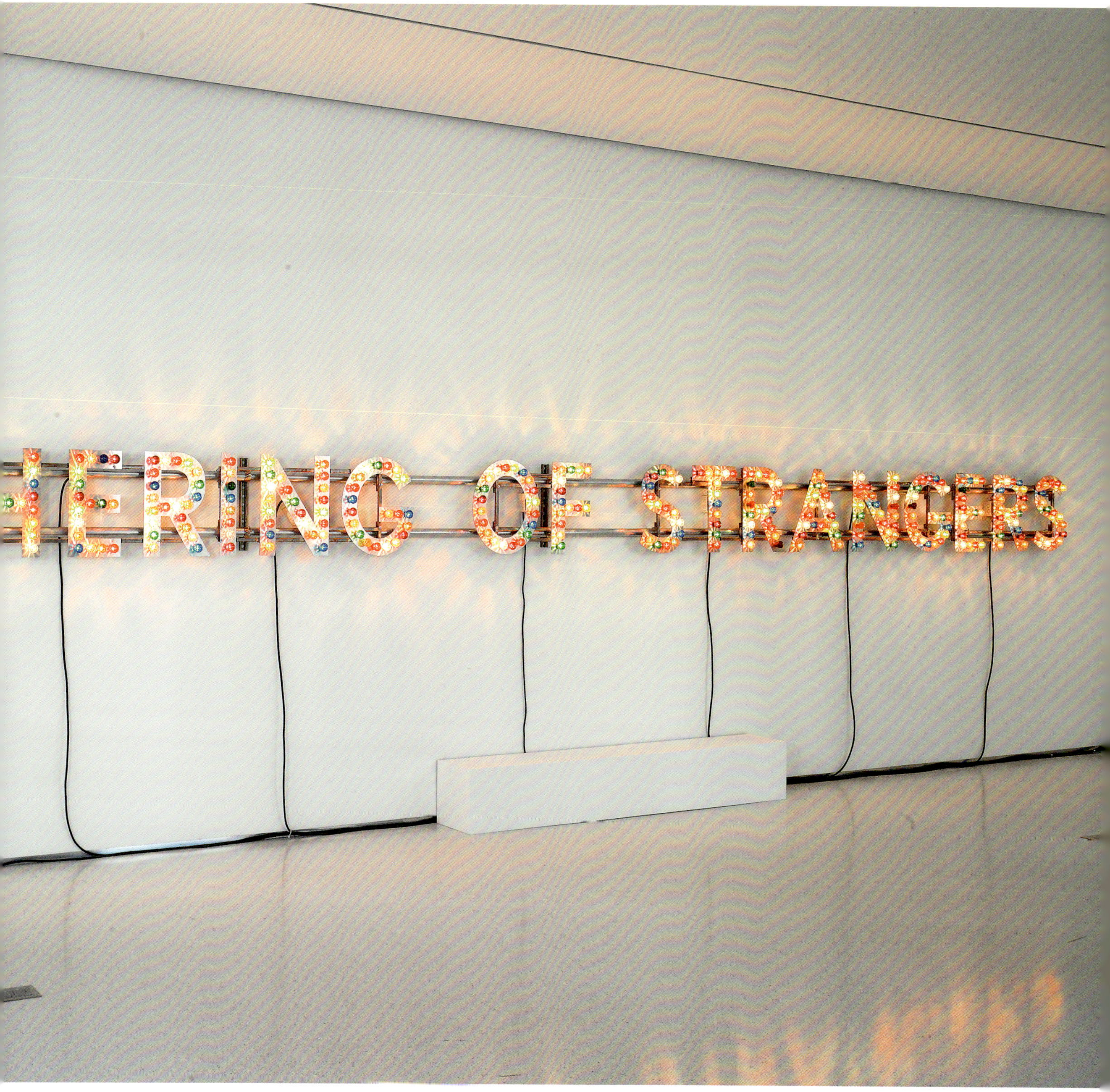
ERING OF STRANGERS

The eighteenth-century satire novella *Candide* by Voltaire follows the disillusioning journey of a sheltered young man—full of parodies, wild humor, and tongue-in-cheek ridicule. The "road stories" involve many a king and queen, politician, thinker, and artist, and land directly on historical events and discussions of the day. Concluding on the very last line, the main character Candide announces, "we must cultivate our garden," as if advising others to act practically and not optimistically when faced with similar disillusionment.

We Must Cultivate Our Garden

Twenty-four thousand pounds per year is said to be the sum of money that a person needs in order to live comfortably in twenty-first century Britain. The protagonist in Voltaire's *Candide* highlights the temptation to fall for a more comparative understanding of happiness. Candide travels the globe in search of happiness, and when he reaches the isolated country of Eldorado he meets children playing with emeralds and is waited on by maidservants of unsurpassed beauty. Candide and his travelling companion decide that their happiness is worthless in Eldorado.

If we stay here, we shall be no different from anybody else; but if we go back to the old world with a mere twelve sheep laden with Eldorado stones, we shall be richer than all the kings of Europe put together.

At the end of the book, after months of tortuous arguments with his famous tutor Pangloss concerning the best way to live life, Candide meets an old man sitting under an arbor of orange trees. The man is happy with his lot; he has twenty acres which he tends with his children and is ignorant of the political machinations of Constantinople and beyond. Candide leaves the farm a changed man: "That old fellow . . . seemed to me to have done much better for himself than those six kings we had the honour of supping with." He returns to his small estate and organizes his life according to the simple principle that happiness is to be found in cultivating the land, relationships, and talents that surround you. His wife Cunégonde discovers she has a flair for pastry making and Brother Giroflée is a good carpenter. Candide concludes that in order to obtain happiness "we must cultivate our garden."

Nathan Coley has mounted these words on a ten-meter-high scaffolding structure where their powerful and complex overtones become explicit. The use of the plural "we" is inclusive, conveying the sense that a joint effort is necessary for an endeavor to have any effect. The imperative "must" lends an active, almost dictatorial tone. The words "cultivate" and "garden" are loaded with metaphorical weight: we can cultivate our minds, our souls, our relationships as well as the soil. Our "garden" might constitute a house, a spirit, a child, or a patch of land.

The intention of Voltaire to allow for multiple interpretations is clear and this is the point that interests Coley. A literal reading of the statement is obvious: tend to your garden and you will feel better about life. A broader,

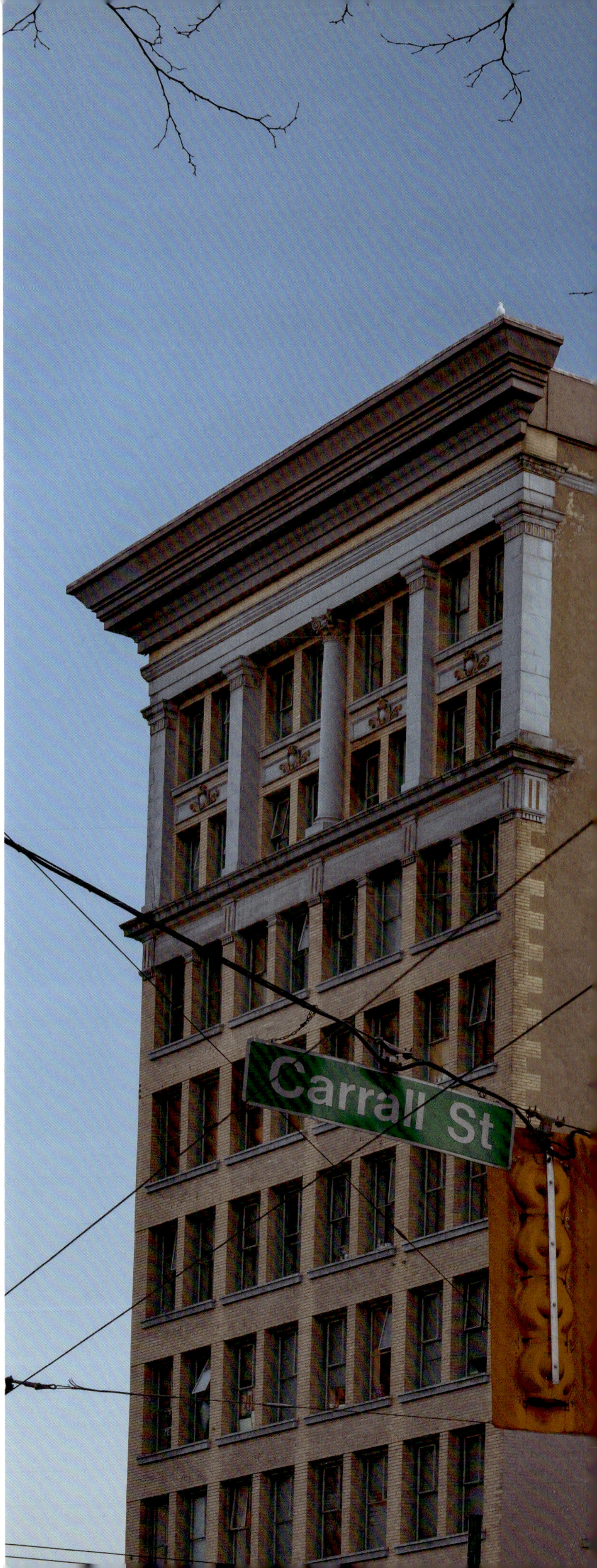

———

We Must Cultivate Our Garden, 2006
Illuminated text on scaffolding
0.45 × 9.9 m
Installation, Carrall Street, Vancouver

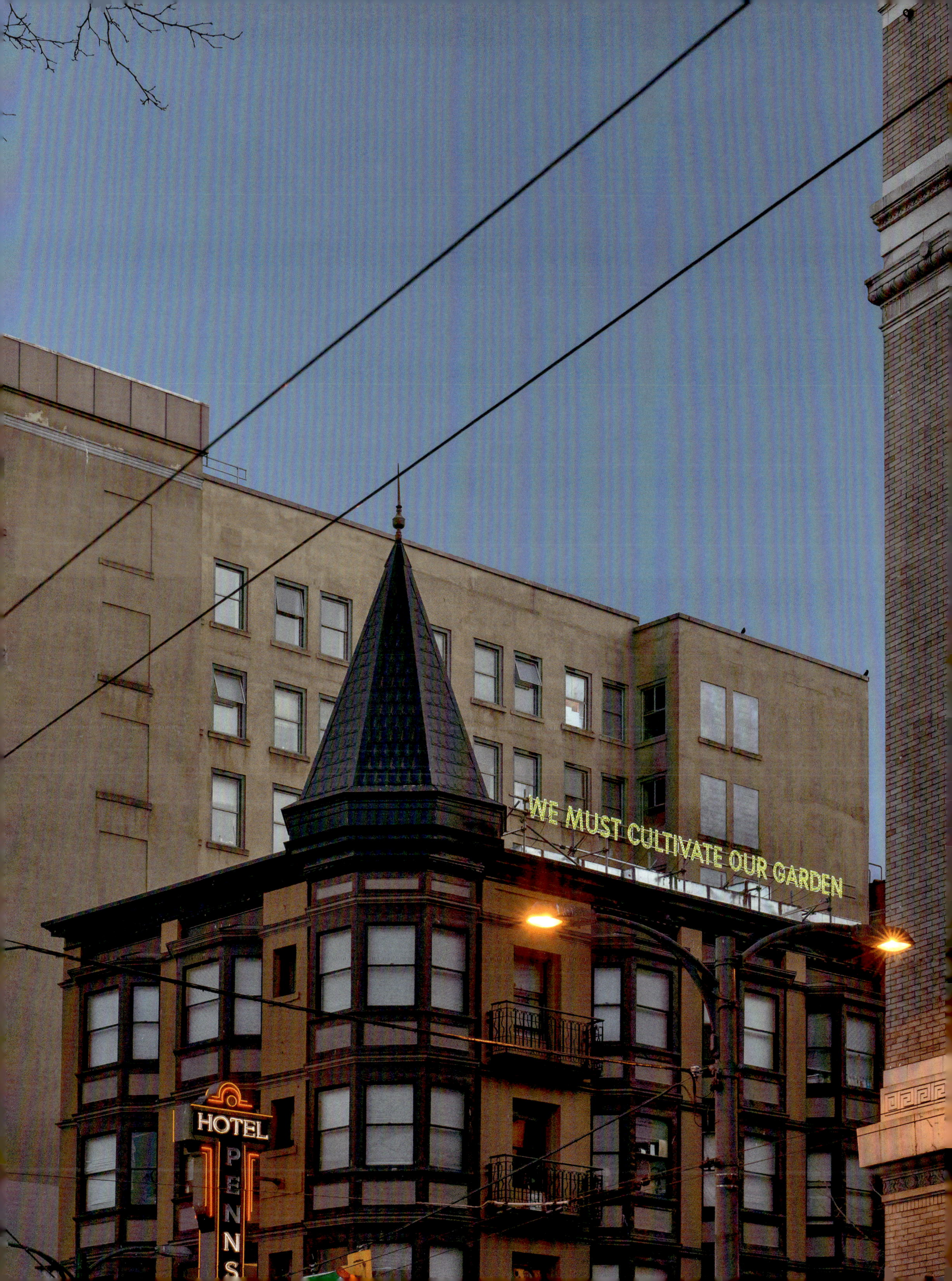
WE MUST CULTIVATE OUR GARDEN
HOTEL
PENNS

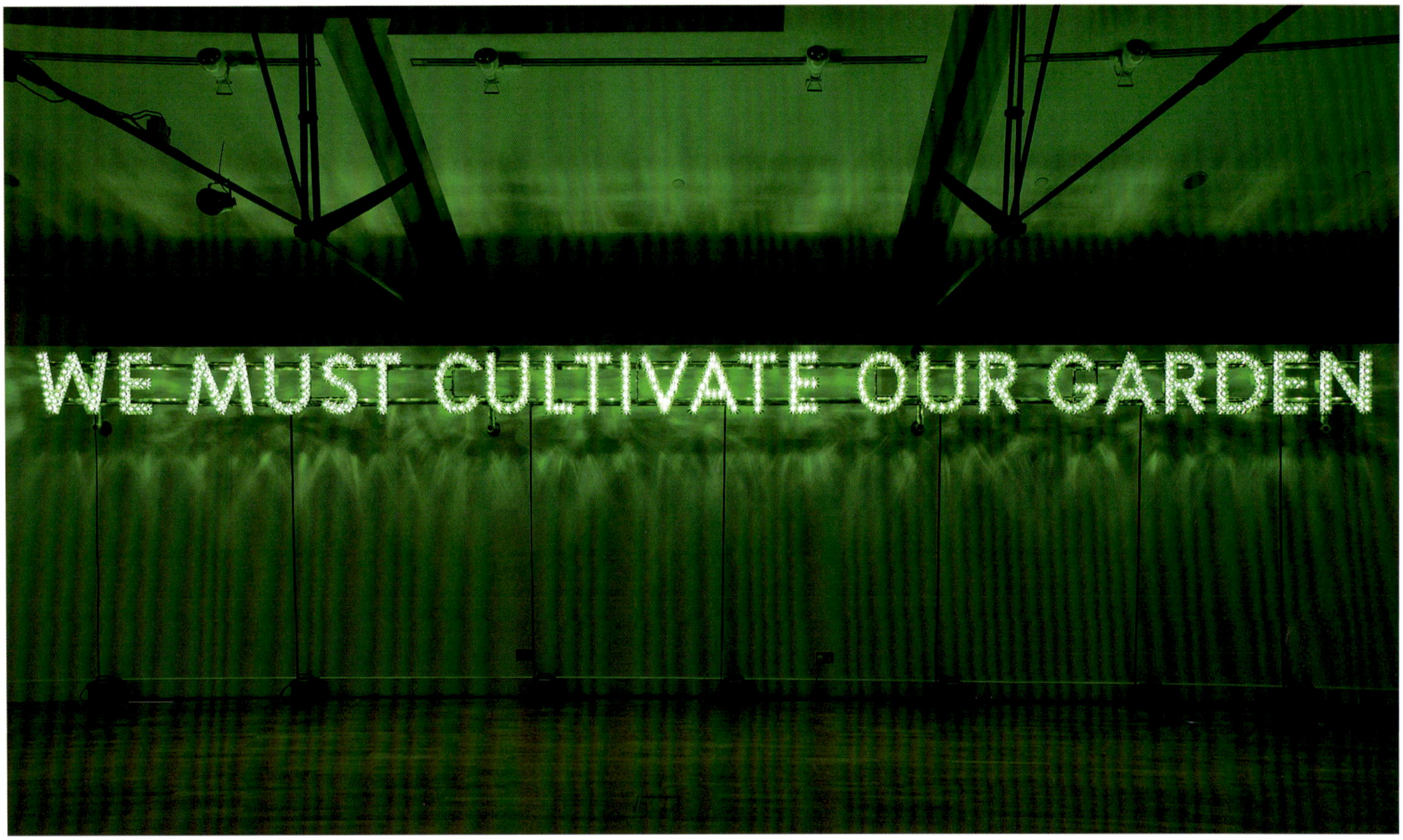

metaphorical reading might yield an anti-church, anti-royalty message which propounds an active, self-reliant approach to life; a belief that a hunger for knowledge and understanding can be satiated through investigation and hard work rather than reliance on fate, tenuous beliefs, or social standing.

The Penguin Classics edition of *Candide* translates "*il faut cultiver notre jardin*" into the rather more limp statement "we must go and work in the garden." While Coley is convinced that he has selected the correct translation, he is interested in the idea that the sentence is open to multiple forms of translation and interpretation. As in all his work, this element of ambiguity is crucial. The onus is placed on the viewer to locate a meaning which interests them. In a recent exhibition on the Isle of Bute, Coley mounted the words "There Will Be No Miracles Here" on a similar scaffolding structure in the grounds of a nineteenth-century gothic mansion, using the same type of fairground bulbs and typeface (designed by James Goggin for the purpose). The statement is derived from a public decree issued in seventeenth-century France in a village persistently troubled by supernatural activity. Such a bold assertion belies its essential tenuousness, leaving the viewer wondering where they can, indeed, be witness to a miracle. The speaker (in this case, the king) is clearly raising himself above the status of God, taking ownership of real and metaphysical space—a somewhat presumptuous position to take, particularly in seventeenth century France when religion was still at the heart of civilized society. At first glance the statement is absurd; on second viewing it is amusingly pedantic and even deflationary in that it seems to close down the possibility of an imaginary space where miracles can occur. But it can also be read as a wholly positive statement with which Voltaire would no doubt have concurred: a plea to citizens to shed their superstitious beliefs in favor of a rational, exploratory, evidence-based approach to life, resulting in a more satisfying and meaningful existence.

The formal elements of the miracles piece are echoed in the Lighthouse installation. In both cases the words are carefully set out on a makeshift scaffolding structure. The first line of "There Will Be / No Miracles / Here" is declaratory and affirmative, the second line is equally declaratory but negative, while the third line emphasizes the location of the statement, presenting a notional boundary within which the diktat must be adhered to. Coley sets out "We Must Cultivate Our Garden" in one line of text where the word "cultivate" is sandwiched between four words, two on either side. This provides the eye with an element of visual harmony but also draws attention to the authoritative tone of the text. The upper case text exaggerates this tone, as does the location of the work in the room. An elevated sign (one

We Must Cultivate Our Garden, 2006
Installation, The Lighthouse, Glasgow, and the De La Warr Pavilion, Bexhill-on-Sea

that is above head height, at least) exudes very different overtones to one that is viewed at eye level. It becomes an injunction which lends an air of authority beyond the grasp of the mortal beneath it. Coley kills two birds with one stone here, as the space below the text provides ample room for a lush and well cared for garden to grow.

In the context of this exhibition, *We Must Cultivate Our Garden* assumes yet another guise. The garden becomes Edinburgh, the city from which, according to some, modern life emerged. *Candide* was first published in France in 1759, when the Scottish Enlightenment was in full swing, and there are many parallels to be drawn between Voltaire's philosophy and those of his contemporaries in Scotland. David Hume and Adam Smith echoed Voltaire's insistence that empiricism and the inductive method were superior to superstition and metaphysics, and that the division of church and state was essential for the creation of a modern state.

Contemporary Edinburgh is steeped in the architectural and emotive fabric of its past. Its distinctive topology lends itself to a type of conservatism that, while conveying a sense of stability, stifles imaginative and physical growth. The medieval castle, perched on its volcanic base and rising majestically above Prince's Street, is an icon that is difficult for any contemporary visionary to compete with. The imposing museums, gardens, monuments, and crescents were all born of the intellectual and economic renaissance that stemmed, in part, from Scotland's political union with England in 1707. While this wealth of history is quite rightly carefully preserved in the twenty-first century, it also provides an insidious backdrop to cries of dissent from traditionalists who, for example, complain of the "blight" to the landscape caused by Enric Miralles's recently completed Scottish Parliament.

If you cultivate your garden with any integrity, you will obviously have to carry out the tedious task of weeding, but you will also need to experiment with new and perhaps exotic plants, some of which will no doubt disappoint, and some which will grow and become firm favorites.

In the broader context of contemporary society, *We Must Cultivate Our Garden* becomes a criticism of the current demand for easy access to everything, where the least amount of physical or mental effort is required to achieve happiness or enlightenment. Government policies which seem to support the idea that elitism is a dirty word are evident in their approach to education and the arts. Voltaire's hatred of church and monarchy would today be replaced, no doubt, by a hatred of a media culture in which teenagers dream of fame for fame's sake and the far corners of the world are reached in the comfort of an SUV.

Finally, the fact that the enlightenment baton was grasped so zealously by the founding fathers of America in 1776 adds an element of poignancy to Coley's installation. The separation of church and state in the constitution drawn up by Thomas Jefferson, James Madison, and Alexander Hamilton with help from, among others, Adam Smith, represented the culmination of Hume and Voltaire's ambitions. This Britain is a country where seventy percent of the population now believes in Satan and the groundswell of support for Creationism (euphemistically called "Intelligent Design") seems to overwhelm all rational thought. Two hundred and fifty years later, it appears to be more imperative than ever that we cultivate our garden.
— *Jes Fernie*

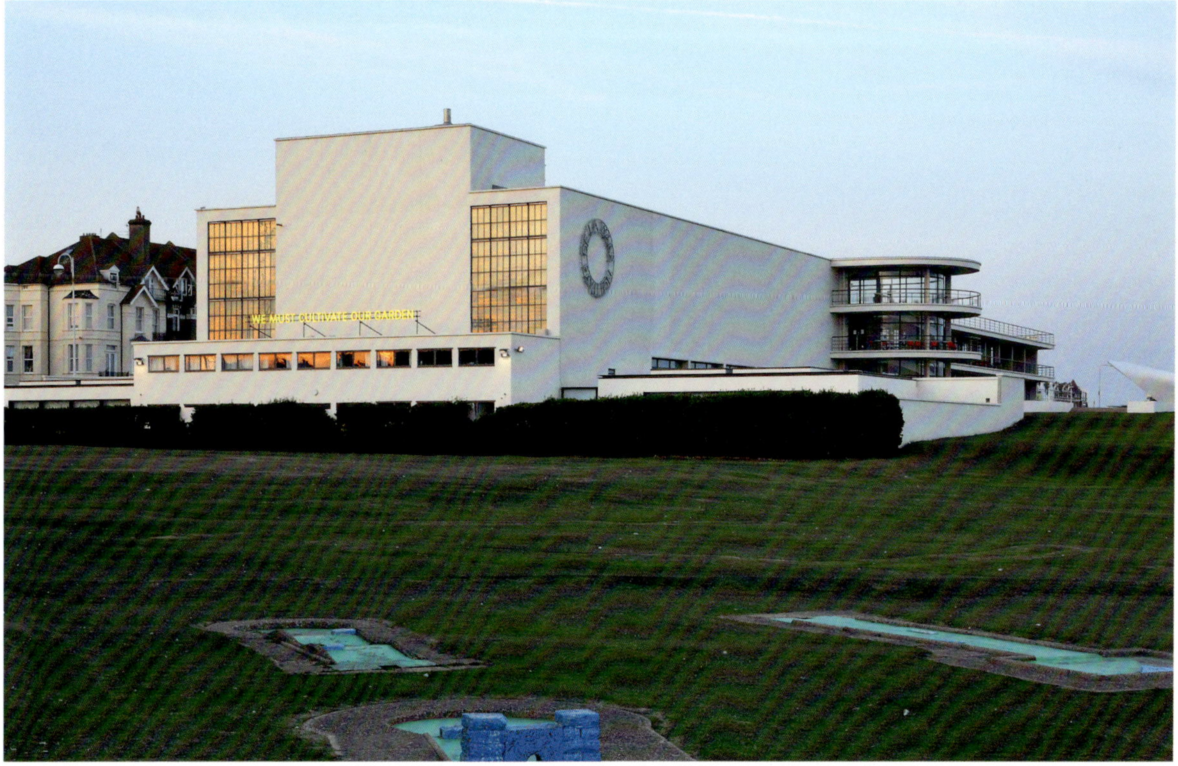

Camouflage Church

Nathan Coley is interested in how the values of a society are articulated in the architecture and public spaces it produces. He uses the immediately identifiable architectural forms of mosques, churches, saloon bars, and holiday homes as a way to unearth our social, political, and ideological value systems. Controlled spaces, thresholds, and platforms become signifiers for the often fraught relationship between church and state; performers and spectators; politicians, monarchs, and subjects.

In 2005, Coley made a series of small-scale models of a church, synagogue, and mosque, which were stripped of their unique characteristics but remained very clear signifiers of their religious types: steeple for church, dome for mosque, and single story for synagogue. The most striking element of the work is the dazzle pattern applied to the surface, reminiscent of the camouflage pattern used to confound the enemy on World War I and II ships. These religious structures are attempting to deny their existence—to appear other than what they are—while also spelling out their religious allegiance through their form.

Coley is playful enough to not be didactic. He is not prescriptive about the kind of questions that he wants us to ask when viewing his work, but there is a palpable sense that he wants us as citizens to be aware of the power structures that define the parameters of our society. With the camouflage series, he may be asking us to consider the position of the church in our increasingly secular way of life; the insidious power that faith still wields while becoming seemingly more invisible, or maybe he is pointing out the conflict between form and surface application—warning us that things are never as they seem.

In 2006, Coley was invited to make a public sculpture in the historically and religiously loaded city of Santiago de Compostela in northern Spain. The context for *Camouflage Church* could hardly have been more rich: the city's cathedral is the final destination of the popular medieval pilgrimage route and is the reputed burial place of one of the apostles of Jesus Christ. This large-scale version of the model has become even more of a sign of itself; the architectural details such as windows and doors are gone, and we are left with a mute generic church installed within a city populated by the architecture of faith in the form of pilgrims, cathedrals, and prayer.
— Jes Fernie

Camouflage Church, 2006
Painted timber
6.5 × 8.1 × 4 m
Installation, Plaza de Cervantes, Santiago de Compostela

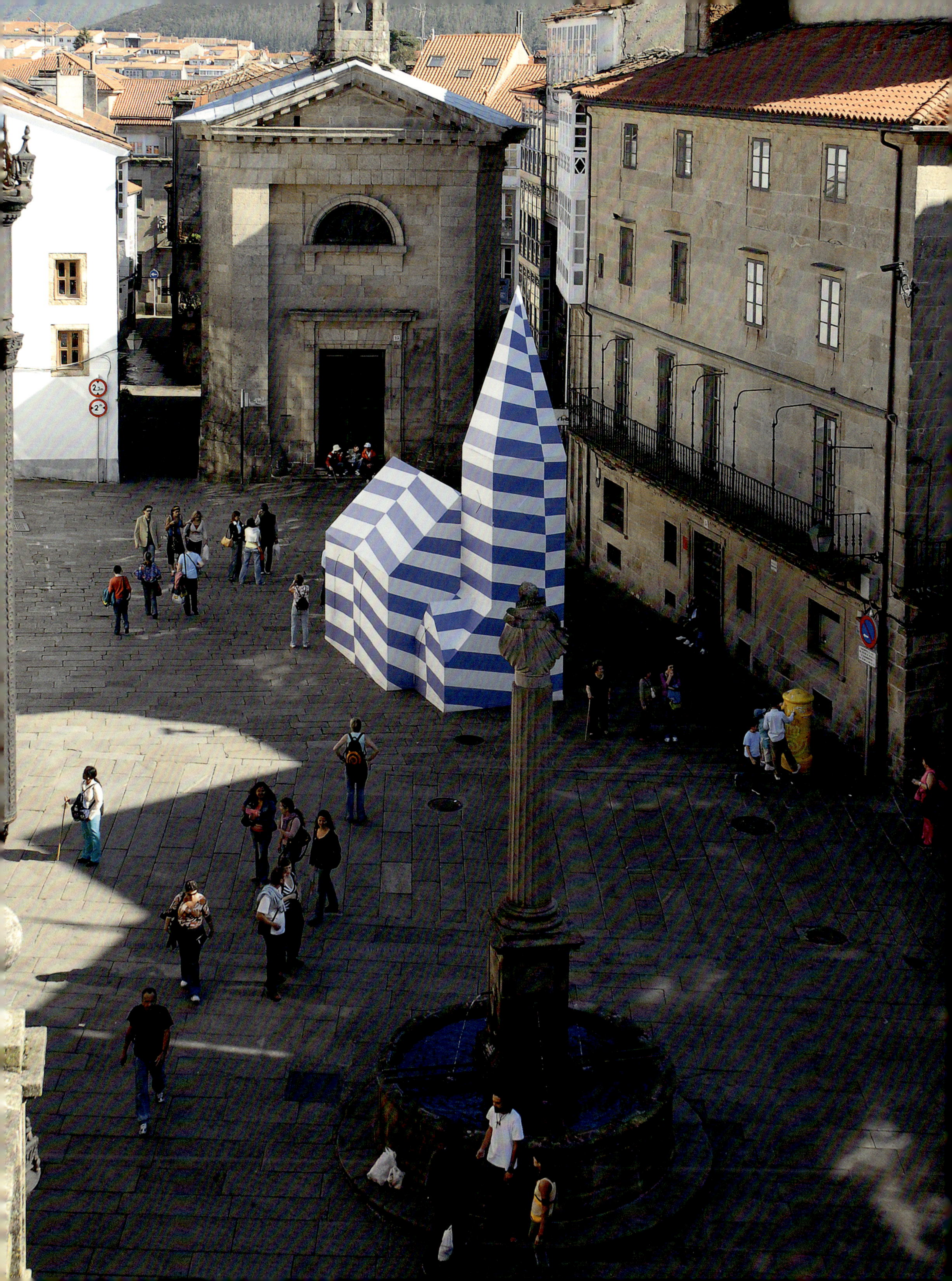

There is a famous case of an entire village in Haute-Savoie called Modseine, which had regularly been the site of miracles and magical practices. One very warm summer in the seventeenth century when these acts of what we would now call mass hysteria were occurring (and the harvest uncollected), a large notice was put up in the town square saying, "There will be no miracles here, by order of the King," just to show that modern legal space considers itself actually superior even to the idea of God having any space.

There Will Be No Miracles Here

Strolling through the eighteenth-century landscaped parkland of Mount Stuart, visitors are unexpectedly confronted by a large illuminated text that proclaims: "There Will Be No Miracles Here." Attached to a free-standing scaffold, six meters high and six meters wide, the words are divided into three lines, giving them the formal appearance of a poem:

THERE WILL BE
NO MIRACLES
HERE

The use of white electric lightbulbs, together with the unusual typeface[1] evokes nineteen-seventies disco glamour as well as fairground aesthetics, at once elegant and tacky, and strangely at variance with the message of the text. This gentle sense of irony is again echoed in the link created between the artificial illumination of text and the prodigious illumination referred to by the text.

Miracles are customarily defined as supernatural events or revelations, which in most religions provide evidence for the divine. To decree that "there will be no miracles here" is to deny, and forbid even, the possibility of divine intervention in this particular site. As declaration of a "miracle-free zone," it asserts God's power to be subordinate to that of the speaker.

Coley's text is in fact appropriated from a historical anecdote, related to the artist by the architectural historian Mark Cousins: "There is a famous case of an entire village in Haute-Savoie called Modseine, which had regularly been the site of miracles and magical practices . . . in the seventeenth century . . . a large notice was put up saying, 'There will be no miracles here, by order of the King,' just to show that modern legal space considers itself actually superior even to the idea of God having any space."[2]

The notion that public space is always controlled by law and authority rather than left unrestricted, open, and free is a concern Coley has addressed in a number of works. The most remarkable of these is *Public Announcement* (1998), which is a direct precursor to the illuminated work at Mount Stuart. On eight sites throughout the Scottish town of Stirling, large screen-prints displayed short historical quotes (including "There Will Be . . ."), each proclaiming power or issuing orders over space considered communal and open. Lacking context and in the absence of stated sources for each, the texts remain ambiguous, but together engender a sense of unease about our understanding of the public realm.

There Will Be No Miracles Here (2006) is firmly anchored in the ancient power struggle between state and church, politics and religion, between the rational and spiritual, the visible and invisible. The decree announces ownership not only of physical space, but also—in an act of flagrant hubris and arrogance—invisible, metaphysical space. The text's command is further highlighted by its setting—in a natural environment, but one cultivated and controlled by man. The urge of a state to make all subjects conform to a single system of interlocking disciplinary regimes requires, as Michel Foucault put it, "power of mind over mind,"[3] and recalls his compelling analysis of the mechanisms of coercion, particularly of total surveillance and control, typical of the panoptic society.[4] Yet at the same time, the work's refutation of the miraculous is reminiscent of Richard Dawkins's categorical secularism and his persistent attacks against organized religion as affront to reason and science.[5] Framed that way, *There Will Be No Miracles Here* reads no longer as polite notification but exposes the determination of an absolute authority to demand obedience, even in matters of personal belief, and the intolerance, fanaticism, and absurdity of such autocratic diktats.

But the text is more ambiguous. If we interpret *There Will Be No Miracles Here* as an example of rationalism versus irrationalism and superstition, then it recalls the bi-polarity of the Enlightenment, a period characterized by Voltaire's ideal of a rational society set against the spirituality of the time. The Scottish philosopher David Hume, for example, argued in his essay "Of Miracles" (1748) that miracles are contrary to our consistent experience of the laws of nature, and that there is therefore a logical obstacle to humans ever proving that events are miracles.[6] *There Will Be No Miracles Here* can consequently also be understood as imperative to depart from superstition and the irrational, to empower individuals to take responsibility for their own action without recourse to, or reliance on, so-called higher powers.
— Andrea Schlieker

Excerpt from the essay "Negotiating the Invisible," 2006

There Will Be No Miracles Here, 2006
Illuminated text on scaffolding
6 × 6 × 4 m
Installation, Mount Stuart, Isle of Bute

Overleaf:
Installation, Tate Liverpool
Collection of the National Galleries of Scotland, Edinburgh

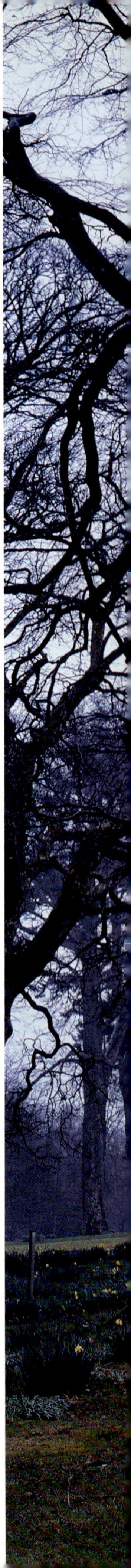

1 The typeface for this work was designed by James Goggin.
2 *Urban Sanctuary—A Public Artwork* (Glasgow, 1997), p. 44.
3 Michel Foucault, *Discipline and Punish: The Birth of the Prison* (New York, 1995), p. 206.
4 Ibid., see "Discipline, 3. Panopticism," pp. 195–228.
5 See Richard Dawkins, *The Devil's Chaplain* (Phoenix, 2003).
6 David Hume, *An Enquiry Concerning Human Understanding,* 1772 (Cambridge, Massachusetts, 1993), section X, p. 90.

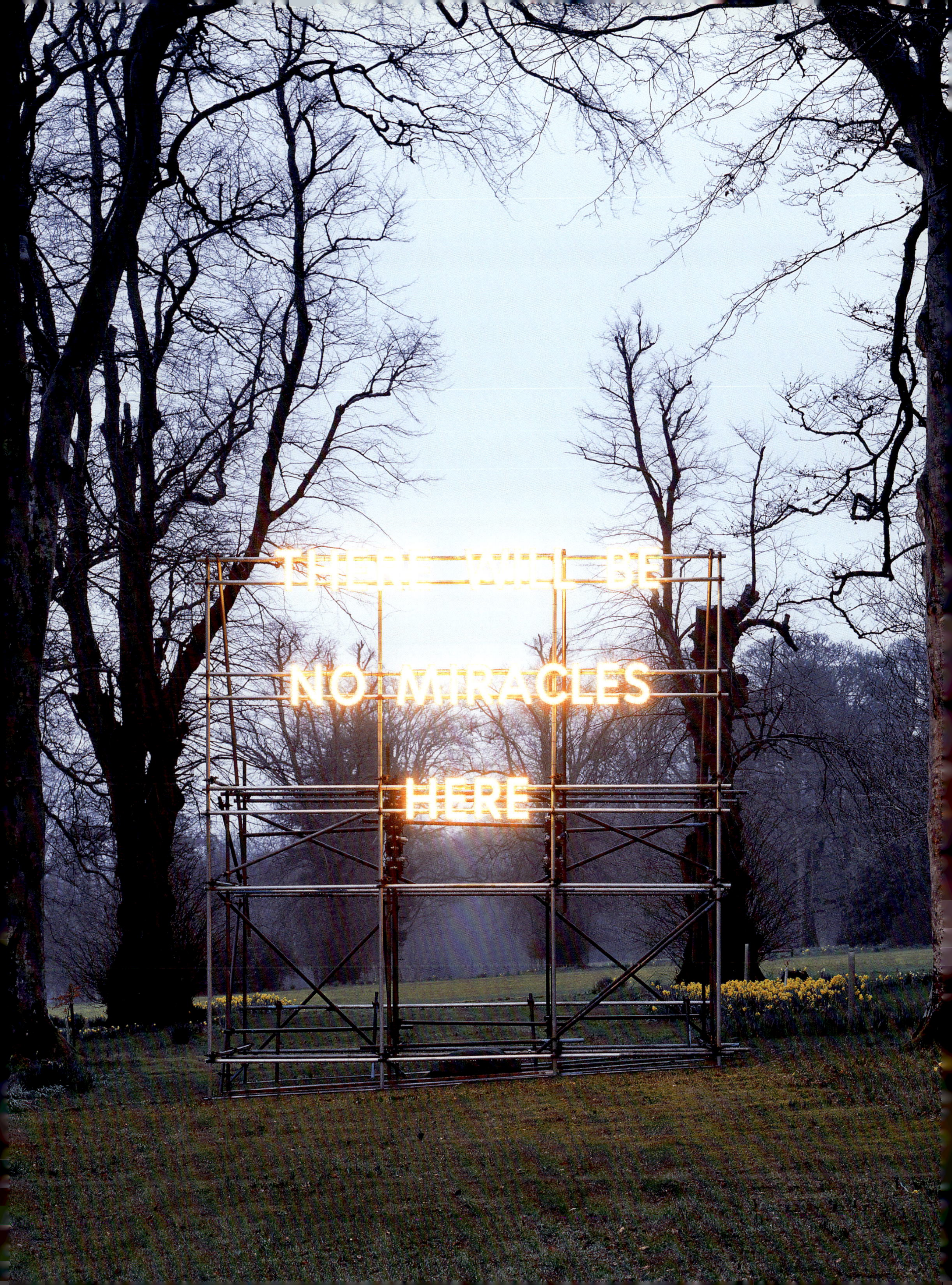
NO MIRACLES
HERE

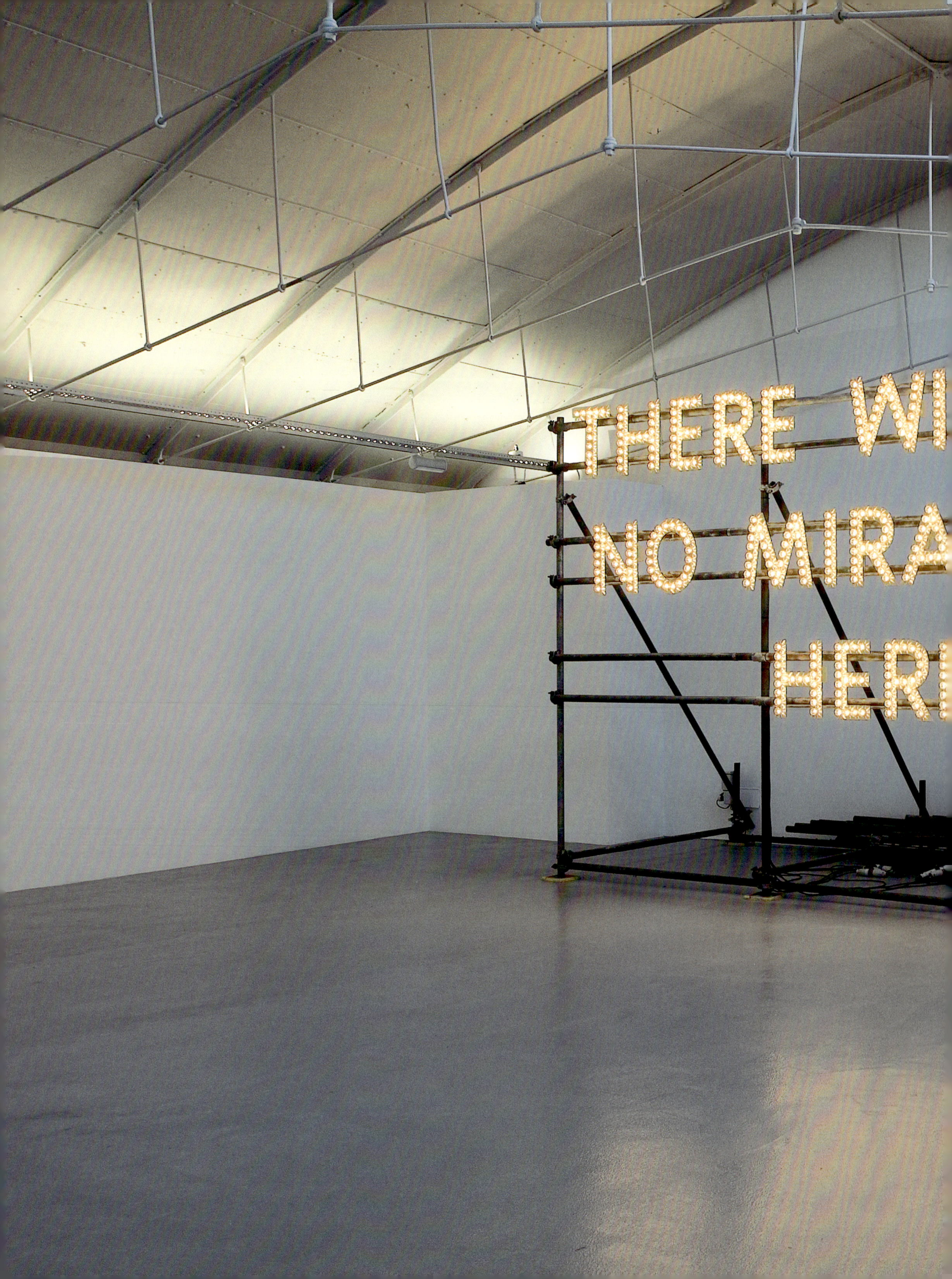
THERE WI
NO MIRA
HER

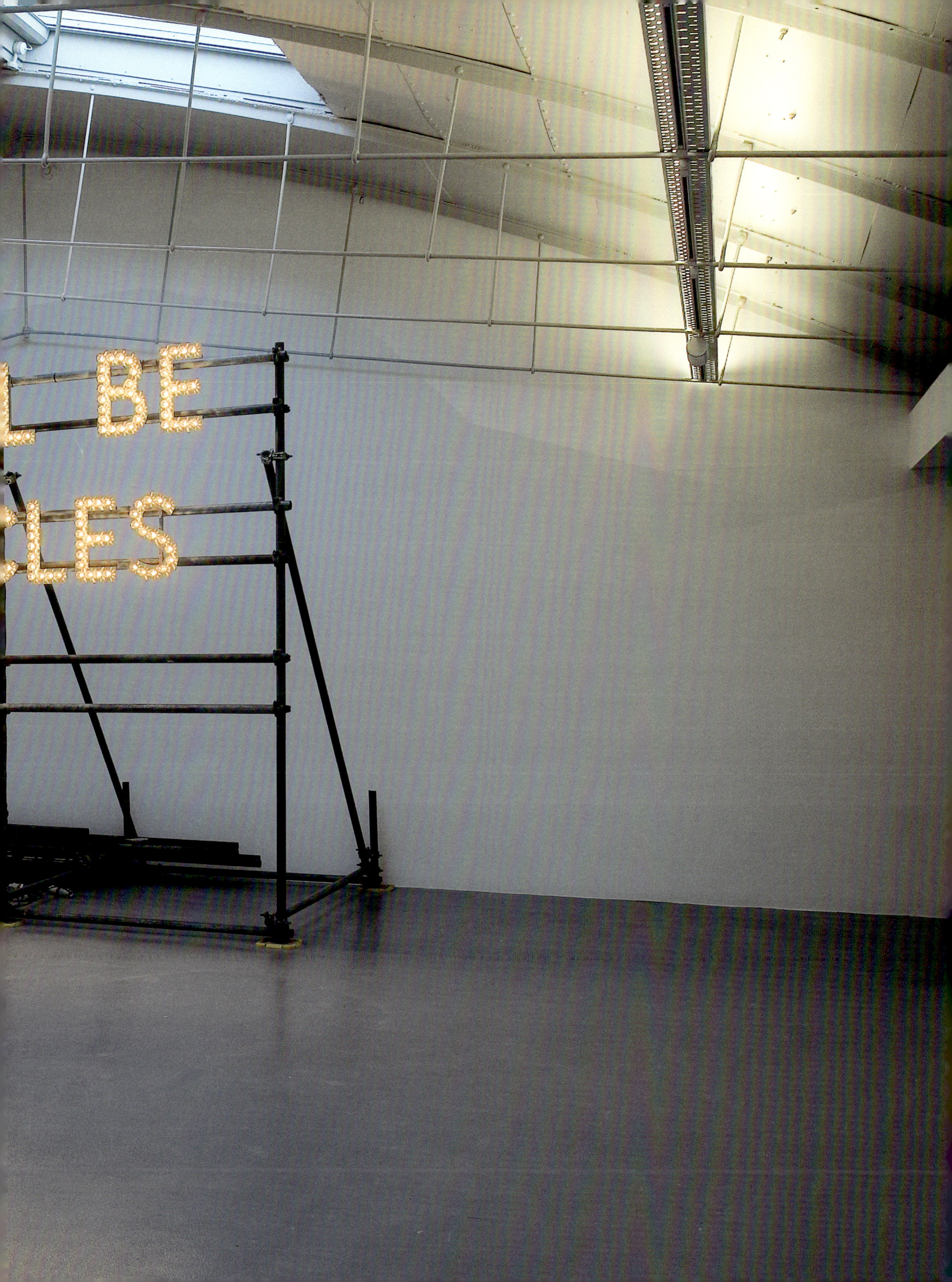
BE
CLES

Camouflage Mosque / Synagogue / Church

A recent film by Nathan Coley portrays the city of Jerusalem, undisputed center of three world religions, by taking us on a journey from the Dome of the Rock to the Wailing Wall and the Church of the Holy Sepulcher. We see worshippers fervently engaged in the minutiae of their diverse and distinctive rituals, compelled by the unique and ancient sanctity of each site. Jerusalem's Church (of the Holy Sepulcher), Mosque (of Al-Aqsa), and Temple (the Western Wall, believed to be the remnant of the second temple)—among the holiest constructed shrines of Christianity, Islam, and Judaism—are here found in closest proximity. Thousands of pilgrims from all over the world are daily brought together by the magnetism and significance of this singular place, yet remain divided by their faiths, each proclaiming its own as the universal truth. This unique matrix of sacred edifices in Jerusalem, and the ardent veneration they elicit, serves as a most formidable articulation of Coley's fascination with visible and material manifestations of the invisible and the elusive nature of faith.

A preoccupation with architecture—especially as a physical expression of religious and political ideas and ideologies—is a leitmotif in Nathan Coley's work.[1] The three world religions and the particular architectural forms they have each engendered are the catalyst for Coley's 2006 work, originally displayed in the Isle of Bute's Mount Stuart Visitor Centre: *Camouflage Mosque / Synagogue / Church.* But instead of grand and elaborate structures we encounter humble, handmade hardboard models of these places of worship, presented on low plinths. The models, with their "boy's bedroom" aesthetic,[2] have been stripped of defining symbols and characteristics (such as crescent, cross, or Star of David). They are rendered as generic rather than specific buildings for each faith, thereby becoming signs for, rather than portraits of, mosque, church, and synagogue.

Yet they are removed even further from any sense of realistic portrayal by the bold horizontal striped pattern which covers each model, and also by different color codings—gold, black, and purple respectively. The pattern has a curious optical effect, making the reading of the architectural model harder, almost denying its form. The specific colors used might have been chosen for their associative value—especially the gold triggers memories of the glittering golden domes of famous mosques, and the purple is reminiscent of ecclesiastical vestments, like the purple cassock of bishops. The stripe effect seems to be a deliberate nod to Op Art and design, to Bridget Riley and Daniel Buren, as well as perhaps to the great Renaissance churches such as Orvieto or Siena, with their remarkable façades of black-and-white stripes.

However, Coley has appropriated the stripe pattern from an altogether non-art and non-religious source: it refers to the so-called "dazzle" camouflage applied to ships during both World War I and II as protection from attack. Devised by Norman Wilkinson, Inspector of Airfield Camouflage, the "dazzle" scheme was inspired by the effect of sunlight on water. Camouflage, derived from the French *camoufler,* meaning "to disguise," is a form of concealment adapted from mimetic strategies in the natural world for use in military action. Artists as diverse as Andy Warhol, Alighiero Boetti, and Hans Haacke have all used camouflage in their work, attracted no doubt by its inherent dual signifier of aesthetics and politics. For Coley it was important here not to "make invisible, but to disguise" these objects "that are trying to deny their existence." At first, the flamboyance and graphic rigor of the works seem at odds with this intent, and it is only when we have identified the pattern as wartime camouflage that this withdrawal into deliberate effacement becomes evident.

To trace the meaning of these camouflaged places of worship it is helpful to consider the nexus of religion and power that Coley repeatedly invokes in his work. For example, we find wartime references in combination with the sacral motif in *14 Churches of Münster* (2000), a video in which Coley had taken his cue from an order to target the churches of Münster, issued to allied bomber pilots in World War II. His book project *Urban Sanctuary* (1997) probes further into this relationship. His investigation (through a number of interviews) of the concept of sanctuary reveals the church's failure to uphold its position as guarantor of refuge and immunity from state legislation in today's secular society. It highlights social, political, and ideological questions about the boundaries of state power, and asks whether any spaces still exist that are beyond the reach of law.[3] As an extension to this enquiry, it can be argued that Coley's *Camouflage* works could be read as subtle metaphors for the increasing loss of authority that religious institutions have suffered in our (Western) secular culture, while their wartime associations also bring to mind geopolitical conflicts triggered by clashing religious beliefs.
— *Andrea Schlieker*

Excerpt from the essay "Negotiating the Invisible," 2006

---

[1] "I'm very interested in the evolution of Christianity, or any religion for that matter, from being a notional concept between scholars to being manifest in buildings and dwellings." Nathan Coley in *Urban Sanctuary—A Public Artwork* (Glasgow, 1997), p. 4.

[2] All quotes by Nathan Coley, unless otherwise indicated, are from conversations with the author.

[3] It is a strange travesty indeed that today's place maintained outside state legislation is not a sanctuary but a prison like Guantanamo Bay.

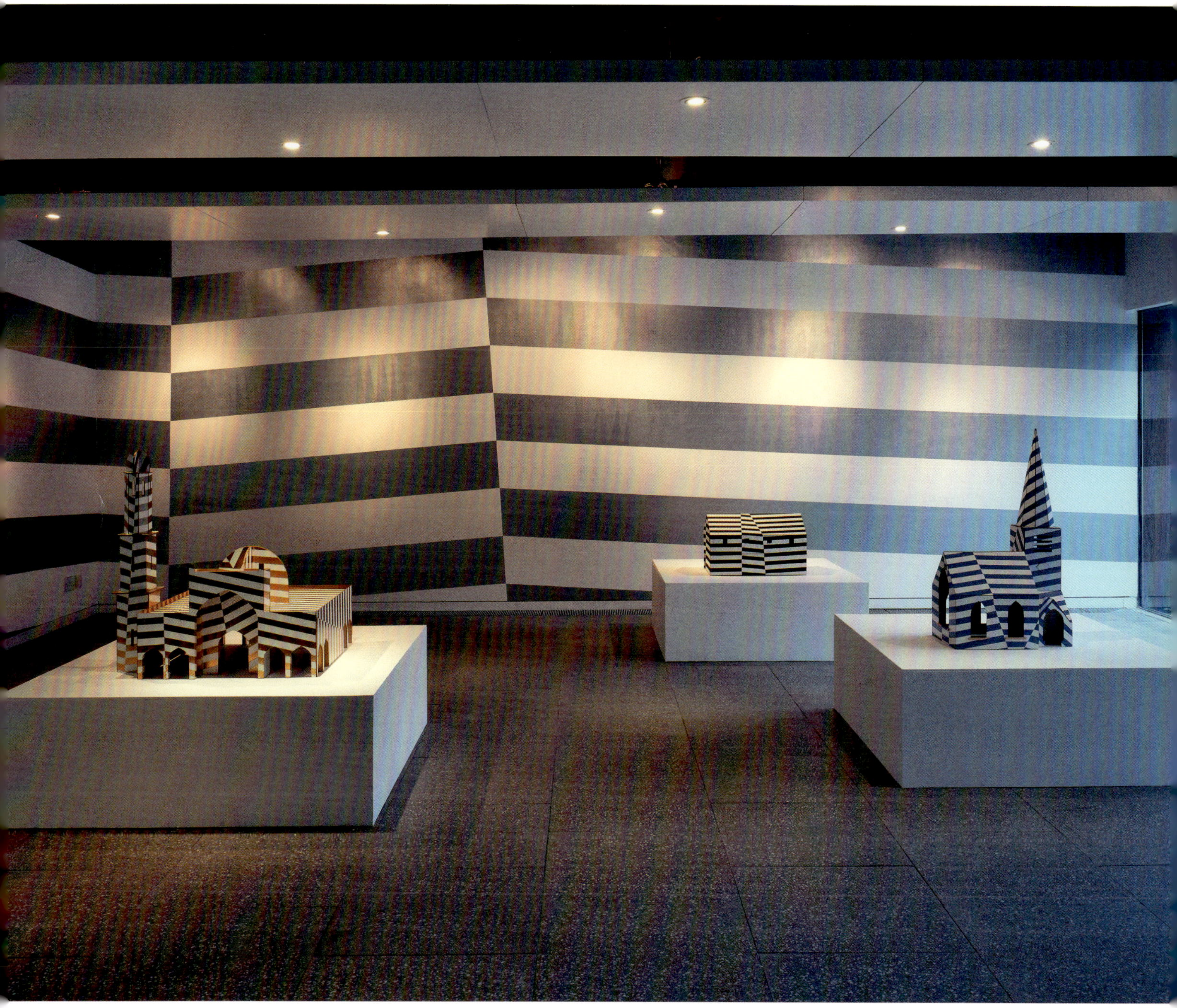

Camouflage Mosque / Synagogue / Church, 2006
Painted hardboard
85 × 82 × 69 cm, 36 × 61 × 41 cm, 91 × 53 × 33 cm
Installation, Mount Stuart, Isle of Bute
Collection of the Frac des Pays de la Loire, Carquefou

Jerusalem Syndrome

This project explores the phenomenon of Jerusalem Syndrome, a rare travel psychosis which afflicts people who find themselves intoxicated by the Holy Land. Those affected can be found at holy sites chanting, singing, and delivering sermons as if living in the time of Christ. Their behavior can range from the benign, such as exhilaration, or a mild nervousness and anxiety, through to the destructive.

Significantly, Coley's work was filmed on location in Jerusalem in November 2004 during the holy month of Ramadan, which coincided with Yasser Arafat's failing health in Paris. The footage captures the daily lives of locals in Jerusalem as well as focusing on the behavior of tourists who visit the holy city, to help give the audience an insight into this rare psychological condition.

By gaining access to areas of the city that are normally off limits to non-Muslim visitors, Coley captures the religious rituals and acts that form part of daily life in Jerusalem, from the delivering of sermons to the kissing of objects of religious significance. In the background, the sounds of the holy city run throughout the film with mosque callers and the shouts of street market sellers to the murmur of everyday life with mobile phones and car horns.

Excerpt from original press release,
Cooper Gallery, Dundee, 2005

Jerusalem Syndrome, 2005
Single-screen projection
20 mins, shot on Super 16 mm film and DVCAM, transferred onto DVD

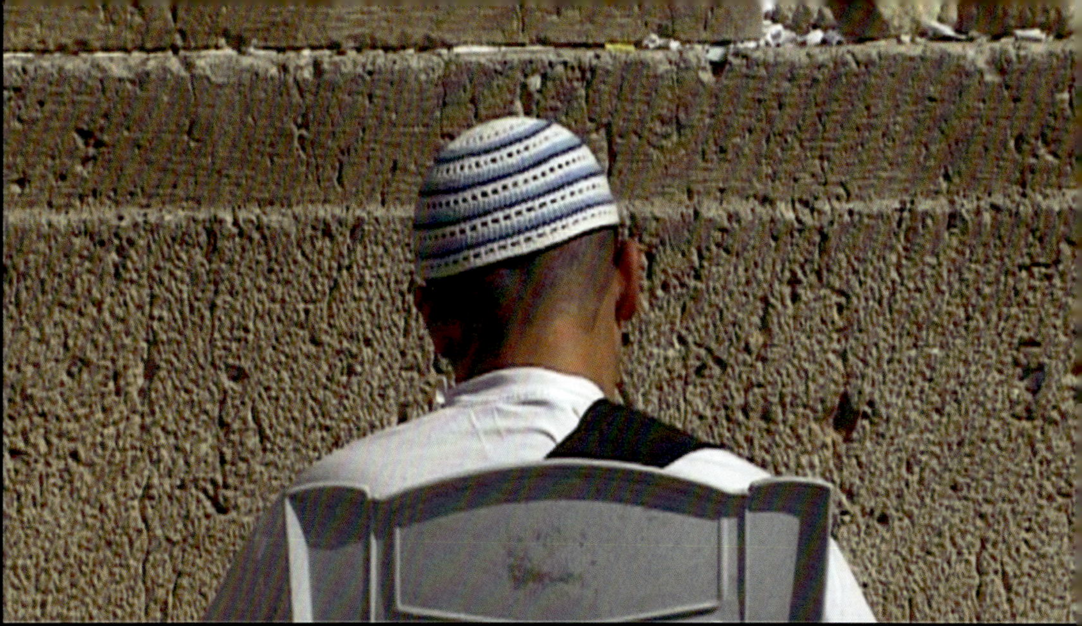
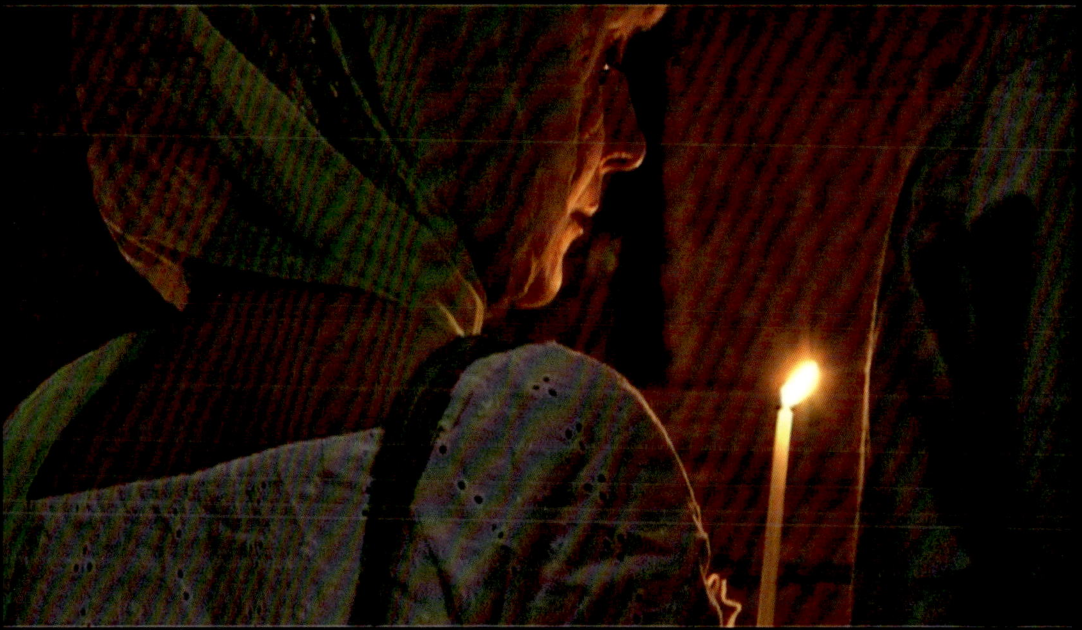
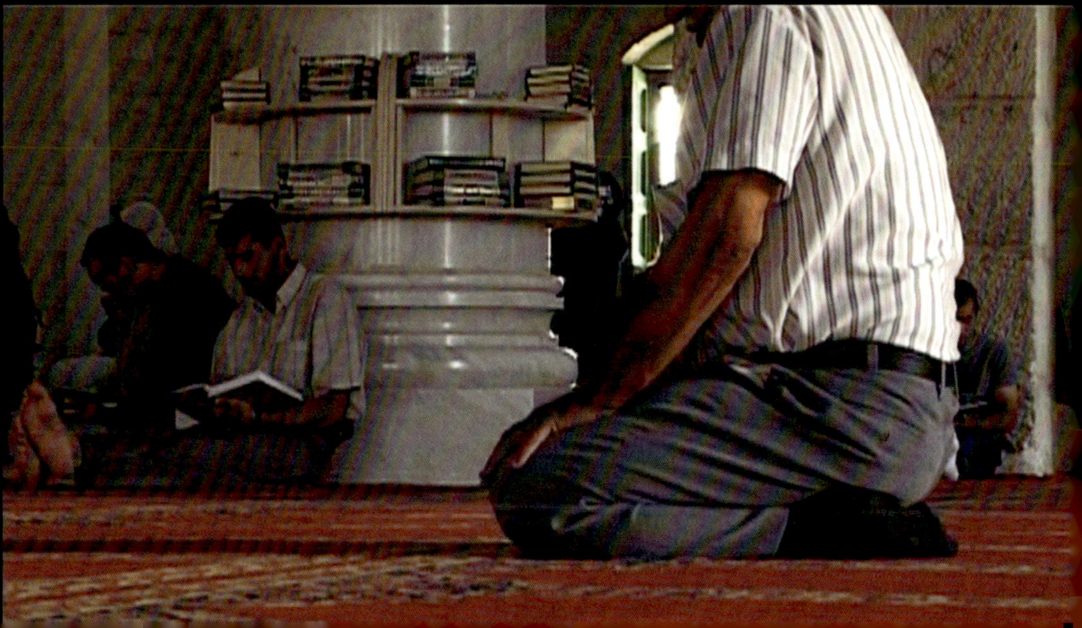

Iceman

Produced for *Thinking of the Outside,* a project in Bristol curated by Claire Doherty in 2005, *Iceman* was located in the heart of the city within the secluded graveyard of St. John's Church. In spite of its central milieu within the city, Coley noticed that the graveyard had been seemingly forgotten: "Right in the center of town, it sits undeveloped, stubbornly unchanged through sixties and seventies modernization, and inevitably lost to the city. With the last burial in the eighteen-eighties, it could be said to be unused. No-one lays flowers or visits a loved one there, and as far as I know, its only real function is to be retained and overlooked."[1] Placing a scaled-down, four-story housing block within the walls of the graveyard, Coley set out to reactivate St. John's by inserting an alien structure within the space.

Coley branded the exterior of the model with a blue graffiti tag appropriated from the side of a building the artist photographed in Dundee. The insignia spells out the word "Iceman," alluding to a colloquial word which denotes a place to buy heroin. By referencing an illegal substance, Coley's use of graffiti disrupts the solemnity of St. John's churchyard. This sense of disruption is exacerbated further by incorporating a highly personalized form of expression in an otherwise private setting; here, Coley explores the role of the individual within the public realm by exploring the significance of vandalism as a marker of identity. As a direct result, Coley highlights the identities of those whose remains lie forgotten within St. John's by drawing attention to the space. Both the signature and the sculpture are *blemishes*; while the graffiti tarnishes the appearance of the model, the structure is an architectural anomaly. Transforming a space left to ruin, *Iceman* considers the increasingly fluid interplay between the individual and the collective, and the role that architecture plays in allowing these two realms to converge.
— *Jonathan Horrocks*

---

[1] Nathan Coley in conversation with Clare Doherty.

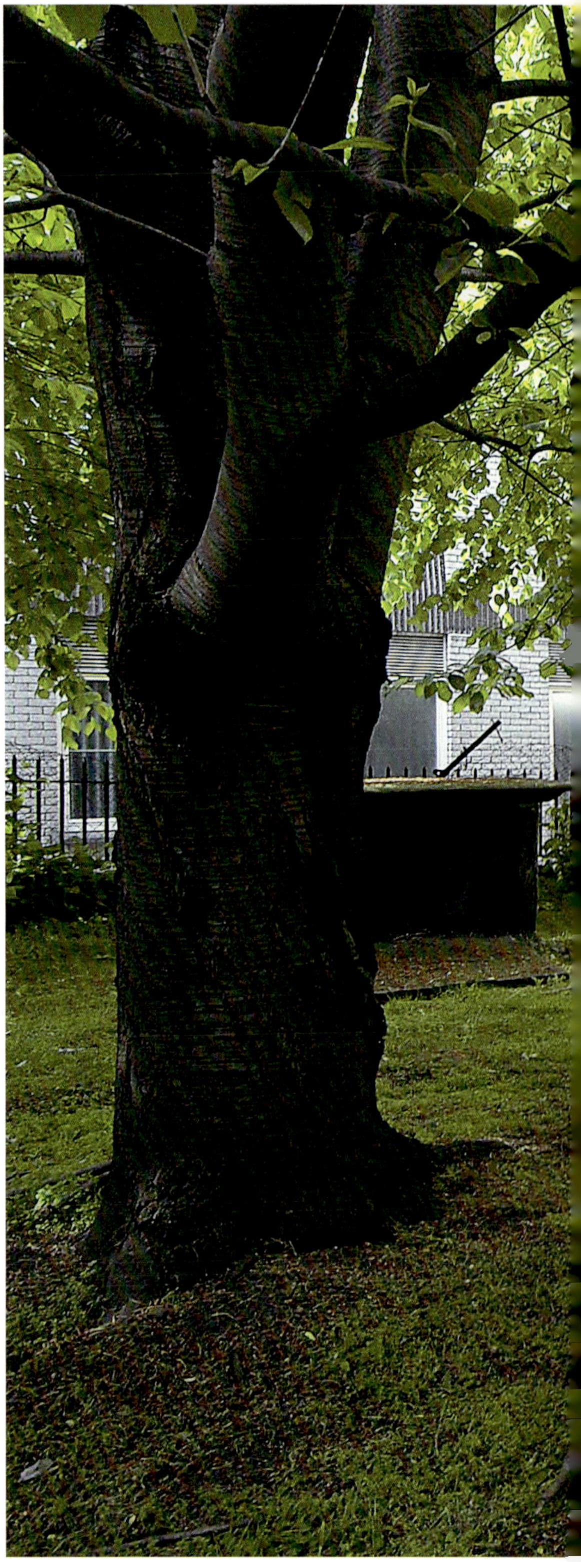

Iceman, 2005
Painted plywood
3.2 × 4.8 × 2.7 m
Installation, St. John's Church, Bristol

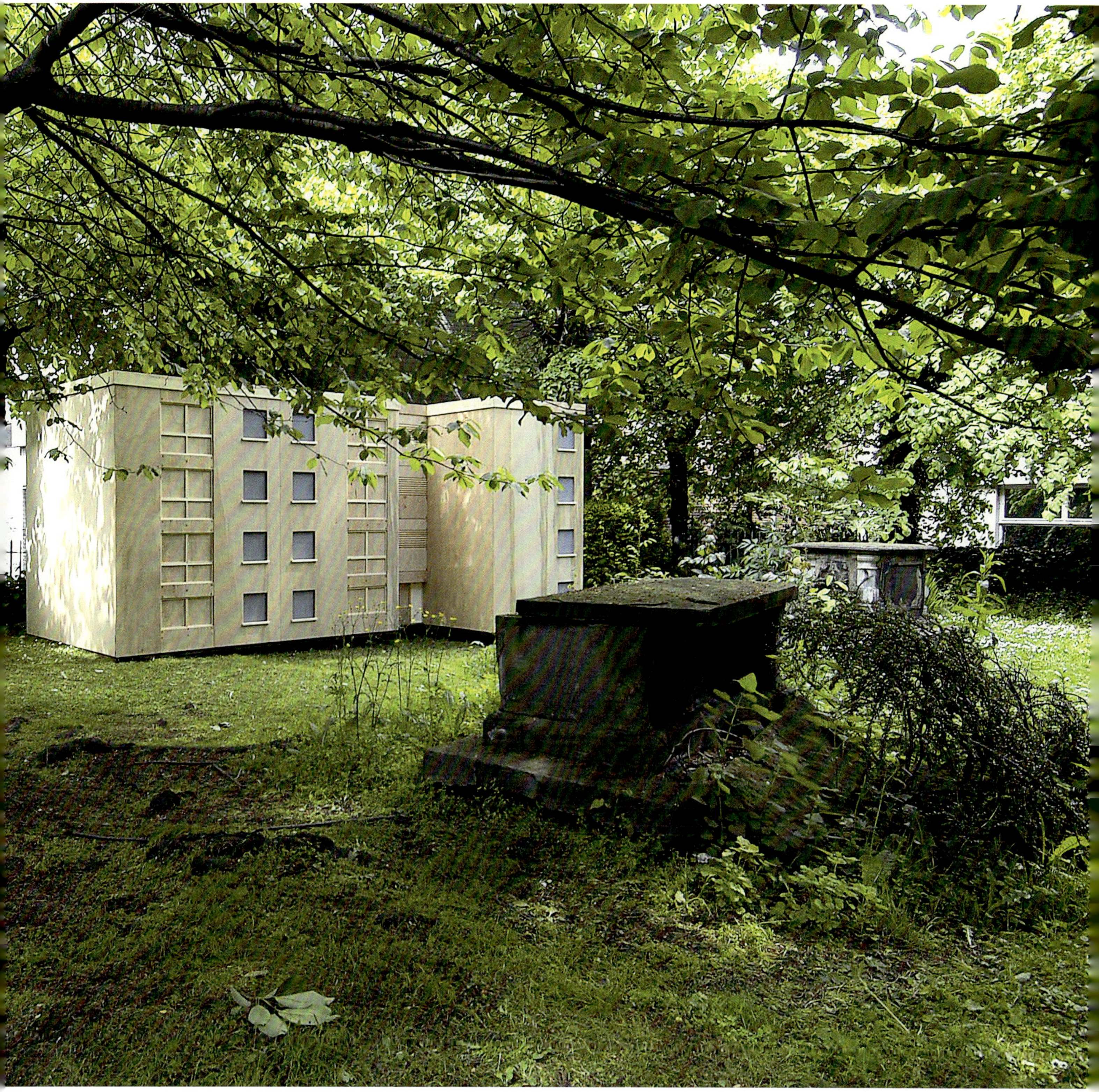

The Lamp of Sacrifice (286 Places of Worship, Edinburgh)

As with *The Lamp of Sacrifice (161 Places of Worship, Birmingham)* (2000), this installation brings together a collection of scaled-down replicas of religious buildings. Using panels of cardboard, Coley re-constructed all 286 places of worship within Edinburgh (as listed in the Yellow Pages at the time), and presented them in direct confrontation with one another by clustering them together within the gallery space. In doing so, the artist highlighted the manner in which religious buildings are characterized by conflicting theological ideologies. The intense amount of labor which went into fabricating each model, both in terms of research and physical construction, manifests the presence of these invisible fractures. The fastidiousness of the work's production also recalls the sacrificial nature of worship which is demanded by religion. Archetypal of Coley's practice, the work demonstrates how the artist uses objects to reveal the conflicting systems of belief through which the space around us is constructed.
— Jonathan Horrocks

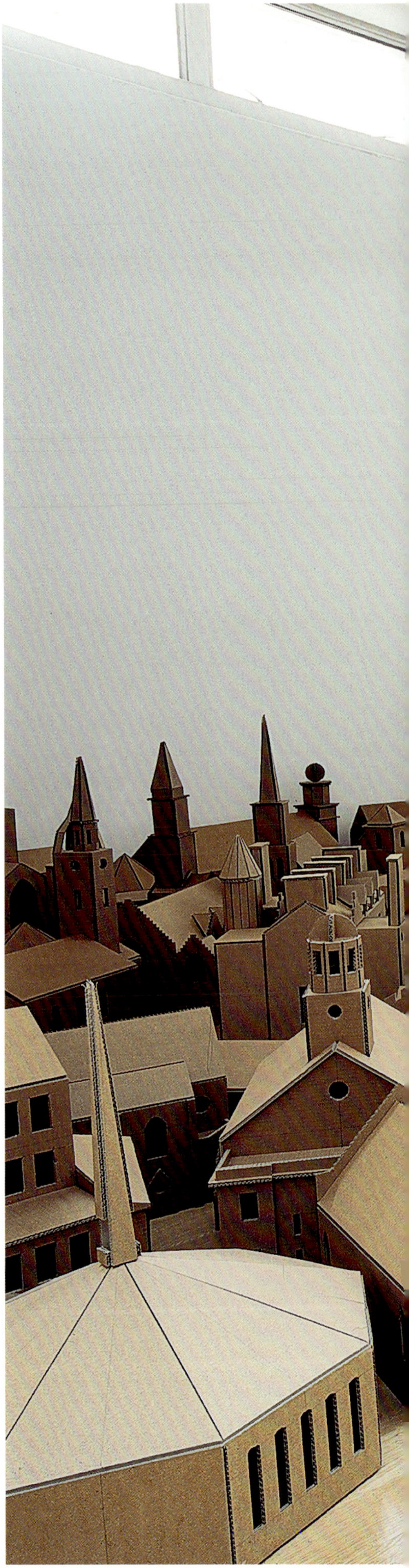

The Lamp of Sacrifice (286 Places of Worship, Edinburgh), 2004
Cardboard
Dimensions variable
Installation, The Fruitmarket Gallery, Edinburgh

Overleaf: Installation, The Dean Gallery, Edinburgh
Collection of the National Galleries of Scotland, Edinburgh

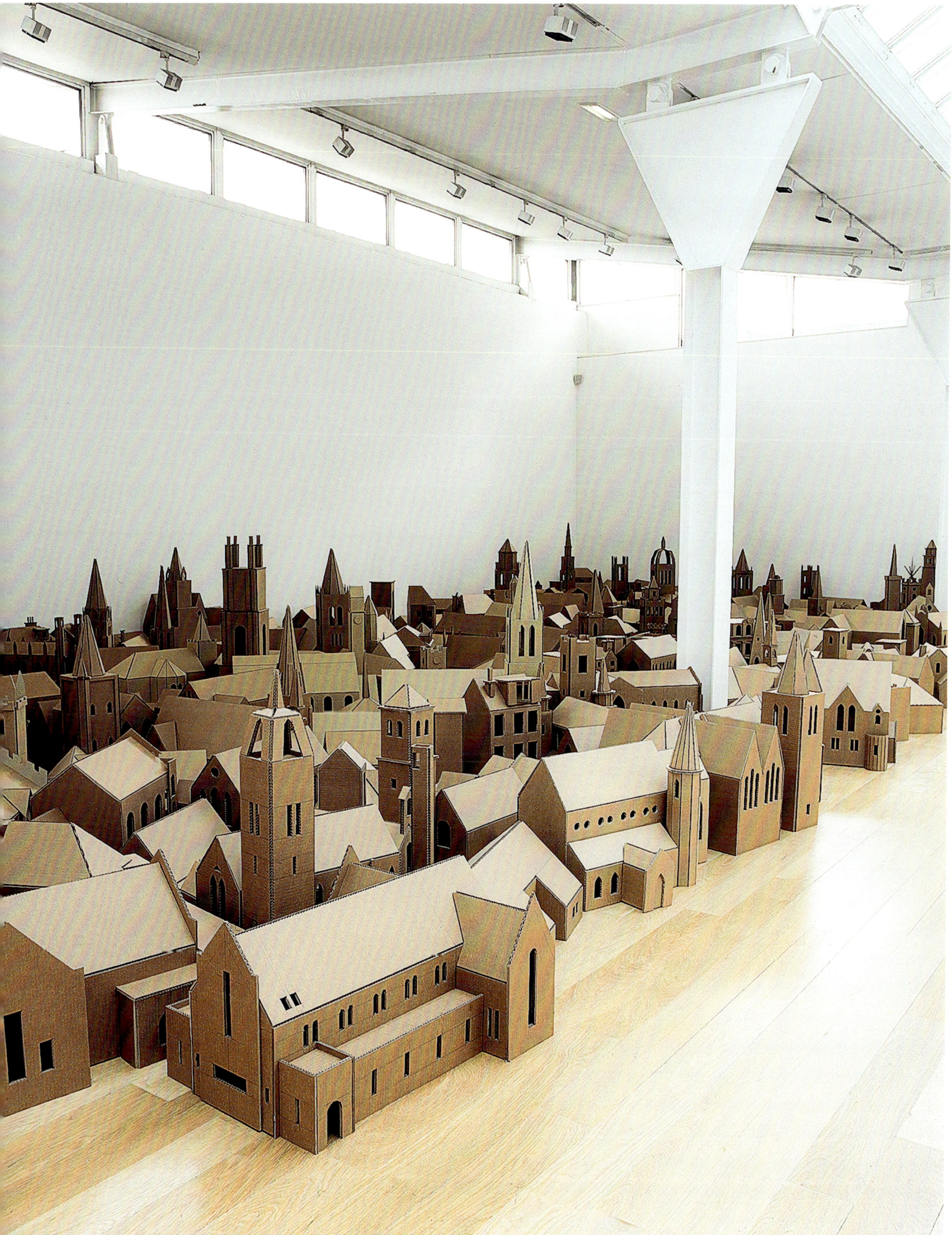

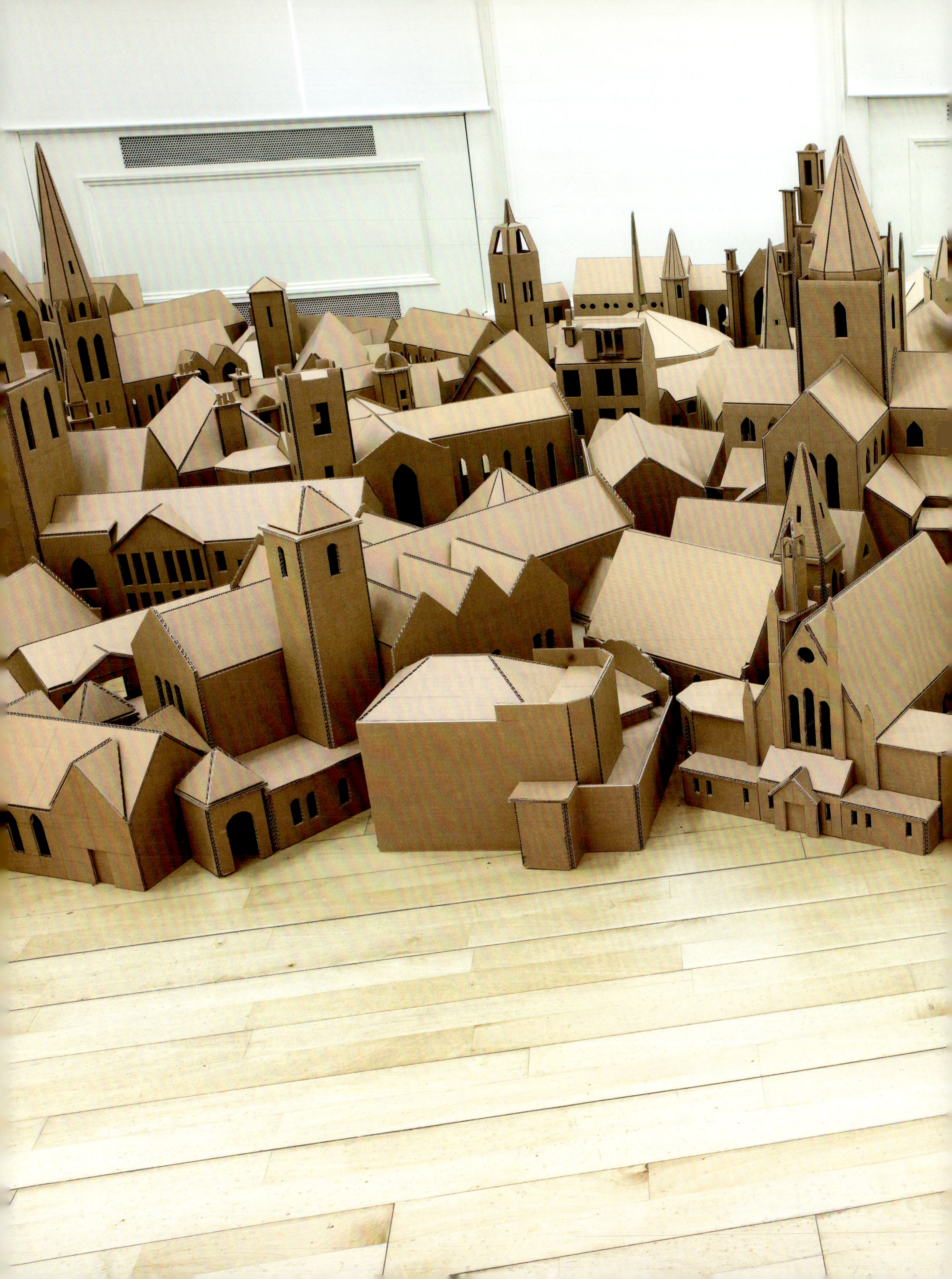

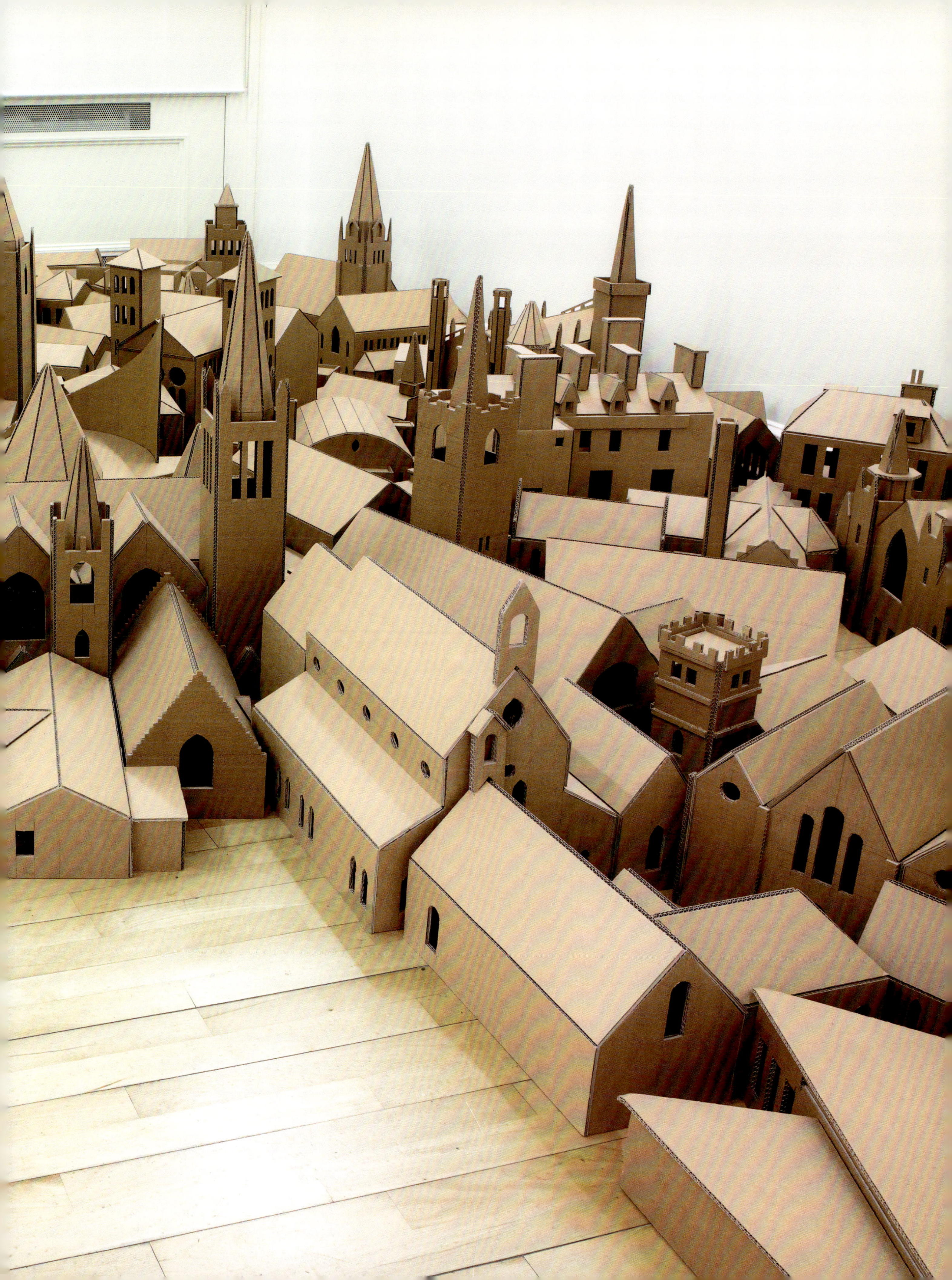

Biography

Nathan Coley

Born in 1967 in Glasgow
Lives and works in Glasgow

Education

1989 B.A. Fine Art (Hons.), Glasgow School of Art

Selected Solo Exhibitions and Projects

2014 *Nathan Coley,* Future Perfect, Singapore
2013 *A Place Beyond Belief,* NDSM-Werf / Nieuw Dakota, Amsterdam
Burn the Village, Feel the Warmth, Pier Arts Centre, Orkney, UK
Nathan Coley, Kunstverein Freiburg, Germany
2012 *Knowledge, Kindliness and Courage,* Contemporary Art Gallery, Vancouver
A Place Beyond Belief, Haunch of Venison, London
A Place Beyond Belief, Kosova Art Gallery, Pristina
2011 *Appearances,* Australian Centre for Contemporary Art, Melbourne
The Ballast Project, Het Scheepvaartmuseum, Amsterdam
2010 *In Memory,* Jupiter Artland, Edinburgh
There Will Be No Miracles Here, Scottish National Gallery of Modern Art, Edinburgh
2009 *Nathan Coley,* Bergen Kunsthall, Norway
2008 *Nathan Coley,* De La Warr Pavilion, Bexhill-on-Sea, UK
46 Brooklands Gardens, Jaywick, UK
Palace, Haunch of Venison, Berlin
2007 *Nathan Coley,* doggerfisher, Edinburgh
We Must Cultivate Our Garden, public art project, Edinburgh
2006 *Nathan Coley,* Mount Stuart, Isle of Bute, UK
Gathering of Strangers, Nottingham Contemporary, UK
Camouflage Church, Santiago de Compostela, Spain
2005 *Jerusalem Syndrome,* Cooper Gallery, University of Dundee, UK
Nathan Coley, Haunch of Venison, London
2004 *There Will Be No Miracles Here,* Fruitmarket Gallery, Edinburgh
Show Home, City Arts Centre, Dublin
Show Home, MK Gallery, Milton Keynes, UK
2003 *Black Tent,* Portsmouth Cathedral, UK
Show Home, North Shields, UK
2002 *Ruskin's Road,* Leidsche Rijn (as part of *Super Utrecht*), the Netherlands
The Black Maria, The Physics Room (as part of *Scape: Art and Industry Urban Biennale*), Christchurch, New Zealand
2001 *Nathan Coley / Bas Jan Ader / Gavin Wade,* Vilma Gold, London
The Italian Tower, Kielder Reservoir, Northumberland, UK
The Land Marked, Centro Cultural de Belém, Lisbon
2000 *International Style,* Architectural Association School of Architecture, London
Nathan Coley, Galerie Rüdiger Schöttle, Munich
1999 *Der Standard,* Museum in Progress, Vienna
1998 *Public Announcement,* The Changing Room, Stirling, UK
1997 *Urban Sanctuary: A Public Artwork,* Stills Gallery, Edinburgh
Demolition in Progress (collaboration with Thomas Bechinger as part of *Blind Date*), Volksbühne, Berlin
1996 *Nathan Coley,* Index—The Swedish Contemporary Art Foundation, Stockholm
1992 *Pure Ideas in a Wicked World,* Crawford Arts Centre, St. Andrews, UK

Selected Group Exhibitions

2014 *You Imagine What You Desire,* 19th Biennale of Sydney
2013 *Mom, Am I Barbarian?,* 13th Istanbul Biennial, Turkey
12th Triennale Kleinplastik, Fellbach, Germany
Call of the Mall, Utrecht, the Netherlands
Homelands, The Harrington Street Arts Centre, Kolkata, India
2012 *Daydreaming with . . . The Hong Kong Edition,* ArtisTree, Taikoo Place, Hong Kong
Mixed Media, Haunch of Venison, London
Crisis Commission, Somerset House, London
Miracles, Art, Science, Religion, Kunsthalle Krems, Austria
2011 *Communities without Propinquities,* MK Gallery, Milton Keynes, UK
Big Brother: Artists and Tyrants, Dinard, France
2010 *Let's Dance,* Mac / Val-Musée d'art contemporain du Val-de-Marne, Paris
Park Liv, Marabouparken, Stockholm
2009 *Mythologies,* Haunch of Venison, London
Nuit Blanche, Paris
The Enlightenments, The Dean Gallery, Edinburgh
Jerusalem Show (Edition 2.1), Al-Ma'mal—Foundation for Contemporary Art, Jerusalem

2008 *Tales of Time and Space,* Folkestone Triennial, UK
Take Me There, Show Me the Way, Haunch of Venison, New York
Oppositions and Dialogues, Lewis Glucksman Gallery, University College Cork, Ireland
The Greenroom, CCS Bard Galleries and Hessel Museum, New York
Persona, Parc Saint Léger—Centre d'art contemporain, Pougues-les-Eaux, France
Rosebud, Kunstverein Lagenhagen, Hannover, Germany
Prospects and Interiors—Sculptors' Drawings of Inner Space, Henry Moore Institute, Leeds, UK
Nothing to Declare, Triennale Oberschwaben, Zeppelin Museum, Friedrichschafen, Germany

2007 *The Turner Prize,* Tate Liverpool, UK
Breaking Steps, Museum of Contemporary Art, Belgrade

2006 *Northern City (Between Light & Dark),* The Lighthouse, Glasgow; Florence
Solitude, Upstairs Berlin
Making History, Tate Liverpool, UK
The Unquiet World, Australian Centre for Contemporary Art, Melbourne
Off the Wall, Scottish National Gallery of Modern Art, Edinburgh
As If Magic, Bethlehem Peace Center, Palestine

2005 *Model Modernism,* Artist Space, New York
British Art Show 6, Baltic Centre for Contemporary Art, Gateshead, UK
Changes of Mind: Transformation and Belief, Haunch of Venison, London
Thinking of the Outside: New art and the city of Bristol, UK

2004 *The Stars Are So Big, the Earth Is So Small . . .*
Stay As You Are, Galerie Schipper & Krome, Berlin
On Reason and Emotion, 14th Biennale of Sydney
Art School, Bloomberg Space, London
Tales of the City, Arte Fiera, Bologna

2003 *Independence,* South London Gallery
Days Like These: Tate Triennial of Contemporary British Art, Tate Britain, London

2002 *Recent Acquisitions,* City Art Centre, Edinburgh
Fabrications, Cube, Manchester
The Gap Show, Museum Ostwall, Dortmund, Germany
Happy Outsiders, Zachęta—Narodowa Galeria Sztuki, Warsaw

2001 *Audit,* Casino Luxembourg—Forum d'art contemporain
Believe, Westfälischer Kunstverein, Münster, Germany
Here and Now, Dundee Contemporary Arts, UK
Making History, Cannock Chase, Staffordshire, UK
Circles 3, Zentrum für Kunst und Medientechnologie, Karlsruhe, Germany
Local Motion, Galerie für Zeitgenössische Kunst, Leipzig, Germany

2000 *Jahresgaben 2000,* Westfälischer Kunstverein, Münster, Germany
As It Is, Ikon Gallery, Birmingham, UK
Contemporary Scottish Artists Books, Printed Matter, New York
Tabley, Tabley House, Knutsford, UK
Salon d'art contemporain de Montrouge, Lisbon
What If, Moderna Museet, Stockholm
Without Day, City Arts Centre, Edinburgh
Continuum 001, Centre for Contemporary Arts, Glasgow
Inside Out, Westfälischer Kunstverein, Münster, Germany

1999 *Blue Suburban Skies,* The Photographers' Gallery, London
In the Midst of Things, Bournville, UK
School Reunion, Wilkinson Gallery, London
Exhibition without an Exhibition, Leipzig, Germany
Threshold, The Travelling Gallery, Edinburgh

1998 *In Visible Light,* Moderna Museet, Stockholm
Strolling, Heide Museum of Modern Art, Bulleen, Australia
Artranspennine98, Tate Liverpool, UK
Nettverk Glasgow, Museum of Contemporary Art, Oslo

1997 *Correspondences,* Martin-Gropius-Bau, Berlin; Scottish National Gallery of Modern Art, Edinburgh
Glasgow, Kunsthalle Bern, Switzerland
A Scottish Collection, Berwick Gymnasium Gallery, UK
Blueprint, Glasgow Print Studio
Wish You Were Here Too, 83 Hill Street, Glasgow

1996 *Girls' High,* Old Fruitmarket, Glasgow
Try, Royal College of Art, London

1995 *Swarm,* The Travelling Gallery, Edinburgh
Cameraless Photography, National Media Museum, Bradford, UK

1994 *New Art in Scotland,* Centre for Contemporary Arts, Glasgow; Aberdeen Art Gallery, UK
Riviera, Oriel Mostyn, Llandudno, UK
Gol! The Soccer Show, Mark Boote Gallery, New York

1993 *Pure Fiction,* Intermedia Gallery, Glasgow
Exposure, Centre for Contemporary Arts, Glasgow
Five from Transmission, Artemisia Gallery, Chicago

1992 *Love at First Sight,* The Showroom, London

	Lux Europae, Edinburgh
1991	*Speed,* Transmission Gallery, Glasgow
	Windfall '91, Seamen's Mission, Glasgow
1990	*Fem fra Glasgow,* Hordaland Kunstsenter, Bergen, Norway
	Dependents, Transmission Gallery, Glasgow

Residencies

2002	Lockerbie, the Scottish Court in the Netherlands
2000	University of West Scotland, Paisley campus, Chemistry Department
1992	Crawford Arts Centre, St. Andrews, UK

Awards

2007	Short listed for Turner Prize
2003	Artist award, Scottish Arts Council
2001	Henry Moore Fellowship, Duncan of Jordanstone College of Art & Design, University of Dundee, UK
	Creative Scotland Award, Scottish Arts Council
2000	Scotland's Year of the Artist, Public Art Initiative Scheme, Scottish Cultural Enterprise, Scottish Arts Council
1997	RSA, Art for Architecture Award
1996	Artist award, Scottish Arts Council

Publications

The Ballast Project (Rotterdam, 2012). Text: Tanja Karreman.
Appearances, exh. cat. Australian Centre for Contemporary Art (Melbourne, 2011). Texts: Brian Dillon, Juliana Engberg, and Charlotte Day.
46 Brooklands Gardens (Colchecter, 2009). Text: Jes Fernie.
Nathan Coley, exh. cat. Mount Stuart (Isle of Bute, 2006). Texts: Andrea Schlieker and Andrew McLean.
There Will Be No Miracles Here, exh. cat. Fruitmarket Gallery (Edinburgh, 2004). Texts: Fiona Bradley and Susanne Gaensheimer.
Urban / Wild (London, 2004).
Francis McKee, ed., *Urban Sanctuary* (Glasgow, 1997).

Acknowledgments

As with all major undertakings, the exhibitions at the Contemporary Art Gallery (CAG), Vancouver and Kunstverein Freiburg, along with this associated publication, are a result of much partnership and shared enthusiasm. The collaboration of our two venues has proved a fruitful and energetic exchange, a model for enabling significant work to be achieved. In our respective cities we are indebted to many individuals who provided key support at crucial times. In Vancouver, we acknowledge those within the city itself, including Councilor Heather Deal, Glen Hodges, Bryan Newson, and Karen Henry, all of whom played a role in the research helping secure necessary permissions for works to be realized. Mark Townsend and colleagues of the Portland Hotel Society could not have been more straightforward and positive in response to our approach to the temporary site *We Must Cultivate Our Garden* on the roof of Hotel Pennsylvania. And Jane Irwin and Ross Hill were equally instrumental through their generosity of time and support in ensuring a rightful celebration of Coley's contribution to the artistic discourse in this part of the world. For this we extend our sincere thanks. We express our appreciation also for the significant multi-year support of BMO Financial Group, a crucial contribution to both the exhibition and this publication.

In Germany, we would especially like to thank the architect Wolfgang Frey, whose infectious enthusiasm brought all those involved in the construction of *Bandstand* to give their best, and without whose generosity and technical expertise this project would have been not been possible. We extend our thanks to Christian Schürhuber and Martin Schmidt from the company Züblin, who were able to match Nathan Coley's intentions for *Bandstand,* producing the sculpture with its immaculate concrete surface. Günter Manthey, Sigrid Hofmaier, and Clemens Back from the Rieselfeld City Council were also tremendously supportive during the preparations for the competition out of which *Bandstand* emerged, and the inauguration of Coley's winning proposal. Special thanks as well go to Marc Doradzillo, whose photographs of *Bandstand* and Coley's subsequent exhibition at the Kunstverein Freiburg are included in this monograph.

Special mention should be made for Jonathan Horrocks, Tom Hunt, Stephanie Schleiffer, Matt Watkins, and others at the former Haunch of Venison, who were able, insightful, and thoughtful companions in all aspects of planning and coordination. Their support and assistance were essential along the way. We thank too Lisa Le Feuvre for her insightful text, drawing out the many strands and nuances of Coley's work, thus providing keen and astute thought into his enquiry.

And so to Nathan Coley, an artist of great thoughtfulness, wit, and intelligence—we thank him for his unstinting attention to the various aspects and opportunities present within the context of each project and situation. The experience of working with him toward the exhibitions, commissions, and this publication has been particularly rich and rewarding. As with many artists we work with, each contributes to our thinking and consideration of the world in differing ways. The conversation is, and has always been, one to savor. For Coley, his intention to always attempt a return to the source of ideas is a significant one, and one we take forward as we seek to inform our decisions and ground our futures in experiences lived.

— Caroline Käding and Nigel Prince

Supporters

Contemporary Art Gallery, Vancouver is supported by

Canada Council for the Arts / Conseil des Arts du Canada

British Columbia Arts Council — An agency of the Province of British Columbia

British Columbia — The Best Place on Earth

City of Vancouver

BMO Financial Group

Kunstverein Freiburg e.V. is supported by

Freiburg im Breisgau

Baden-Württemberg

Sparkasse Freiburg-Nördlicher Breisgau

Graphic design: Matt Watkins
Copyediting: Sandra-Jo Huber, Hatje Cantz
Production: Julia Günther, Hatje Cantz
Reproduction: LVD Gesellschaft für Datenverarbeitung mbH, Berlin
Typeface: Regular
Paper: Hello Fat Matt, 150 g/m^2
Binding: Lachenmaier GmbH, Reutlingen
Printing: Offset Druckerei Karl Grammlich GmbH, Pliezhausen

Front cover illustration: *A Place Beyond Belief,* 2012
Installation, National Gallery of Kosovo, Pristina

Back cover illustration: *In Memory,* 2010
Permanent sculpture, Jupiter Artland, Edinburgh

Published by
Hatje Cantz Verlag
Zeppelinstrasse 32
73760 Ostfildern
Germany
Tel. +49 711 4405-200
Fax +49 711 4405-220
www.hatjecantz.com
A Ganske Publishing Group company

Hatje Cantz books are available internationally at selected bookstores. For more information about our distribution partners, please visit our website at www.hatjecantz.com.

ISBN 978-3-7757-3675-6
Printed in Germany

Photo credits:

Andrew Curtis: frontispiece, pp. 14, 62–63, 64–65, 66, 67, 69, 70–71, 72–73; Scott Massey: pp. 06, 34–35, 36–37, 38, 39, 116–17; Atdhe Mulla: front cover, pp. 09, 32–33; Keith Hunter: back cover, pp. 04, 10, 55, 56, 58–59, 76–77, 78–79, 80–81, 82–83, 86–87, 88–89, 90–91, 124–25, 128–29; Peter Mallet: pp. 13, 42–43, 44–45, 46–47, 48, 49, 52–53, 85; Gary Kirkham: p. 15; studioNathanColey: pp. 17, 20–21, 22, 23; Marc Doradzillo: pp. 24–25, 26–27, 30–31; Jannes Linders: pp. 40–41; Ruth Clark: pp. 51, 103, 104, 105, 106, 107, 109; Donald Nesbit: p. 61; Thierry Bal: pp. 94–95; Gunter Lepowski: pp. 97, 98–99, 100; Peter Dibdon: p. 119; Enrique Lista: p. 121; Jamie Woodley: pp. 132–33; Alan Dimmick: pp. 134–35.

For their assistance in the making of this publication, Nathan Coley would like to give special thanks to:

Katrina Brown, Celia Davies, Charlotte Day, Brian Dillon, Claire Doherty, Juliana Engberg, Jes Fernie, Jonathan Horrocks, Tom Hunt, Caroline Käding, Tanja Karreman, Lisa Le Feuvre, Rory Mitchell, Darren Pih, Nigel Prince, Michael Rooks, Andrea Schlieker, and Matt Watkins.

And further thanks are due to:

Kitty Anderson, Susanna Beaumont, Jon Bewley, Tom and Jo Bloxham, Fiona Bradley, Joost ten Bruggencate, Stephanie Camu, Jonathon Carroll, Amanda Catto, Ruth Clark, Sophie Crichton Stuart, Gavin Coley, Hester Coley, Hannah Coley Brown, Luke Collins, The Common Guild, Max Delany, Susan and Alistair Duff, Tony Dunworth, Charles Esche, Karen Garka-Prince, Derek Gerrard, Neil Gillespie, Glasgow Sculpture Studios, James Goggin, Simon Groom, Derek Harte, all the staff at Haunch of Venison, London, Alan Haydon, Huib Haye Van der Werf, Tim Heatherington, Simon Hopkins, Keith Hunter, Jane Irwin and Ross Hill, Brian Johnstone, Senan Kellecher, James Lavelle, Maria Lind, Colin Lindsay, Hazel McEvoy, Iain McFadden, Andy McGeorge, Donald Nesbit, Stephen Palmer, Hector Pottie, Erzen Shkololli, Stephen Snoddy, Calum Sutton, Jonty Tarbuck, Robert and Nicky Wilson, and Judith Wylie.

studioNathanColey
www.studionathancoley.com

This publication has been supported by

Contemporary Art Gallery, Vancouver

Kunstverein Freiburg

Creative Scotland

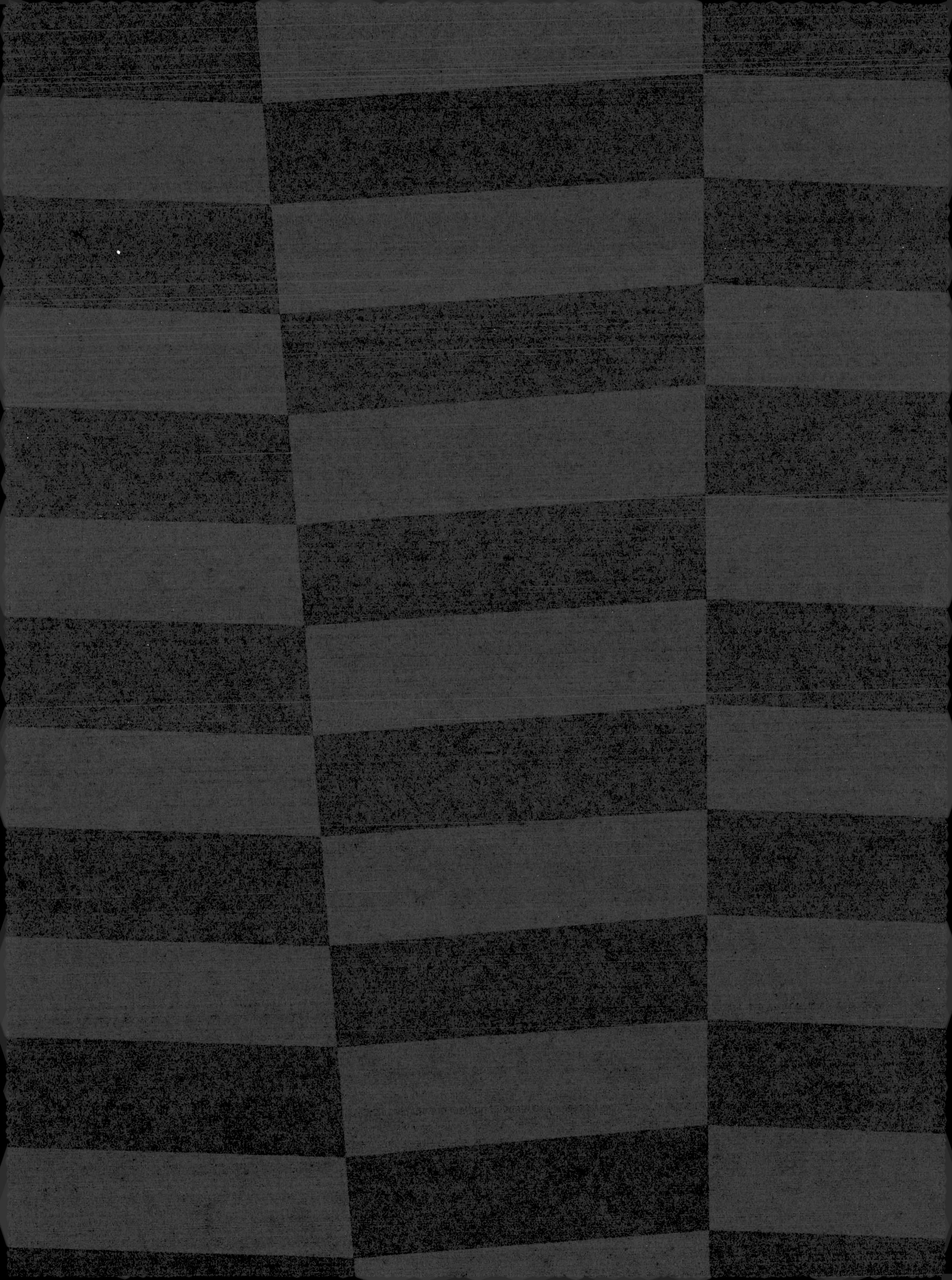